W9-DFK-945

GREAT MEN

Psychoanalytic Studies

Edward Hitschmann, M.D.

Foreword by
ERNEST JONES

Edited by
SYDNEY G. MARGOLIN
with the assistance of HANNAH GUNTHER

INTERNATIONAL UNIVERSITIES PRESS, INC.
New York   New York

UNITY SCHOOL LIBRARY
Unity Village WITHDRAWN
Lee's Summit, Missouri 64063 by Unity Library

Copyright 1956, by International Universities Press, Inc.

Library of Congress Catalog Card Number: 56-6978

Second Printing, October, 1956

Manufactured in the United States of America

BF
175
.H5
Cop.2

Contents

v

Foreword

DR. HITSCHMANN and myself, who started practicing psychoanalysis in the same year, are the oldest living exponents of Freud's work. This, however, is very far from being the only bond I have with him. From the beginning we were close friends, and no shadow has fallen on our friendship. I have always followed his numerous and valuable contributions to psychoanalysis with keen interest and had the honor of editing the translation of his first book on the subject.

At the end of the first decade of this century psychological studies of various famous literary personalities began to appear. The earliest were by Hitschmann, Sadger and Stekel, but the only ones which Freud approved were those by Hitschmann, whose taste and discrimination Freud praised highly. Freud himself considered that pathographies, i.e., medical studies of the morbid conditions that had affected various famous personages, were of very little value in throwing light on their personality and consequently on their works. He considered, however, that a psychological, and still better a psychoanalytic, investigation of the manner in which their minds had developed from the earliest beginnings would throw much light on the motives that impelled them toward their various acts of creation and would in this way illuminate the inner meaning of their productions. Such studies, therefore, would be of value to the literary critic as well as to psychologists in their studies of exceptional personalities. Among such studies those by Hitschmann will long retain an honored position, and it is gratifying to know that some of the most important are being collected in this volume in an accessible form.

ERNEST JONES

Editorial Preface

More often than not, the task of literary editor is primarily part of the craft of putting a book together. It can happen, however, that the nature of the work to be edited and escorted from the desk of the author to that of the publisher and printer offers more than the exercise of technical competence. Dr. Hitschmann's present collection of his extraordinary biographies of famous people is such a book. Here is the work of a mature scientist whose role in the history and development of psychoanalysis is established and universally acknowledged. Consequently, I must express profound appreciation for the honor and privilege of participating in the publication of Dr. Edward Hitschmann's book.

Dr. Hitschmann's treatment of the biographical subjects and of the creative activities encompassed within these covers discloses the dimensions of his uncommon erudition. For not only does he comment with originality in the areas in which his subjects were outstanding, he discusses with exceptional historical sense the cultural setting in which these unique individuals lived and became famous. Hovering over all this information like a giant scanning device of modern physics, is Dr. Hitschmann's comprehensive and comprehending view of psychoanalysis. He writes simply and informatively of the concepts of his science.

He is that rare person, within his special field, whose hardy vitality and undimmed creativity permit him to span the whole of psychoanalysis, from the very beginnings with Freud up to the present time, several generations later. Thus, we must say that Dr. Hitschmann is and always has been contemporaneous with psychoanalysis.

This book, which is an outstanding example of applied psychoanalysis, is of the greatest interest for several reasons. It illustrates, in a way not hitherto available in one volume, the method by means of which psychoanalytic psychology can be applied to supplement the other essential techniques that are required for the writing of biography. Consequently, biographers concerned with the nature of their art will find much to ponder and study in Dr. Hitschmann's principles of procedure and in the theories which he applies in a most exemplary way.

Dr. Hitschmann's special interest in the nature of the creative process has led him to concentrate on these aspects of his subjects wherever possible. By means of his methodology, he is able to demonstrate that the aesthetic experience as well as revelation and love can be critically and etiologically studied without resorting to metaphysics. His ability to treat these subjects in the realm of lucid discourse should commend his studies to philosophers and others who are interested in theories of knowledge and in the more profound processes of the human mind.

For the student of psychlogy in general and of psychoanalysis in particular, we have an array of relative rarities—namely, elegantly presented psychoanalytic case histories. One can see and, so to speak, hear at work one of the most experienced psychoanalysts of our time. It might be argued that the voices of the dead subjects are not heard and that only Dr. Hitschmann speaks. The reading of the biographical supplements, however, will demonstrate the richness and variety of sources from which an extensive documentation has been drawn. For, as Dr. Hitschmann points out, his subjects "have spoken through their work," have left many biographical memoirs and, because of their fame, have stimulated many recorded observations by their contemporaries.

Finally, and not the least, for those readers whose interests are in the subjects themselves, new light on their personalities will be observed. Through the discipline of his psychology and his appreciative sensitivity, Dr. Hitschmann has brought his subjects closer to all of us without degrading them; he has rendered them more human and showed the links between their soaring creative genius and our comparative earth-bound activity.

It is no disservice to the art or science of psychoanalysis to emphasize that a personal psychoanalysis provides a progressive and corrective revision of one's own biography. By the same token, the application of the psychoanalytic method to the subject of a biography will have a similar influence on his life picture. That this should be so becomes apparent upon reflection.

The patient undergoing psychoanalysis tells the story of his life. He attempts to chart out the forces, the determining circumstances and experiences of his past. For the most part such biographical accounts consist of the recalling of events and associated circumstances, all more or less strung out along an axis of time. In most instances this history initially is a line of buoys in a sea of amnesia. Because buoys are markers that indicate danger as well as safety, the points that are remembered by the biographer-patient more often than not involuntarily are designed to give safe passage to the self-esteem and self-image of the voyager.

The self-image contains among other things the inherent psychological and biological impulses and traits specific for the human species and, therefore, universal in all individuals. Among these we would list certain causes of mental pleasure and pain, the tendency to form the same or similar symbols for the same basic ideas and events, and various drives in the service of self-survival. There are also the values, that is, expectations as to what is pleasurable or unpleasurable peculiar to the time and culture of the biographer and of the subject, even when both are the same as in psychoanalytic patients and autobiographies, by means of which all aspects of the self-image are involuntarily judged. Moreover, the vested personal interests of the biographical observer of which he may or may not be aware, participate almost like undetected optical faults in a lens, thus unwittingly and systematically distorting the image when those parts of the lens are used.

This distortion takes on the form of commission or of omission —that is, of the recall of disguised memories or of forgetting. What directs the storage of events, fantasies, emotions, wishes in those caverns of the mind where they are accessible to recall, and what forces render them unavailable are characteristic for the particular individual. Inasmuch as psychoanalysis describes the mind in terms of structure and function, it can be said that the mind has a screening filter which determines what may pass to consciousness, how much of it and—in so far as we treat our past and our memories plastically—what shape it will have. It would seem that a major purpose of this filter is to prevent the pain of the unacceptable from overwhelming the sense of integration and purposeful will on the part of the self-observer. The psychoanalyst attempts in his patient to discriminate between the possible defects in the so-called "filter" and to estimate the energy of the psychological material for which the filter proved to be inadequate.

Our patient or biographical subject, generally speaking, lacks the awareness and the insight into the intensity of these drives on the one hand, or a conception of the mechanism which has so inadequately restrained them. After all, he who is psychologically ill is least able to know himself; although he may be more capable of reporting about himself in an insightless way. Psychoanalysis, more than other systematic psychologies, is the unique method for studying the domains of the repressed in which these forces reside and of the barriers which so selectively determine the way in which these forces may become manifest —that is to say, the unconscious and the defenses of the personality.

This property of psychoanalysis as a penetrating and uncovering investigative tool is one of its most powerful assets and yet capable of exciting the greatest repugnance. Is it not understandable that the breaching of repressing forces which strive for equilibrium of the personality—even by the measured and exquisitely controlled techniques of psychoanalysis—is threatening to some? There is a level, of course, at which even the sturdiest among us would be affected. Consequently, it is often the timing, appropriateness and intensity of the uncovering interpretation which determines whether we shall be enlightened or repelled or overwhelmed. Thus, the application of the science of psychoanalytic psychology combined with the art of tact and taste, makes the psychoanalytic formulation effective as well as accurate.

Dr. Hitschmann, because he is a scientist, has rigorously applied the methods of psychoanalysis to the biographical data of the subjects of his book. Because he is also an artist, it is precisely these aspects of tact and taste which cause his theses to develop both with logic and a sense of growing illumination. The experience of revelation that will inevitably accompany the reading of these fascinating biographical supplements, as Dr. Hitschmann calls them, will be in relation not only to new insights about their famous subjects, but especially to the methods which he used so remarkably. As a result we have a collection of exceptional case histories, scientifically considered and weighted, artistically presented, which are concerned with subjects of never-ending fascination—namely, creative activity and the lives of great people.

Introduction

WHEN at an advanced age, I joined the flight from my country, without possessions and with my surviving friends and family scattered, I found some compensation in learning to know the two great English-speaking nations, and to admire each for its own qualities. To quote the words of a brilliant English lady about her glorious country: "England is eminently just, generous and humane."[1]

Now that my psychoanalytic biographical studies are to be published in the English language, I should declare first of all that they were written between the years 1912 and 1948, and that the majority are not of the most recent vintage. They were a kind of private luxury, a hobby indulged in by a physician, an internist, with a general European education in the humanities who, from the beginning, was interested in both internal medicine and psychiatry.

I was introduced to the small circle of Freud's pupils in 1905. My first psychoanalytic contributions which were made before this group dealt with the psychology of friendship, a pathographical investigation of Nietzsche, and with my personal initial resistance to certain aspects of psychoanalysis.[2] I was always a bookish man, and to me Freud came to represent a model of the broadest general education, with an outstanding knowledge of

[1] Mrs. Heather Lynch Piozzi in the Preface to her book, *Anecdotes of the Late Samuel Johnson* (1894).

[2] In 1911 Dr. Hitschmann published the first textbook of psychoanalysis under the title, *Freud's Neurosenlehre* (Verlag F. Deuticke, Vienna). An English translation was published in 1913 (*Freud's Theories of the Neuroses*, Nervous and Mental Disease Monograph Series, New York) with a Preface by Ernest Jones.—When Robert Barany recommended that the Nobel Prize be given to Freud, the latter wrote that this book represented the then outstanding summary of psychoanalysis. [Editor.]

3

literature, aside from his special scientific field. We had a common meeting ground in our admiration for Goethe, his life and his work. Freud commended my knowledge of Goethe's early childhood in his paper, "A Childhood Recollection from *Dichtung und Wahrheit.*"

No doubt, unconscious identification with the master gave me the impulse to write interpretative analytical papers as he had done in so exemplary a fashion in his publications on Moses, Leonardo da Vinci, and Dostoevsky. The subjects of my own published studies, some of which form the basis of this book, included: Gottfried Keller, Goethe, Knut Hamsun, Selma Lagerlöf, Max Dauthenday, Swedenborg, Johannes Brahms, Franz Schubert, Franz Werfel, and William James. The latter's *The Varieties of Religious Experience* inspired me to apply the psychoanalytic science to subjects which he treated.[3]

Once, when Freud described a curriculum to be taught by a faculty of a psychoanalytic institute, he thought that there should be included such subjects as history of civilization, mythology, psychology of religion, and literature.[4] I would enlarge Freud's curriculum by adding the "science of biography." Granting the obvious value of psychoanalysis as a treatment for neurotic disturbances, yet, as Dr. Greenacre points out, "it would still seem that its greater and wider contribution lies in problems of human behavior, whether in the fields of psychology and medicine, or in

[3] Dr. Hitschmann published his studies with the derivative title, "New Varieties of Religious Experience. From William James to Sigmund Freud" (In: *Psychoanalysis and the Social Sciences,* Vol. 1. International Universities Press, Inc., New York, 1947). [Editor.]

[4] Freud advocated an extensive general education for the psychoanalyst: "If a psychoanalytical faculty were to be set up, a notion which today may seem a fantasy, much would have to be taught in it which is also taught in a medical faculty. Besides depth psychology, that is, the psychology of the unconscious which will always be the main subject, some biology would be required; the science of sex in its widest sense; and some knowledge of the clinical pictures dealt with in psychiatry. On the other hand, the analytical curriculum would include subjects which are far removed from medicine and which a doctor would never require in his practice: the history of civilization, mythology, the psychology of religion, and literature. Unless he is well oriented in these fields, the analyst will be unable to bring understanding to bear upon much of his material." (Freud, *The Question of Lay Analysis.* W. W. Norton & Company, Inc., New York.)

related fields of sociology, education, and even literature and history."[5]

In 1900, Freud's *Interpretation of Dreams* appeared, and in 1905, *Three Contributions to the Theory of Sexuality*. Early in 1900, the famous psychiatrist P. J. Moebius published a pamphlet, *The Hopelessness of all Psychology*. He stated: "Psychology must either remain arid and superficial or invoke the aid of metaphysics . . . It is possible to observe the working of the mind at only one point,—in one's own self . . . The concepts of instinct and unconscious, gained through comparative animal psychology, lead to the destruction of a more exacting human psychology." Freud's genius and the new areas he explored in the field of human psychology have so completely revolutionized this "hopelessness of psychology" that psychoanalysis may now be regarded as the essential element in the science of man. From Freud, psychology has learned the methods and principles of making patient, painstaking observation of the minds of others, whether healthy or sick. The patience and the tenacious curiosity of the laboratory physiologist who uses his instruments to perceive beyond the naked human senses, that same patient wisdom and methodology have become the mental instruments of the psychoanalyst in the study of human behavior. The analyses of many thousands of subjects have opened up all this new knowledge since the day of Moebius' pessimistic declaration.

From Charcot, Freud had learned "to look at things until they begin to speak." For more than fifty years, we analysts have been asking the question, "What is on your mind?" The method is to suggest nothing, merely to ask for free associations. These are the unprejudiced and uninhibited verbalizations of everything that passes through the mind, such as memories, fantasies, wishes, impulses, confessions, dreams, emotional displays, to mention a few. The technical device of free associations not only yields forgotten memories and hidden tendencies, but also reveals how character traits and behavior function in the service of mental

[5] Dr. Phyllis Greenacre, "Psychoanalysis and the Cycles of Life." Freud Lecture, The New York Academy of Medicine, 1953.

health and illness. Free associations are rarely, if ever, random or chaotic. Psychoanalysis has demonstrated that they tend to be mobilized around themes which can be directly or indirectly disclosed.

This method became fruitful thanks to two discoveries of Freud, the insight into transference and resistance, and the scientific interpretation of dreams. The latter, in Freud's own words, contained "the most valuable of all the discoveries that it has been my good fortune to make." And he remarked: "Insight such as this falls to one's lot but once in a lifetime."[6] Many other discoveries have followed in the next five decades, such as the deeper knowledge of the instincts, child psychology and ego psychology. The result is that, while we still do not know what the mind is, we do know, on the basis of a brilliant and productive working hypothesis, *how it functions*. Today, supported by anthropology, sociology in the broadest sense as well as by biology, psychoanalytic psychology has given new direction and impetus to the scientific approach to human behavior, to the knowledge of mankind.

Thus, Freud gave us the interpretation of dreams, the technique of free associations, and the analysis of day-to-day behavior. This penetrating and uncovering insight of psychoanalysis can contribute to even the best and most extensive biographies. The complex interacting factors that make up all the situations of the subject's life are considered in the light of psychoanalytic psychology. These include the onset of his artistic productivity, the nature of his skill and of his accessibility to creative inspiration. Existing autobiographical attempts of such subjects, of course, are of the greatest value. In addition to these, dreams—even invented dreams—furnish most revealing material. Neurotic symptoms, phobias, hallucinations and other frank symptoms are very indicative. And as all my subjects are writers and artists, they have, of course, spoken through their work.

There may be other means for further investigation. It might

6 Preface to the Third (Revised) English Edition (1932), *The Interpretation of Dreams*. *(Standard Edition*, Vol. IV, p. xxxii.)

be useful, for instance, to explore the economy of an individual's activity and productivity in relation to sexual abstinence. The conflicts between narcissism and object love, between consuming love for work and an inclination toward leisure, might also be investigated. I would propose a new kind of group analysis, i.e., comparative analysis of the biographies of individuals in given fields, for example, writers, philosophers, painters, musicians, to mention a few. Perhaps we might find in certain events such as bodily defects or the early loss of a parent or sibling a common origin for the tendency to be productive. A collection of biographies, all written from one point of view (which would have to include anthropological and sociological factors) might bring about greater progress in the "science of man."

Biography, which was enriched by this development, has begun to acquire a different meaning. It is no longer "the history of the life of a particular person." To us it means a recorded personality, especially his psychology, development, function of his soul, heredity, constitution, childhood, defense mechanisms, his instincts and their vicissitudes, the ego, the superego—in short, the understanding of a man's work, character and personality. A "man-record" would be a better word for it. Because the Twentieth Century contains an accelerated interest in and understanding of psychological life, the disciplines of psychoanalysis, anthropology and sociology together represent a "science of man" as never before. The dynamics of the creativity of the unconscious mind in the form of dreams, fantasies and works of art are being registered. The practicing analyst studies personalities as part of his method of therapy. He records these data in his files. Material of this kind, obtained by psychoanalysis, is necessary for the man-record of a great and productive individual. Thus, biography is psychoanalysis, and every psychoanalyst collects data for a man-record (*Menschenbild*), that is to say, every psychoanalysis is a biography.

Samuel Johnson, whom Clifford with some justice calls "the father of modern biography," stressed that domestic privacies and minute details of daily life should be included in biography.

He praised Sallust for writing of Catalina that "his walk was now quick and again slow." Johnson condemned "eulogies and uniform panegyrics," and wrote that "nobody can write the life of a man but those who have eaten and drunk and lived in social intercourse with him." Boswell, whose relationship to Johnson qualified him as his biographer for just these reasons, declared: "Should I have omitted his frailties? If I delineate him without reserve, I do what he himself recommended both by his precept and example." Johnson and Boswell were among the most interesting characters I have ever studied, and I wrote psychoanalytic biographies of them.

Works of art, in so far as they represent fantasies, autobiographical details and characteristic subject matter of a given artist, lie within the concept of free association and in many instances psychoanalytic psychology can be applied. The essence of the psychoanalytic method is to uncover the unconscious and to demonstrate the modes by means of which the unconscious retains its contents, while powerfully determining behavior. This methodological consideration perhaps more than anything else distinguishes the psychoanalytic biographer. It determines his selection and weighting of biographical data, as well as their handling. This quality, however, in no way justifies a claim of superiority in the difficult and often elusive art of biography. It is an application of a scientific method for the purpose of obtaining and exploiting data not available otherwise. The non-analytic biographer, through his art, innate skill and methodical study of his subject, can and may intuitively draw the same conclusions as the analyst, but more often than not, these are stated declaratively and are persuasive through empathy. This artistic achievement is not available to the analyst unless he combines with his method the art of the great biographer. The biochemist or pathologist, in addition to his skill in his specialty, may have within himself the capacity to practice the highest form of the art of medicine. I would like to say here that I consider Ernest Jones' biography of Freud a model of modern biography, both in its interpretation of collected information and in its profound understanding of the development of a complex mind.[7]

Not infrequently the work of a given biographer will be praised or condemned if psychoanalytic concepts have been utilized. This basis for criticism would seem to contain an inherent absurdity. It would be like criticizing a given astronomer because his approach stresses mathematical astrophysics rather than optics and spectrum analysis. Such short-sighted controversy would cease if it were realized that different techniques provide different bodies of information, each of which illuminates different aspects of a given subject, whether in a biography or in astronomy. The realistic ground for such disputes lies in the appraisal of the validity and in the correctness of the application of a given method.

The biographer can and should use many methods of which psychoanalysis is but one. He is above all a historian in his collection and verification of data. If he thinks of it at all, he must decide for himself the degree to which his own value judgments and prejudices enter into the process of collecting, verifying and weighting. He may attempt to cross-check his outlook by sociological, ecological and other cultural examinations of his subject's environment. Even here, however, the biographer must deal with a systematic distortion introduced by his own character structure and by the ideologies to which it responds.

A search for common denominators in these psychoanalytic supplements of biographies yields some valid findings. Among these are the obvious facts that they were the output of a single psychoanalyst, namely myself, and that the concepts of psychoanalytic psychology were applied in their formulation. Of perhaps even greater significance, however, was the evocation of several questions of fundamental importance to the writers and readers of biographies. What determines the choice of a subject for a biographer? What is a given author's incentive in writing such a study? And finally, what motivates the reader's interest in

[7] *The Life and Works of Sigmund Freud,* Vols. I and II. Basic Books, New York, 1953, 1955.

such publications? To the extent that some famous biographers are subjects of this present volume, an effort to furnish some answers may be justified. This is not to say that the famous subjects of biographical studies necessarily have common character structures. No greater difference in character, for instance, could exist than between Goethe and Samuel Johnson—but even Carlyle's famous essays deal with both of them equally.

The joys of writing such analytical biographies are many. There is the intellectual sense of a satisfaction that is achieved by knowing more than others, and the keen aesthetic gratification of developing and elaborating a clue as Freud did in his study of Leonardo; of gaining insight into a whole life, and the life of a great man at that. This is a rare experience for an analyst who, as a physician, deals primarily with sick people or with students. Psychoanalysis as a method of treatment, like other medical curative procedures, is not invariably successful. Unfortunately, therapeutic success is not always a consequence of diagnostic accuracy. To paraphrase a statement by Karl Marx who said: "Philosophers merely give the world different interpretations, but the real task is to change it," I would say: "Psychoanalytic psychology can give a neurotic personality different interpretations, but the real task is to change it."

I should not forget to explain the special feeling of pleasure that is reserved for the analytic biographer whose application of psychoanalytic psychology may yield basic information. By way of illustration, let me mention the fact that Schubert's first texts for songs deal with patricide; that Dauthenday, when he broke with his father, was converted from deism to pantheism. Knut Hamsun's orality and mother fixation appear in his associations to a mountain slope in outdoor nature: "This place," he writes, "is in reality not a slope of a mountain, but a breast, a lap . . . so soft it is . . . a large slope full of tenderness and helplessness, like a mother it allows all to be done with it." In the case of Gottfried Keller, there is a particularly significant dream which he recorded at the age of twenty-seven. It provides the classical proof for his fixation to his mother's breasts and for his orality. He dreamed: An unknown young girl lures him into going home with her to her garret. The indescribably bosomed girl makes him feel extraordinarily comfortable. "I did not wonder when suddenly from her there developed two girls, one on either side of me. They were both completely similar, differing only in age, as if one were an older sister and the other a little younger." One of them offers him her white young shoulders to caress; but at that moment they are frightened by some witchlike old women gliding down from the roof who compel the girls to leave him alone.—This dream which reveals inhibited sexual wishes and anxiety, yields the interpretation that the duplication of the girls means two breasts. In erotic dreams, two girls or two sisters regularly symbolize the two breasts. In Keller's novels, moreover, the theme of "*Zwiehan*"—that is, "*zwei haben*," "having two"—plays a recurrent role. Brahms, the confirmed bachelor, throughout his life fluctuated in his sexual interests between idealized love objects and degraded sexual objects. In his case, this was not merely the consequence of a mother fixation; there is also the known fact that in the inn for sailors, where his father played music, prostitutes used to take him on their laps and fondle him.

Most of these supplements to the life histories of famous personalities date from a time when Freud wrote: "We know that we have not as yet exact certainty as to the aetiological conditions of neurosis. The precipitating occasions are frustrations and inner conflicts: conflicts between the three great psychical agencies [id, ego and superego], conflicts arising in the libidinal economy by reason of our bisexual disposition, conflicts between the erotic and the aggressive instinctual components. It is the endeavour of the psychology of the neuroses to discover what imparts a pathogenic character to these processes, which are a part of the normal course of mental life."[8]

For us to attempt, in our biographical studies, to gain insight into a personality and the motivation of its activity is no easy task. Freud, on the occasion of receiving the Goethe-Prize, had to

8 From Freud's paper, "Libidinal Types" (*Collected Papers*, Vol. 5, pp. 250–251. Hogarth Press, London, 1950).

confess: ". . . that we have not yet been very successful in the case of Goethe. This is attributable to the fact that as a poet, Goethe not only indulged in much self-revelation, but was also carefully reticent despite the fullness of autobiographical details." In this connection, we cannot but recall, says Freud, the words of Mephistopheles (Faust, Part I):

> "The best that you can know with all your labour,
> You dare not tell the striplings raw."
> ("*Das Beste, was du wissen kannst,*
> *Darfst du den Buben doch nicht sagen.*")

Other psychoanalytic pathographers report in various ways this very same limitation. J. B. Wisdom published his paper on Berkeley's philosophy with the regret "that only little is known of his childhood or of his relation to his parents or siblings." According to the author, Berkeley's fundamental conflict lies in an ambivalent attitude to feces which he regarded as both "good" and "bad." Though the bad aspects, felt as "poison," predominated at the more conscious levels, this "matter" could be abolished "by a subjectivist philosophy of 'esse est percipi.' " A childhood reconstruction shows childhood diarrhea.[9]

Drs. E. and R. Sterba, in their study of *Beethoven and His Nephew*, cannot refer to childhood at all. The authors restrict their record of interpretation in this way: "We hardly err to assume that 'polarity' and 'antithesis' in Beethoven's work correspond to the conflict between the male and female principle . . . This conflict was certainly one of the most important dynamic motivations of his creation . . . All extension of our understanding of artistic creation must depend upon an insight into the fundamental structure of the psychological content and dynamics of the artistic personality."[10]

In his biographical study, *Leonardo da Vinci, A Psychosexual Study of an Infantile Reminiscence* (1910), Freud admitted: ". . . the nature of artistic attainment is psychoanalytically in-

[9] J. B. Wisdom, *Philosophy and Psychoanalysis*. Philosophical Library, New York, 1953.

[10] Pantheon Books, New York, 1954.

accessible to us." And he continued: "Even if psychoanalysis does not explain to us Leonardo's artistic accomplishment, it still gives us an understanding of the expressions and limitations of the same." Psychoanalysis is able to prove that human love and morality can be understood without the help of explanations based on mystical or divine intervention. Romantic love needs no more than an admixture of narcissistic enjoyment with its biological basis;[11] and we know that our morality stems, through a psychic mechanism, from identification with parental authority and not from God. Dreams are not sent from heaven or hell. Similarly, it should be possible to explain creative imagination and inspiration without alluding to divine powers. Goethe once said to Eckermann: "Every productivity of an exalted kind, every great thought of consequence which bears fruit, is beyond human powers, is above earthly powers. Man has to consider it as an unexpected gift from above, a creation of God." Since then we have learned much about the unconscious, which Goethe had imagined and used: "Man cannot remain for long in a conscious state or in consciousness; he has to take refuge in the unconscious, for that is where his roots are."[12] We have learned much about our ego and about narcissism, and are able to understand the narcissistic source of our pleasure in moral deeds, our joy in self-love. Is it not a function of the early developing ego of the individual to satisfy its narcissism by being capable of being moral, by being capable of love, and finally by being able to create?

To come back to the subject of my first biographical study, Nietzsche, I may mention that no complete analysis of him exists. This may be due to the uncertainty as to when his organic brain disease (general paresis) began to influence his thoughts. Yet

11 In "Freud's Concept of Love" (*International Journal of Psycho-Analysis,* Vol. 33, 1952), Dr. Hitschmann developed the thesis of the communality of religious ecstasy, esthetic experience and romantic love. [Editor.]

12 We must surmise that Goethe's term "unconscious" is not equivalent, psychologically speaking, with the psychoanalytic concept of the unconscious, except in the sense of "unawareness." Goethe did not at any time postulate a systematic psychology. [Editor.]

Nietzsche's inspired reports of his own introspections indicate
that he had taken some tentative steps along the path that Freud
subsequently explored so extensively. I would like to quote some
of Nietzsche's remarks:

> "I did that," says my memory. "I couldn't have done
> that," says my pride and remains obdurate. In the end mem-
> ory gives way.
>   The degree and nature of sexuality in man extends to the
> highest reaches of his spirit.—For the longest period, con-
> scious thought has been regarded as the only form of
> thought. Only now is the truth dawning on us that our ac-
> tivity for the most part runs its course, unconscious and un-
> felt.
>   When the origins of religion, art and ethics will be de-
> scribed in such a way that they can be completely explained
> without taking recourse in any assumptions of metaphysical
> interference, then even the most profound interest in the
> purely theoretical problems of "the thing in itself" and in
> "the phenomenon" will cease . . .
>   If it is the fate of genius to be understood for a time by
> only a few among mankind, these few may yet feel that they
> are in marked measure complimented and honored, for it is
> vouchsafed them to see the light and to derive warmth from
> it, while the mass of mankind is still standing and freezing
> in the cold fog. Yet these few do not reach their appreciation
> of genius without an effort; on the contrary, they have to
> struggle vigorously against all powerful prejudices and their
> own opposing views; so that, when they win through to vic-
> tory, they have, as it were, a conqueror's claim on genius.

My interest in another philosopher, Schopenhauer, was
aroused by chance when I was in my teens. My grandfather, a
homeopathic physician, gave me two volumes of Schopenhauer's
works, the *Parerga* and *Paralipomena,* with the remark: "I do
not like the work of a man who hated women." I diligently read
the writings of this highly educated and temperamental man
and one result of these studies was the essay, "Psychoanalysis of a
Philosopher," which was published in 1913. I was able to show
why Schopenhauer developed into a philosopher, and why he
formulated the principles of *his* particular philosophic system.

Schopenhauer's awareness of and conflicts with the drives known to psychoanalysis as aspects of the oedipus complex, may have contributed to his withdrawal from women and to his implacable hostility toward his father. The anxiety and guilt aroused by his tabooed erotic interest in his mother may very well have reflexly occurred in relation to other women as well. Consequently, for him all women were associated with these most disagreeable of affects and therefore repelled him. It should be emphasized, however, that these feelings of guilt and anxiety, and his compulsory flight from women were all determined by his intense unconscious love for his mother in relation to whom his father was invariably a successful and aggressive rival. Because the youthful Schopenhauer repressed his unacceptable longings and converted them into their opposite, that is, hatred and withdrawal, he was able to challenge and attack his father without internal criticism and without reference to his mother. These two themes, the rejected but desired mother and the challenged but feared father, together with his intolerance for any source of guilt and anxiety, are basic concepts which appear symbolically in Schopenhauer's philosophic system.

In the *Dialogue on Religion,* Schopenhauer's argumentation is similar to that of Freud in his *Future of an Illusion.* One partner in the dialogue predicts "euthenasia" for the future of religion. "Religion will take its leave of European humanity like a nurse whom the child has outgrown. Philosophy and science will then be instructors and tutors." For us, it is analysis that succeeds to the inheritance. Our metapsychology with its understanding of the dynamics of the psyche, with its reality testing, agrees with Schopenhauer's conclusions.

Let me quote one more statement of Schopenhauer because it demonstrates his understanding of repression and reaction formation.

Men of genius often have violent desires; they are prey to feelings of sensuality and anger. But they do not commit violent crimes . . . because they recognize the idea behind these . . . that these constitute the goal; this knowledge gains supremacy over the strong will and diverts it—the same happens in the saint,—and thus no crime is committed.

My analytic study of Schopenhauer concluded with these sentences: "He who would venture forth to seek a man who is healthy enough to be a philosopher would fare as did that messenger of an ailing king who went to search for the shirt of a happy man to restore his master's health. For when he at last found a happy man, a shepherd, the shepherd did not own a shirt. The man who would be healthy enough to be a philosopher simply does not become a philosopher." Now, many years later, I would like to change that last sentence: "The man who would be healthy enough to become a philosopher, does not do so—he becomes a psychoanalyst instead."

Nietzsche, originally the greatest admirer of Schopenhauer, later perceived the defect inherent in all philosophy through his psychological insight into the personal and subjective conditions of all philosophizing. "Gradually," wrote Nietzsche, "it became clear that every philosophy hitherto has contained an involuntary confession of its creator, a kind of unconscious memoirs. Philosophy always creates the world according to its own pattern. It cannot do otherwise. Philosophy is itself this tyrannic instinct, the spiritual will to power in its creation of a world, the causa prima." Nietzsche stated that when art, religion and ethics are traced back to their origins, one is able to understand them without having recourse to metaphysical conceptions. He went on to develop this further, pointing out the hopelessness of all philosophical systems. It is apparent that Nietzsche came to realize that philosophy functioned as an intellectualized defense against knowledge of the personal and unconscious self. This effort at repression was not completely successful for it appeared to determine the form and content of the philosophical system or of the so-called "philosophy of life." Logic, therefore, by compelling an ordered process and selection of thoughts, becomes a discipline against unplanned insight by an involuntary association of ideas. Nietzsche not only realized such mechanisms in the work of philosophers but discovered them with greater immediacy through his own introspection. It was through the latter that he expressed formulations which were precursors of the super-ego and defense mechanisms of psychoanalytic psychology.

With regard to psychoanalytic observations of the biographies of philosophers, it might be mentioned that Schopenhauer and Nietzsche and many others remained unmarried. Schopenhauer called attention to this circumstance and compared himself to other genuine philosophers who had remained single, such as Cartesius, Leibnitz, Malebranche, Spinoza and Kant. Why did so many philosophers remain unmarried? We are not yet suf-ficiently informed about the significance and consequences of an unmarried life. Neither do we comprehend enough about the equivalents of orgastic satisfaction in nongenital character struc-tures. It is apparent, therefore, that the psychoanalytic biogra-pher should have full knowledge of sexuality in its broadest and most particular aspects in order that he may both understand his subject and learn from him.

My application of psychoanalytic psychology to the biographi-cal data of famous creative individuals has two purposes. The first is more general and is part of the endeavor to comprehend the subject of the biography in terms of the dynamic forces of his de-velopmental experience. The second, however, is a more special interest of mine, namely, the nature of the creative man and of the creative process. It is an old hope of the human mind to dis-cover the origin of creative imagination. If we still do not know it, we can at least say that an important contributing factor ex-ists in the form of a discernable set of certain conditions. The main value of psychoanalytic psychology for this investigation lies in its ability to structure meaningfully highly complex and diverse biographical information. That is to say, cause and effect relationships can be established between the data of infancy, childhood and adult life by the application of psychoanalytic principles. In my opinion, other systematizations of human psy-chology have not as yet acquired a comparable degree of theoreti-cal and practical development.

The individuals who become the subjects of biographical study possess traits, achievements and other personality properties which have set them apart. It seems characteristic of man to dramatize and elaborate the unique and the extreme within himself and his environment. For example, mythology in one sense is comprised of the biographies of various deities or of culture heroes in terms of their effects on the human individual, his needs, his impulses for good and evil, his gratifications and his frustrations. The gods and their agents can be viewed as externalized representations of these basic mental and emotional aspects of the society that invented them. The myths, dealing as they do with every phase of man's birth, life and death in his environment, provide the illusion of magical and symbolic control of fear and danger as well as of pleasure and reality. These special properties of the myth as an archaic biography can be observed in the biographer's study of an individual man. The subjects of biographies, like the gods of mythology, express the unique and the exceptional in the nature of man. It is rare that a so-called "average man" is studied, except as a case in a statistical process. Yet the "average man" will arrest the attention of some if his biography exposes and describes that intimate behavior which, although universal, is conventionally experienced in the greatest privacy. In such examples, the biographer's and the reader's interest is directly voyeuristic and exhibitionistic, that is, an erotic or pornographic indulgence.

The unanswered question as to the origin of the creative imagination naturally is of utmost interest to the psychoanalytic biographer. We have learned that we are all creative in dreams to some extent, depending on the varying degrees of imagination, elaboration and dramatization, both in the dream and in its retelling. We know that dreams have more meaning than is manifest in them, that in particular they tend to provide fulfillment of wishes, even as do the simpler daydreams. Of this we are sure. Many a song, many a poem, even the solution to difficult scientific problems have been found in dreams. Creation tends to be experienced in two phases. In the first, the creator is driven;

he is in an exceptional state. This is what we call the moment of inspiration. The ecstasy of the creative state has been variously described as divine, pathological, superhuman. Actually, nothing comes suddenly into existence in the mind. Everything is slowly developed, in a particular, individualistic way. That moment of inspiration is most probably the moment of narcissistic acknowledgment of something which has been unconsciously prepared for a long time. The second phase is no longer exceptional, it is elaboration.[13] In my biographies I attempt to describe the determinants and preconditions of creative inspiration in my subjects. Psychoanalysis has taught us the significance of the unconscious, of the love life, of dreams; the importance of relationships within the family, of the personalities of parents, relatives and servants, and of fantasies, sexual experiences, punishments.

Several of my biographical subjects show a traumatic experience in early childhood as a possible source of their creativity. All were excessive daydreamers—and often were rebuked and punished for it. Many show a certain bisexuality or femininity or at least some conflict in masculine or feminine identification. Their productivity can be compared to the act of childbirth.

Daydreaming alone does not make anybody creative. It is the giving up of excessive daydreaming with the guilt feelings that it engenders which harnesses the creative powers. It is the activity after passivity, the narcissistic impulses to communicate and to win an audience—in a way the antithesis of withdrawn indulgence in fantasies. Here I would like to mention the confession of a well-known writer who explained his success in life in comparison to the much lesser achievements of his younger brother by the fact that he gave up masturbation while the brother continued this practice. The brother always asked him to tell him stories before falling asleep.

Which medium of expression the productive ego will choose is directed by the inborn talent, for instance, a special gift for

13 See Ernst Kris, *Psychoanalytic Explorations in Art*. International Universities Press, New York, 1952.

visual observation. But it is influenced by the accessibility of tools in the home, such as musical instruments used by the parents, or paint, or paper and pencil. By way of illustration, I observed and described the development of a young sculptor who as a small child had the habit of kneading his feces. His intelligent parents provided him with clay. He was able to use this substitute material without any guilt feelings and soon showed great talent as a sculptor of animal figures.

A general impression to be derived from most of my biographies is the significance and "the importance of the father for the fate of the individual." This quotation, a caption that comes from Jung, contains his involuntary confession of his defection from psychoanalysis which was determined by the fact that his father was a clergyman. I found among my subjects that the father was always the most important person who was decisive for the destiny of the son—not only the main influence, but indeed the origin of all biography, of all life and of all inspiration. He is the leader, the authority. It seems as if these creative artists were productive through identification with the father who, as the bread-winner, represented achievement through work. We know that the relationship with the father, however, is always ambivalent. The wish to function like the father coexists with the hatred that stems from the oedipal situation, the breaking away from the father, or an unconscious search for a better father, as exemplified in the lives of Eckermann and Boswell. Freud considered the death of the father the most important experience in the life of a man. In his biographical studies he throws light on two outstanding father figures: Moses and Leonardo da Vinci.

One of the most interesting and illuminating observations was the influence of the son's early relationship with his father on the development of religiosity. Freud stressed this when he said an individual's attitude toward religion depends on "what subsisted in childhood." He referred not only to cultural indoctrination but also to the dynamic events which evoked habitual reactions toward father figures. There are many examples of this influence of the father: Franz Werfel was converted to religion because of his guilt feelings over his rebellion against the father. Gandhi's ethics, as has recently been pointed out again in India,[14] were greatly influenced by his guilt feelings; at the time of his father's death he enjoyed the fulfillment of his love with his young wife. Swedenborg, the son of a bishop, was for the greater part of his life a positivist, in opposition to his father. In later years, in the grip of a psychological illness, he returned to the father in the form of God.

In early years in Vienna, Freud recommended that we read William James' *Varieties of Religious Exprience*. I would paraphrase this title and refer to the contents of this book as "the theory of relativity of religion." I was very impressed by the problem of revelation, an intrapsychic phenomenon which represents the regression to the father. This religious experience is reported both by Albert Schweitzer and Alfonse Maeder, the Swiss psychoanalyst who turned from psychoanalysis. The description of their revelations are practically identical and both remark on a warm sunny morning as part of the setting for their experience. Why a warm sunny morning is associated with the regression to a word of Christ learned in childhood, and with the decision for intensified moralistic behavior should be investigated. The vision of fire appeared in the revelations of Moses and Mohammed. There is much to suggest that this symbol represented incestuous excitement over the mother, which was warded off by revelation of and identification with God, the father. By these means, the unconscious erotic wish for the mother is symbolically experienced while the punitive aggression of the father is accepted by totally submitting to his omnipotence and omniscience.

A very interesting example of a similar experience of a sudden insight is reported by the physicist and philosopher Ernst Mach:

14 N. K. Bose, "Some Facts of Psychoanalytic Interest of Ghandhi's Life." *Samiksa,* Vol. 6, 1952.

I have always considered it very fortunate that at an early age (when I was about fifteen), in my father's library I came upon Kant's *Prolegomena zu einer jeden künftigen Metaphysik* [*Prolegomena for Every Future Metaphysic*]. This essay made a tremendous indelible impression on me, such as I never felt again in all my subsequent philosophical readings. About two or three years later, I suddenly realized the futile role which the "thing in itself" plays. *On a beautiful summer day* during vacation, the world, including my own ego, suddenly appeared to me to be one coherent mass of sensations, only more strongly interconnected within the ego. Careful reflection came later, but that moment was decisive for all my work.[15]

Mach's sudden impression, as in the cases of Maeder and Schweitzer, with which a sunny summer day was associated, appears to have been a revelation, by means of which he was able to discard metaphysics and the "thing in itself."

Boswell became a psychopath because—like many psychopaths —he could not identify with his vain, cold and egotistical father. In his search for a better, kinder and superior father he came to write the most famous biography in the English language—about his fatherly friend, Samuel Johnson.

The loss of the mother's love when a new sibling was born was certainly a traumatic experience for Schopenhauer. After his sister's birth the mother neglected him. His strict father did not understand him. Girls rejected him. He decided that he, for one, did not want to live his life. He preferred to think about life. Later, his mother refused to let him live with her and degraded the honor of the family by taking a lover. Knowing all this, can we not understand Schopenhauer's well-known hatred of women? Schopenhauer proved to be the finest specimen for a psychoanalytic biography. I was able to establish the reason why he turned to philosophy, and why it was precisely *that* system of philosophy. The will in Schopenhauer is nothing other than his stern father and the latter's energy. His ethical system came into

15 Ernst Mach, *Die Analyse der Empfindungen und das Verhältnis des Physischen zum Psychischen* (*The Analysis of Emotions and the Relationship of the Physical to the Psychical*).

being through reversion, a reaction formation to his own aggressiveness and malice. His denial of the will and his ideal of quietism can be explained in like manner, as Nietzsche was penetrating enough to detect. Like most philosophers, Schopenhauer betrays essential characteristics of an obsessional neurosis. He shows the same interest in dreams and in mental illness as does psychoanalysis. Schopenhauer wrote: "What is the greatest pleasure that is possible for man? The intuitive knowledge of the truth." Freud, in *Civilization and Its Discontents,* arrived at a similar conclusion. But Freud referred to scientific activity as a contribution to the progress of mankind.

It is obvious that with the years there will be other investigators who will confirm and correct much that is contained in these biographies. To some extent this has already occurred. My character study of Eckermann, for instance, was supported and expanded twenty years later by my colleague Kurt Eissler, who emphasized Eckermann's moral masochism.[16] Not many biographies show us the tragic end of creativeness in old age. In the case of Knut Hamsun, his son described his father's tragic last days. They correspond with Shakespeare's "sixth age" in *As You Like It:*

<blockquote>
This sixth age shifts
Into the lean and slipper'd pantaloon,
With spectacles on nose and pouch on side,
His youthful hose, well saved, a world too wide
For his shrunk shank; and his big manly voice,
Turning again toward childish treble, pipes
And whistles in his sound. Last scene of all,
That ends this strange eventful history,
Is second childishness and mere oblivion,
Sans teeth, sans eyes, sans taste, sans everything.
</blockquote>

Alfonse Maeder who, as previously mentioned, gave up psychoanalysis, has recently published a book, *The Way to Psychic*

---

[16] K. R. Eissler, "A Clinical Note on Moral Masochism: Eckermann's Relationship to Goethe." In: *Drives, Affects, Behavior,* ed. R. M. Loewenstein. International Universities Press, New York, 1953.

Health, in which by "giving a vital relation with religion," he promises to cure the patient, sometimes in two or three sessions. I have already cited N. K. Bose's work about Gandhi in which my hypothesis is supported.

The analytical biographer gets to know many typical characters. The *exceptional* character has been described by Freud. This type, conditioned by early physical defects for which he holds others responsible, believes all through life that he may demand compensations. I found such a character in Samuel Johnson.

When I came to London in 1938, Samuel Johnson was the most widely quoted historical personality. As an infant, infected by his tuberculous wet nurse who was engaged due to the stinginess of his father, he partially lost his sight, became hard of hearing, and had scars of scurvy all over his neck. He was too poor to complete his studies at Oxford. Is it not understandable that this introverted boy, inhibited by the defects of his senses, was given to daydreaming and, as son of a bookseller, was considered a "born" writer? Aside from his aggressiveness, he showed the manifestations of no less than three neuroses: tic, depression and compulsion.

One of the best examples of the value of psychoanalytic insight for biography concerns the Swedish Nobel Prize winner, Selma Lagerlöf. Crippled by poliomyelitis in childhood, she was excluded from the carefree games of her siblings. Her mother neglected her in favor of the gentler, more beautiful older sister. Selma was in love with her kind romantic father. Thus isolated, she became introverted and read avidly the legends and sagas of the heroes of her country. Daydreaming became useless, and at last she decided to show those who seemed so critical that she, too, could accomplish something. Her ambition could not help but turn her disadvantages into assets, until one day something she had accomplished—be that a sketch, a story, a line of poetry— was accepted by someone. She now gained a reason for existence, recognition and love were hers. The hatred toward the mother, the jealousy toward her siblings were rendered harmless in this sublimated form. Her inborn gift was her heightened capacity for remembering, so helpful to the writer. In her four volumes of childhood reminiscences she describes an instance of visionary remembering at the age of fourteen. She feared she would go crazy and felt "split" for a time; but the sensation subsided and she became normal again. She suffered from a phobia, believing herself persecuted by cruel birds (mother images). Never in her life was she free from anxiety, not even while writing.

Freud described other typical characters. There is the *demoniac* character who to his own disadvantage repeats all through life the same reactions without correction, and appears to be dogged by an implacable fate. Close investigation reveals that this type unconsciously molds its own fate. We then assume that a repetition compulsion creates a character such as this. Ferdinand Lassalle, the German labor leader, who lived in the period of Bismarck and Marx, in a demoniac way repeated in subsequent phases the struggle for his beloved mother and the father-son rivalry. He obeyed the compulsion to rescue the victimized in his lifelong intervention for the rights of Countess Hatzfeld, a motherly woman, in opposition to her husband. The compulsion to rescue came to light in his intention to liberate the oppressed Jewish people; and it appeared in an even more intensive form in Lassalle's polemic struggle in behalf of the proletariat. There is in existence a diary of the fourteen-year-old Lassalle which betrays at this early age his highly developed narcissism, his precocity and militant nature.

Essentially different is the constellation in the case of Goethe. We can imagine only positive and advantageous circumstances for the development of this universally interested and talented genius. Freud pointed out that Goethe could have opened his autobiography with this remark: "My strength is rooted in my relation to my mother." He explained that Goethe's confidence in his success and conquest was based on the fact that he was his mother's undisputed favorite. Besides, he outlived a younger brother and seemed not to regret his death.

The interest in the neuroses of the great has waned, pathographies are no longer in fashion. Maybe the additional discoveries of psychoanalysis during the last twenty years have not yet been taken enough into account as far as biographies are concerned: the new theories about the ego, the pregenital phase with its orality and our understanding of constitutional defense mechanisms. Countless observations have been made in connection with these developments, but why these complexes either become "pathogenic" or cause productivity, that is something we still do not know, and thus far neither sociological nor anthropological observations can help us find the answer.

Those scientists who only recognize what they can measure and weigh do not want to have any part of psychoanalysis. All we know about the etiology of the neurosis is the patterns of interaction of heredity, inborn gifts, environment, personality of parents, characteristics of siblings, the place in the chronology of siblings, traumatic experience, etc. Psychoanalysis in its progressing thoroughness is providing us with insight into these special constellations.

1

Freud in Life and Death*

FREUD is buried and his followers or pupils will see or hear him nevermore. What did he look like? men will ask. Such a great man must have been of serious and solemn countenance, some may argue. As a man who knew all the foibles and wickedness of people, he certainly must have been severe and inaccessible. What did he really look like, what was his appearance? One who knew mankind and all its types so thoroughly would scarcely wear a curly head and a wild growing beard like a philosopher, a broad-brimmed hat like a painter; he would hardly look like a narcissistic dandy or shabby like a miser.

Freud looked artless, not striking, like other intellectuals or physicians. He used to wear a well-fitting suit of fine quality, always with a black tie—he seemed not to waste much time on his appearance. He was never solemn or withdrawn, always friendly and encouraging, in a word—human.

It is a pity that it is so difficult to change the neurotics profoundly. Most people come to the psychoanalyst too late, in a too advanced state of their illness. Freud smilingly liked to quote the skeptical sentence: "Three things are impossible: to rule, to educate, and to cure." Experience had taught him that it was not possible to rebuild a human mind in a short time, to change a character. He warned of "furor therapeuticus." For him, working with a patient had to bring new knowledge, and he pitied those psychotherapists, and laughed at these who, attempting to use suggestion, repeat all day long the same recommendation. He wanted thoroughly to understand. Music did not interest him because he regarded it as an unintelligible language. Above everything, he was an inquirer. Had it been necessary, he would have devoted himself to research only, without prospect of healing.

* First published in *American Imago*, Vol. 27, 1941.

He left behind him the deepest, most protracted, but in severe cases the unique method for curing. He compared psychoanalysis —dealing with the unconscious—with digging out, excavating, toiling underground. Excavations of antiquity decorated the desk and cabinets in his working room. In contrast he saw in all metaphysics a wild goose chase, leaving reliable ground; credulity and faith instead of knowledge through deep-digging investigation. Science, knowledge, *logos*, were his gods. In *The Future of an Illusion* he refused to accept religion in place of science. When I once told Professor Freud about the progress in my biographical work concerning the Swedish writer Selma Lagerlöf, he considered it a natural progress that the poetess, who later became so religious, was as a child full of guilt feelings. "It is the same thing," he said, smiling. Anna Freud told me that her father had read the manuscript and praised it—this was during the last months of his life—which I appreciated very much, as well as his word "excellent" written on a proof of my book that gave the first compilation of *Freud's Theories of Neuroses*—a sheet I still preserve.

This is not the place to judge Freud's work. I only intend to report some human traits of his character. He enjoyed witty sayings. When he was reproached with the fact that some of his early pupils later showed a perhaps not unobjectionable behavior, Freud remarked: "Does one know today with whom Columbus went when he discovered America?"

The conception of "sublimation" dawned on him when he was told that the famous surgeon Dieffenbach as a student had cut off the tails of dogs. He had a similar impression when he saw a cartoon in a journal which in the first picture showed a girl as a shepherdess of geese and in the second as guarding a flock of young girls. This image seemed to him better than some weighty definitions by one of his pupils. He sometimes complained that he was taken too literally by his followers. He wasn't dogmatic. He was in favor of an indulgent and kind training and used to advise his own children before guests came: "Don't stick to your company manners!"

His learning was very extensive. In early years he was well versed in several languages and won Charcot's intimate friendship by translating his lectures. It is less well known that Freud was so perfect a student of English that he was chosen to translate a volume of John Stuart Mill's works into German.

Freud felt strongly in the matter of social progress, but he rejected terror and revolution. With grief and uneasiness he watched brutality and servility develop in Europe, and the horrors of war. He hoped to see Eros victorious over Thanatos, the death instinct, but he did not live to see it. How long would he have had to live to see it?

In 1932, in his *New Introductory Lectures,* Freud predicted the English-German war. Bleriot and Zeppelin, he understood, had broken through the protecting isolation of the sea. When in 1938 the National Socialists came to Vienna, persecuted and robbed Freud, destroyed the new Psychoanalytic Institute and the neighboring editorial office together with all books, Freud could still accept the generous invitation to come to England which he had always highly esteemed. There he could finish his last work, *Moses and Monotheism,* and in spite of his illness, go on working with pupils. But the neoplasm was progressing and, suffering from severe pains, brave and patient, Freud died, tenderly nursed by his daughter Anna. Thus a life came to an end which had been so heroic in so many directions.

It is natural to ask the question: Why was the life of this benefactor of mankind burdened for so many years with such suffering? The searcher for determinate relationships must attempt to illuminate with scientific insight the problem whether the tragic end of his life was altogether "accidental."

Psychoanalysis is still a young science and not yet fully utilized. It is clear that the specific cause of a death also depends upon the constitution of the individual. But the connection between particular innate impulses and death has not yet been considered. Let us, for example, consider an individual with an intensive oral impulse. As an infant, he may have sucked his finger and may later develop into an inveterate smoker. If greediness also develops, he may become fat and acquire a tendency to drinking and so damage his heart. We do not know much about an organic basis for such strong innate impulses. But the possibility of a *surmenage* of the organs concerned exists. We know, for instance, of the development of neoplasms on the lips of pipesmokers. Of course, we are not yet in possession of a sufficient number of systematic observations.

As psychoanalysts we have to take into consideration psychic and unconscious aspects, such as displacement of the impulse, sublimation, etc.; feelings of guilt as consequence of overindulgence of an impulse. Excesses in a certain direction, and comparison with more frugal individuals may favor hypochondriac and self-reproaching feelings. If there is really an organic effect of such an instinctive activity and a tendency toward localization in certain organs, the psychical side must play an important part. Excessive indulgence of impulses may produce an illness or a neoplasm in a certain organ. But we must be very careful in our new assumptions; their assertion should be supported by statistics. At least we ought to investigate the causation of death in peculiar cases. Being interested in the cause of the death of Professor Freud, we would like to be able to ask him, since he was in his writings, as he said, "more sincere and candid than is customary with people who describe their life for their contemporaries or for posterity."

Freud died from a neoplasm of the mouth which began as an "epulis" on the basis of a leukoplakia oris caused by excessive smoking. He was a passionate smoker, and smoking accompanied his painstaking work. We have learned from him that such excessive smoking is evidence of a strong oral impulse. Anyone who knows psychoanalytic characterology, will find in his nature and unusual gifts several traits which prove this. Moreover, Freud published one of his own dreams which contributes more interesting material. This dream is one of the additions to later editions of the *Interpretation of Dreams,* but it certainly occurred before his neoplasm appeared, perhaps between the years 1915 and 1918. Freud partly interpreted the dream himself. He used it to illustrate his new conception of dreams of self-punishment. The wish which they fulfill is not an unconscious wish coming from the repressed impulse material; it is rather a wish of the ego, reacting against the impulses, satisfying the superego (conscience). The recognition of these dreams and their interpretation adds an important new aspect to our theory of dream interpretation. This is the dream:

> I tell my wife I have some news for her, something very special. She becomes frightened, and does not wish to hear it. I assure her that on the contrary it is something which will please her greatly, and I begin to tell her that our son's Officers' Corps has sent a sum of money (5,000 k.?) . . . something about honorable mention . . . distribution . . . at the same time I have gone with her into a small room, like a store-room, in order to fetch something from it. Suddenly I see my son appear; he is not in uniform but rather in a tight-fitting sports suit (like a seal?) with a small cap. He climbs on to a basket which stands to one side near a chest, in order to put something on this chest. I address him; no answer. It seems to me that his face or forehead is bandaged, he arranges something in his mouth, pushing something into it. Also his hair shows a glint of grey. I reflect: Can he be so exhausted? And has he false teeth? Before I can address him again I awake without anxiety, but with palpitations. My clock points at 2:30 A.M.

[Freud continues:] To give a full analysis is once more impossible. I shall therefore confine myself to emphasizing some decisive points. Painful expectations of the day had given occasion for this dream; once again there had been no news for over a week from my son, who was fighting at the front. It is easy to see that in the dream-content the conviction that he has been killed or wounded finds expression. At the beginning of the dream one can observe an energetic effort to replace the painful thoughts by their contrary. I have to impart something very pleasing, something about sending money, honorable mention, and distribution. (The sum of money originates in a gratifying incident of my medical practice; it is therefore trying to lead the dream away altogether from its theme.) But this effort fails. The boy's mother has a presentiment of something terrible and does not wish to listen. The disguises are too thin; the reference to the material to be suppressed shows through everywhere. If my son is killed, then his comrades will send back his property; I shall have to distribute whatever he has left among his sisters, brothers and other people. Honorable mention is frequently awarded to an officer after he has died the 'hero's death.' The dream thus strives to give direct expression to what it at first wished to deny, whilst at the same time the wish-fulfilling tendency reveals itself by distortion. We have indeed no idea what lends it the requisite motive-power. But my son does not appear as 'falling' (on the field of battle), but 'climbing.'—He was, in fact, a daring mountaineer.—He is not in uniform, but in a sports suit; that is, the place of the fatality now dreaded has been taken by an accident which happened to him at one time when he was ski-running, when he fell and fractured his thigh. But the nature of his costume, which makes him look like a seal, recalls immediately a younger person, our comical little grandson; the grey hair recalls his father, our son-in-law, who has had a bad time in the war. What does this signify? But let us leave this: the locality, a pantry, the chest, from which he wants to take something (in the dream, to put something on it), are unmistakable allusions to an accident of my own, brought upon myself when I was between two and three years of age. I climbed on a foot-stool in the pantry, in order to get something nice which was on a chest or table. The foot-stool tumbled over and its edge struck me behind the lower jaw, I might very well have knocked all my teeth out. At this point, an admonition presents itself: it serves you right—like a hostile impulse against the valiant warrior. A profounder analysis enables me to detect the hidden impulse which would be able to find satisfaction in the dreaded mishap to my son. It is the envy of youth which the elderly man believes that he has thoroughly stifled in actual life. There is no mistaking the fact that it was the very intensity of the painful apprehension lest such a misfortune should really happen that searched out for its alleviation such a repressed wish-fulfillment [Freud, 1900, pp. 504–505].

This dream, reported by Freud as a sample of a dream of self-punishment, punishing the dreamer for illicit gratifications, is the reaction to painful day residues. It punishes the envy and death wishes against the son and brings in the memory of an accident in early youth of the dreamer, caused by taking food by stealth, certainly an evidence of greediness on the part of the little boy. There are some surprising details: the exhausted son, who is growing old, seems to have a teeth prosthesis, which Freud himself had to wear after his more serious operation (1923).

We now have the following assumptions for the development of the neoplasm. The injury on or near the lower jaw in early youth, the inveterate smoking which the doctors blamed as the original cause of the neoplasm, the tendencies for self-punishment for envy, an oral character trait. The localization may thus become intelligible.

We now turn to the problem of the death impulse. The ingenious conception of the imposing antimony, Eros and Thanatos, *Lebens- und Todestrieb,* was a product of the later years of the great thinker (1920). That the organism, the cell, should not die from being consumed but should have a genuine impulse to perish was the most criticized aspect of this conception. The neoplasm, a phenomenon mostly of older age, shows cells of an intensive growth, but in the end they all die and kill the whole organism, even after they have been operatively removed. All these circumstances may have impressed Freud, and the preoccupation with death may have strengthened the conviction. Here Freud also found a place for the aggression impulse which he recognized in later observations. In *Civilization and Its Discontents* (1930) we read: "I no more understand that we could have overlooked the ubiquity of the non-erotic aggression and destruction and could have failed to concede to it its due position in the interpretation of life." Freud admitted that for a long time he called sadism what was only aggression impulse and that he underestimated the importance of this latter impulse which now takes its place alongside the death impulse and represents the principal cause of guilt feelings. A famous discoverer in psychology confesses in his seventy-fourth year that he has been mistaken! What tragic greatness in such a confession! At that moment psychoanalysis became more true—and more decent.

One who has seen Freud suffer from the difficulties and pains of this fatal disease through many years may be allowed to postulate reasonable causes for the misery which destroyed the old age of this great and till his end productive genius. It was his wise experience that if to cure is not always possible, to understand the origin is always worth while.

If these considerations result only in a stimulus to new investigations, I am satisfied. Is there a connection between innate impulses and a disposition for a certain illness and the causes for death, a certain localization of an illness? What more could be learned of psychical and unconscious connections?

Let me point out two places in Freud's work where, between the lines, he spoke about himself: " . . . he who has been the undisputed darling of the mother retains throughout life that victorious feeling, that confidence in ultimate success which not seldom brings actual success with it" (Freud, 1917). And further he said that the culturally most valuable character "combines independence of external factors and regard for the requirements of conscience with the capacity for energetic action" (Freud, 1931).

Freud's independent work and his magnificent discoveries are proof of his sublimation with a powerful activity as well as never failing self-confidence. A human man with superhuman achievements!

Absorbed in his psychoanalysis the author has found the blessing of a life work.

2

Schopenhauer*

ATTEMPT AT THE PSYCHOANALYSIS OF A PHILOSOPHER

> *Schopenhauer idealized compassion and chastity because he suffered most from their opposites.*
>
> —NIETZSCHE

PSYCHOANALYSIS has made several successful attempts to penetrate not only the psychic life of normal and neurotic people, but also the psychology of poets and artists. To some extent the philosopher belongs in this category. Not all philosophers can be considered exact scientists; the creative philosopher who builds his own system is far closer to the creative artist than the material with which he works would indicate. In the history of philosophy we repeatedly come upon independent spirits who feel the unconscious urge to construct their own system which would interpret the world and explain the mysteries of existence —and which according to their own conviction actually provides a definitive solution to these problems (metaphysicians). Every one of these creative philosophers had his followers and left his imprint on a certain era. In this respect the history of philosophy recalls the history of religion.

Only atheists are interested in the latter; and as we survey the various philosophic speculations that followed each other through thousands of years, we cannot help but feel skeptical towards all these systems which proved to be transitory after all. This transitoriness is revealed by the very fact that each philosopher disavows his predecessors, unless he can reach greater heights by standing on their shoulders. In the last analysis, this

* First published in *Imago*, Vol. 2, 1913.

transitoriness is explained by the fact that every product of the mind—if it is not the result of consequent scientific research—is permeated by the subjectivity of its creator and must show tendencies which of necessity have their source in the personality and psyche of the individual; this psyche, in turn, is the singular product crystallized out of heredity, disposition, and a particular era.

What all these philosophers have in common is—to put it briefly—their philosophizing; this peculiar, irresistible urge to devote their life and thoughts to the interpretation of the world, and the processes of coming into being and passing away of the individual as well as the cosmos; to gain recognition by teaching this interpretation to their fellow men—instead of living like ordinary human beings and taking for granted what life has to offer. The philosopher stops at those early problems of life which give the child cause to ponder: the problems of birth and death, good and evil, aim and purpose of one's own existence. These early subjects of childhood inquiry continue to occupy the philosopher; the researcher transfers his interest to another field and thus facilitates his social adjustment. The philosopher ponders life instead of "living" it.

Along with the transference to other fields, the scientist succeeds to a great extent in sublimating his infantile interests and inquisitiveness; the philosopher reveals by his endless doubting, searching, struggling, that he is never done with the primary problems and "suffers" from them all his life. Of course, there is no sharp demarcation line between these two types, but rather many shades in between. There have always been philosophers who devoted themselves mainly to epistemological science or to physical and mathematical problems, or took these as their point of departure; others merely used the methodology and findings of these sciences for their own purpose and remained faithful to the basic problems of philosophical thought. The psychoanalyst is familiar with other types of humanity, too: those who cannot cope with their instincts and psychic complexes, who cannot enjoy life like healthy people, and either succumb in the struggle as neurotics, or reach higher goals as poets and artists.

Child psychology has taught us that at a certain age the child, just like the philosopher, begins independently to investigate where he himself, and maybe his siblings, came from, i.e., the problem of the process of coming into being and passing away. This infantile instinct of inquisitiveness is later revived in a more intellectual form in the typical philosophic inclinations of the adolescent reaching manhood. In the philosopher, this quest seems to become fixated, just like any other phase of development may become fixed. In every philosopher we find mystical and artistic elements and, in some, neurotic features. This is also true of poets, and would point to a common origin of the abnormal or disproportionate configuration of instincts which, according to disposition and talents, may result in inferior or superior types of various categories. Freud explained the final outcome of this configuration in the following way: if that which is imperfectly repressed becomes manifest in symptoms and thus occasionally breaks through into consciousness, it leads to neurosis; if its flood overwhelms the consciousness, it leads to psychosis.

The artist has the good fortune to be able to express his unconscious wealth of fantasy in a manner that gives pleasure to himself and others. The philosopher is different. He, too, seeks to comprehend, in his struggle for psychic self-preservation, his inner strivings in general terms, valid for all mankind; but it does not fulfill his wishes directly, as the created world of fantasy does the poet's; he interprets the world in his own image so that his weakness as well as his superior strength is justified. Thus he achieves the satisfying and soothing feeling that he fits into this (his) world. He tries to integrate his basic disposition—be it optimistic or pessimistic—with the quality of the external world and projects his inner tensions upon the outside world in symbolic forms, often concealing them behind their opposites. "The philosopher himself decides not only the answers he will give, but also the questions he will ask"—indeed, questions and answers of the original thinker are "so much a unity within themselves, so much the intellectual expression of a self-sealed being that question and answer merely represent a subsequent division of the thought process" (Simmel, 1907). In this sense the originality of a system parallels the individuality of its creator.

Schopenhauer is an excellent example for everything said above. He is especially well suited to demonstrate the close connection between philosophy and personality, traced back to their instinctual roots. Hardly any other thinker shows so many peculiar and striking features in his nature and in his work (pessimism, asceticism, contempt for women). No other has—and we have his own testimony for this—so obviously created unconsciously and intuitively. He himself considered his philosophy a work of art. Hardly one other has so tenaciously and consistently held fast for the rest of his life to a system that was fully developed at the time of his early manhood. Few, if any, before him have thought and written so much about themselves. And since the days of antiquity no philosopher had considered the importance of sexuality—which we today recognize as the force that shapes the psyche—or treated it with such candor.

Almost all of Schopenhauer's predecessors had considered man as a rational being. Schopenhauer was the first to establish a fundamentally new concept. He emphasized and popularized his theory about the primacy of the blind driving will in the individual and in the world. This theory again can be traced back to his own overly powerful instinctual "Anlage." This has long been recognized by Schopenhauer's biographers, such as Volkelt, Paulsen, Moebius. It can also be shown that the dichotomy into Will and Idea stems from a deeply felt "duality in his own nature." Paulsen found this discord recurrent in all of Schopenhauer's philosophy. We can see the psychological source in the conflict between powerful instinctual urges and their repression by an intellectualizing counterinstinct (Denial of the will), and in the contrast between conscious and unconscious. It can further be shown that Schopenhauer's respect for asceticism and saintliness stems from his own sensuality which was so difficult to subdue; that his profound pessimism, the low esteem in which he held mankind and the world, came primarily from his own frame of mind; that his ethics of compassion are a reaction against his malicious and cruel nature; and, finally, that his longing for pure knowledge springs from despair about the continually torturing demon of passion.

The main purpose of this essay is to offer the most exact proof for these interrelationships. This cannot be done without giving an outline of Schopenhauer's life and a sketch of his character. We cannot ignore anything concerning his instinctual life which we have learned from him or about him; neither must we neglect his neurotic and eccentric traits. Then we shall attempt to trace his system to his personality—following it all the way to its instinctual roots—in as great detail as possible. This intriguing example will serve two purposes: it will prove the value of psychoanalytic investigation for the understanding of philosophic genius; and it will reveal Schopenhauer's intuitive recognition of the unconscious; he was a precursor of the psychoanalytic science.

HIS LIFE AND PERSONALITY

First of all, let me point out that the biographical data needed for a specific psychoanalytic investigation have to include not only incidents of events and environmental influences, but first and foremost the innate psychic forces that motivate the individual and the reactions they cause. Many a seemingly unimportant detail will acquire great significance through a shift in emphasis, as it were; a dream, a note tossed off on the spur of the moment, will provide an important clue; peculiarities, eccentricities, neurotic features, can be used as successfully as actual experiences if we know how to interpret psychological material. This is typical for the psychoanalytic approach. It presupposes a knowledge of psychic mechanisms. These mechanisms were first observed in sick people but could be verified for the most part in the average healthy person and applied to the gifted and to the genius. If this study is successful, "The individual's behavior is explained by the interaction of constitution and destiny, inner power and external forces" (Freud).

From this point of view, we psychoanalysts pay special attention to the generally neglected period of infancy, no matter how scanty the data may be. We take particular interest in the manifestations of instinctual life;[1] in the relationship to parents and siblings. This relationship which corresponds to the special characters and destinies of the parents, explains many of the later reactions better than the overrated heredity. Inherited characteristics are not the sole cause for a child's resemblance to his parents; out of love, the child wants to be like the parents. There is a form of imitation that is really an unconscious putting-oneself-in-their-place, an empathy which Freud called "identification." Another point that is frequently overlooked is the unconscious hostile attitude toward one parent which is prompted by love for a close relation, such as mother or sister. Later on, during adolescence, the original affection will return, often in exaggerated form.

The deepest and most lasting impression upon the child is, of course, made by the parents, by the loving mother and the seemingly almighty father. For the newborn infant these are giant figures who love him, nurture him, and punish him. Though this infantile attitude of love, respect, and overestimation is periodically replaced in the adolescent by the hostility that stems from childhood jealousy, and is destroyed by the reality figures of the parents, the unconscious retains that romantic childhood attitude in which the father is seen as a divine omnipotent ruler, the mother as a sublime gracious fairy. And yet, at the same time,

[1] Schopenhauer, too, subscribed to the prepsychoanalytic view that the child has no sexuality (cf. *The World as Will and Idea*, II): "The mischievous work of genitality is still dormant. Childhood is the period of innocence and happiness, the paradise of life because this evil-fraught instinct is absent. The basis for that happiness is the fact that in childhood our whole existence centers around perception rather than the will. This explains the child's clear, innocent gaze." For a psychoanalyst this view is nothing less than a proof of a very rich infant sexuality which has been repressed.

one or the other parent is also a hostile power because in the relationship of children to their parents sexual attraction and aversion come to the fore, in that the son loves the mother and sees in the father an intruder, while the daughter would like to belong to the father and finds this place already occupied by the mother.

Accordingly, objective reports about Schopenhauer's parents have their value, but a final analysis of his character can only be made by considering his own view of people and things.

The Family

If we start with an investigation of Schopenhauer's family background, we note first of all some prominent characteristics in his forebears. The most prominent is perhaps a vigorous, brutal energy, and a far-reaching, ruthless urge for action. Both the grandfather and the father show such drive for action, ambition, pride and efficiency. A violent disposition was evident in his paternal grandmother. Both she and a paternal uncle ended in insanity, while another was feeble-minded since youth. Heinrich Floris Schopenhauer, the father, was tall, strong, and ugly. As a child the son, who was below average height, thought him a giant. Later, he complained that in the course of his education he suffered much from his father's severity. The father had always been irascible and stubborn and became more and more irritable and violent with age; his pedantry was unbearable; occasionally he let himself go in violent outbursts, but it never took too long before he "regained his senses." At the age of fifty-eight he fell through a warehouse opening into a canal and was drowned. The son, as well as his biographers, suspected suicide.

At the age of thirty-eight he had married Johanna Trosiener, the daughter of an equally irascible, unmanageable, violent man who was an enterprising businessman. She was nineteen years his junior, and married the much older, ugly, though highly respected man after an unhappy love affair. She never really loved him, but she always spoke of him with respect. Descriptions of her vary from biographer to biographer, but it seems certain that she was intellectual rather than emotional, and that in her relationship with her children she always had her own interests in mind. As a widow she came to know many famous men and developed into an accomplished woman of the world. She discovered her talent as a writer, and wrote diaries and several novels that were well thought of at the time.

During their married life the couple showed a restlessness and an almost morbid desire to travel which seem to indicate a lack of contentment and happiness. The friends she made after her husband's death, the extensive social life she led, are evidence that in the somber marriage of convenience she had missed the gaiety and joy of life she had been used to in her parents' home. Her friends became more important to her than her son. One of her friends was a mediocre poet named Mueller, alias Gerstenberg, with whom she had been living since 1813, that is to say, she had rented him a part of her apartment and took her meals with him, just as she previously had done with von Fernow. Young Schopenhauer quarreled with Mueller, and his mother wrote him the "letter of farewell." It seems plausible that the son had accused his mother of immoral relations, though she was forty-seven at the time. Mueller, it is true, was only thirty-three. But this conflict between mother and son goes much farther back and at that time only reached a climax.

It seems certain that in the first period of maternal happiness the boy, who was born after three years of marriage, when the couple lived quietly in the country, received a great deal of tenderness from his mother, maybe even too much, especially since the mother was never completely satisfied by her marital life. It also seems certain that later the boy did not get enough affection at home, otherwise he would not have referred to the two years he spent with a business friend of his father in Havre (at the age of ten to twelve) as "by far the happiest" part of his childhood, as he did in his curriculum vitae. Three years later his parents sent him away again, for several months, this time to a British clergyman. His mother wrote him clever, pedagogical letters, but they clearly betray her irritation and dissatisfaction with her son's inflexible, vain, and brusque behavior;

they cannot have inspired a kindlier attitude toward his mother, especially since her criticism may have been at least partly justi- fied. Later letters, written at a time when he could at last indulge his scientific bent and his intellectual conceit was rapidly grow- ing, show a much stronger opposition to her son's nature. She could not help but admit that he possessed intellect, education and feelings, but she continued:

> All your good qualities are overshadowed by your over- bearing intellectualism which renders them useless for the world, and only because you cannot control the urge to know everything better, to find fault everywhere except in yourself, to improve and criticize everything. This attitude of superiority offends the people around you, for nobody likes to be improved and enlightened by force, least of all by such an unimportant individual as you are as yet. You, your- self, have still so many faults, and no one will stand for your finding fault with them, in your dogmatic, deprecating man- ner, when you announce like an oracle that this is the way it is, without even suspecting the existence of any objection [Gwinner].

When the nineteen-year-old Schopenhauer returned to Wei- mar, the question was raised whether he should stay with his mother. She refused:

> For my own happiness it is necessary to know that you are happy, but not to witness it. I have always told you how diffi- cult it would be to live with you, and the closer I watch you, the more it seems to me that these difficulties are growing— for me at least. I cannot help but admit that as long as you are the way you are, I would make every sacrifice, rather than live with you . . . I cannot agree with you on any- thing that concerns the outside world. Your ill humor de- presses me and is out of tune with my own gay spirit . . . every time you visited me even for a day we had violent scenes about nothing . . . and every time I started to breathe freely again only after you had left. I felt oppressed by your presence, by your complaints about things that are inevi- table, by your sombre mien, your bizarre opinions which you pronounce like the judgments of an oracle, without permitting any objections . . . You may dine with me on my

social evenings, if you can refrain from your unpleasant disputes which make me cross, and from your lamentations about the folly and misery of mankind [Gwinner].

Mother and son were simply not made for each other. "He reproached her with not honoring the memory of his father; he did not believe she ever loved him, and consequently could not believe in her love for him, either." He worried "That his father's estate might fall into his mother's hands and be squandered by her and that he, who did not feel qualified to earn a living, would be responsible for the care and support of his immediate relatives" (Gwinner).

When he was twenty-five and a doctor of philosophy, he again made an attempt to share his mother's apartment in Weimar; but he found no home there. At the slightest provocation violent scenes developed between mother and son, exceeding all bounds of decency, which finally led to a permanent break. It can be assumed that they never saw each other again, although the mother lived for another twenty-four years.

If we look at this growing aversion for her son, we have the right to conclude that there must have been some deep-seated differences in their personalities. The mother liked to display her own intellectual interest and superiority; she liked to be courted and admired. Oddly enough, she described one of her "dear friends" in a letter to her nineteen-year-old son: "If I wanted to go out, he escorted me; if I wanted to play chess, he played chess with me; if I wanted to be read to, he read to me; if I wanted to hear music, he sang and played the guitar; if I wanted to play 'quatre mains,' he played 'quatre mains' with me; if I wanted to paint, he sat for me; if I wanted to be alone, he left. I shall never again find such a *cicisbeo*." Certainly her morose, stubborn son, so vastly superior intellectually, and aware of this superiority, did not fill these requirements!

If we look at Schopenhauer's utterances about his mother, it seems hard to believe that he ever might have been an affectionate son, and yet there is reason to assume that in his earliest childhood he had been. Later on, according to R. v. Hornstein, he held her responsible for the father's suicide and for the family's financial decline. Full of irony he relates how his father approved of his wish to learn to play the flute; "but," he continues, "my poetic mother, the 'bel esprit' of Weimar, was opposed to my desire: 'some day he will have enough money to have somebody play the flute for him.'" When Schopenhauer heard L. Feuerbach's unfavorable comment on his mother: "A rich widow, she makes a profession of being erudite. A writer. She talks a great deal, and very well; is sensible; but has no heart or soul. Self-satisfied and eager for applause, smug"—he let it pass.

Schopenhauer's view that a person inherits the intellect from the mother, the will from the father, may have been based primarily on his own experience. Cultured, well read, literarily active, in constant touch with poets and men of letters, the mother most probably was originally a model for the boy; but later, under the influence of his growing hostility and the turning away from the maternal authority which offended his manly pride, he considered her a superficial blue-stocking. For in the meantime he had left *belles lettres* far behind, turning to serious scientific work. When he gave his mother his thesis "On the Fourfold Root of Sufficient Reason," she was not proud, as other mothers would have been, but said mockingly: that must be something for druggists. Hurt, Schopenhauer retorted that his works would still be read when there would hardly be a copy of her writings to be found in any attic. Whereupon her quick repartee was: "The entire edition of your works will still be available." His contempt for the mother image, polluted by suspicion of her faithlessness, grew to such an extent that it became impossible to live with her.

We can assume that this turning away from the mother was a reaction to his original love for her when the father, after his death for which she was partly to blame, became reinstated as the infantile ideal. A character such as Schopenhauer's cannot carry into manhood the dependence—with perhaps some masochistic coloring—on a person whom her sex rendered inferior in his eyes.

This impulse probably contributed to his generalization from the hatred for the mother to his hatred for women in general.

In advanced years Schopenhauer related that as a six-year-old child, while his parents were out for a walk, he was suddenly overcome by the fear that they might have abandoned him for ever. The very fact that he told this incident late in his life, shows the intensity of the experience. This anxiety feeling, which was frequently repeated, shows the child's ambivalent relation to his parents (the oedipus complex). Let me mention something at this point to which I shall refer later—that this childhood anxiety developed into neurotic anxiety and often manifested itself in his later life in morbid form.

In contrast to the mother, his stern father who insisted on having his way and was unyielding in his opposition to his son's plans, must have appeared as the enemy in early childhood. Schopenhauer's view that the world is created by a devil rather than a God, is associated with his impression of his father's severity. But in later utterances, the dead father appears again as the extravagantly praised ideal, the picture of a strong character, a provident, unforgettable man. We may assume that when Schopenhauer lost his father at the age of seventeen, he reacted to this event with a depression; that his love for the father was reactively strengthened, and that this was caused by remorse and guilt about his disobedience and lack of affection, and even hostile feelings and desire for revenge.[2]

Schopenhauer's Peculiar Character

Schopenhauer's peculiar character, with its oddities great and small, which is of course expressed in his work, has made his personality very familiar. If his work were not so impressive, if the grave, powerful and profound traits were not predominant and did not reveal such a strong, steadfast and impetuous person-

[2] It is in this light that we have to consider the enthusiastic, rapturous style of the drafts for a dedication to the second edition of his chief work. It is characteristic of the ambivalent attitude of the son toward the father that Schopenhauer was never satisfied with this dedication and kept changing and rewriting it—and in the end did not publish any one of these dedications.

ality, some of his characteristics might make him appear eccentric, even comical. We shall consider in detail especially that which is striking, eccentric, peculiar in him, those instances where his mode of life, his appearance, his social manners and customs deviated from the norm. It is part of the modern method to point out and interpret neurotic features in men of genius; we cannot indulgently overlook them.

Let us look at the boy as he spends his childhood in his refined home and on journeys undertaken with every comfort. We have sketched the picture of his parents; many reports tell us that the marriage was not very happy, beset by many quarrels; we may assume that a joyous mood rarely prevailed. The father's brusque, stern manner, which the son remembers even late in his life, must have weighed heavily on the house and on the boy. For this reason the two years he spent in Havre seemed to him the happiest time of his youth and he praises the man who took the place of a father as a "dear, kind, gentle man." "Obviously," says Moebius, "what made the boy happy was not only the real kindness he encountered there, but also the separation from his family; both his father's peculiarity and his mother's worldliness made life difficult for him." Moreover, the actual home life had frequently been disrupted by the many travels with his parents and by long sojourns in foreign cities. Even in his early childhood a melancholic brooding became noticeable, and a depression which he himself described as discholia.[3] This becomes clearly evident for the first time in his travel impressions. In 1807 his mother writes in a letter to him: "I know only too well that you had very little of the lightheartedness of youth and that a strong inclination to melancholic brooding was your sad share of your father's inheritance." At thirteen and fourteen the serious lad showed a passionate urge to study science which the father had to reckon with. He tried to win the boy over to the practical side of life by traveling ("my son shall learn from the

---

[3] In the beautiful chapter "On What Someone Is" in the *Aphorismen zur Lebensweisheit* surprisingly much space is given to the importance of the emotional predisposition of the individual for his life's happiness, which would point to Schopenhauer's own experiences.

book of life," he said).[4] But various impressions he received during his journey (1803) only intensified his dark moods. He visited the ruins of the Roman amphitheatre at Nîmes, and his thoughts were drawn, as he wrote in his diary, to the "thousands of human beings, long since decayed," and the brevity of human life. In the Bagno of Toulon the inexperienced youth was horrified at the fate of the convicts; another time he lost all pleasure in traveling when the carriage passed some wretched huts and debased human beings. These melancholy moods, the brooding over death and transitoriness which we find so often in the early history of neurotics have to be brought in close relation to Schopenhauer's morbid anxiety states which were manifest from his youth to his old age.

We know that he had attacks of anxiety when he was six years old. A mood of anxiety pervaded his whole life, and in later years feelings of anxiety overcame him not only during the day but in his dreams, too. Gwinner speaks of an almost manic anxiety which sometimes befell him for the most trivial reasons with such force that he experienced some most unlikely, barely possible misfortune as if it had actually happened. As a youth he was tormented by imagined illness and quarrels. While studying in Berlin, he thought for a time he had consumption. Fear of smallpox drove him from Naples, fear of cholera from Berlin. In Verona he was seized by the fixed idea that he had taken poisoned snuff. When he was about to leave Mannheim in 1833, he was overcome by an indescribable fear without any reason at all. For years he was haunted by fear of criminal action, of losing his property, of his inheritance being contested by his own mother. If there was some noise during the night, he would start up from his bed and reach for his sword and pistols which he always kept loaded. Without any apparent reason he was continuously worried and looked for and found dangers where none existed. In

---

[4] It might be conjectured that this remark, if it was made early, and left an impression on the boy, was misunderstood by him and gave him the impulse to turn to philosophy. Cf. Schopenhauer's words: "Scholars are those who derive their knowledge from books; but the thinkers, the men of genius are those who have learned directly from the book of life."

later years this morbid excitability seems to have diminished, but he did have relapses. He tormented himself and his surroundings with his suspiciousness. His valuables were so well hidden that despite the instructions he gave in his will in Latin, some articles were extremely difficult to find. Since his second journey to Italy, he kept his accounts in English and used Latin and Greek for important business notes. To guard against thieves he chose deceptive headings: his securities were labeled "arcana medica," the coupons of his dividends were kept in old letters and notebooks, and heavy gold pieces were hidden under the inkwell on his desk. He never entrusted himself to a barber's razor; he carried with him a leather vessel to avoid contagion when drinking water in public places. He locked away the mouthpieces and bowls of his pipes when they were not in use. Out of fear of being considered dead when in a trance, he stipulated that his remains be left unburied beyond the usual time.

A poem written at the age of twenty is very characteristic for these nocturnal anxiety feelings:

> In the middle of a stormy night
> I awakened in deep anxiety;
> I heard the storm rage and I heard the storm howl
> Through yards, through halls, and along the towers . . .
> I was seized by a great fear
> I felt so lost, so alone and forsaken
> In vain I sought to recall the joy
> We had felt only yesterday . . .

Another passage describes the experience and its application side by side:

> When in oppressive, horrible dreams anxiety reaches a climax, this in itself awakens us and all those monsters of the night vanish. The same is true of the dream of life, when the highest degree of anxiety forces us to end this dream [*Neue Paralipomena*].

Here anxiety is directly related to the fear of death. There is another passage in which the fear of death is described as life's terrible companion:

There are moments when death, if we concentrate our thoughts on it vividly, appears in such frightful shape that we cannot understand how it is possible to have even one peaceful minute with this prospect before us and that we do not spend our life in lamentations about the necessity of death [*Neue Paralipomena*].

Finally, let me quote the words of *Neue Paralipomena* which are extremely characteristic for the psychology of every victim of anxiety:

If I have nothing to make me anxious, then I become anxious about this very fact; for I feel there must be some cause, only it is hidden from me. Misera conditione nostra!

This anxiety began as pavor nocturnus, recurred in pathological anxiety equivalents, pervaded his dreams and accompanied and embittered his whole life. It has to be understood as a morbid manifestation which, according to medical observation, is closely connected with processes of repression of infantile sexuality. We are accustomed to relate such anxiety in childhood to the process of detachment from infantile self-gratification and repression of death and love wishes directed toward parents and siblings. We find it especially pronounced in people with a violent disposition that is inhibited toward the outside world and turned against the ego. Schopenhauer did have such a disposition. He himself reports about his childhood that his sexual drive was excessively strong; and he boasts about his extraordinarily hot temper (Gwinner). A poem he wrote when he was eighteen shows clearly how much he suffered from this powerful instinct. It mirrors the struggle against the sensuality he felt to be reprehensible.

O sensual delight, O inferno, O love, insatiable and unconquerable. From heaven's heights you have drawn me, and thrown me down into the dust of this earth. Here I lie in chains. How I yearn to soar to the throne of the Eternal, be reflected and mirrored in the noblest thought, be cradled

in fragrance, fly through space, filled with devotion, filled
with wonder . . . But thou, bond of weakness, thou draw-
est me down, thy myriad threads constrict me, and all my
upward striving is in vain [*Neue Paralipomena*].

From numerous passages in his private notes, letters and other
writings, the biographer Damm concludes "how enormously
Schopenhauer suffered from this secret scourge, how conscious
he was that a passion for the female sex, for sensual pleasures
repeatedly enchained him and threw a dark shadow over his
character . . . Even in his youth he sought to overcome these
instincts: now he plunged zealously into his business commitments, now he tried to find diversion in reading . . . in attend-
ing theatres and concerts, in playing the flute, in long walks and
in sailing. But nature asserted itself. Finally he was overpowered
by disgust at the whole existence and sank into deeper and deeper
melancholia." Throughout his life he suffered from this "demon" and it was "with jubilant joy that I greeted the beginning
of that stage of life when the desires have gone to sleep" and he
is redeemed. An analogy suggests itself here with the need for redemption that plays such a great role in his philosophy. The
strong sense of guilt is in keeping with this strong instinct, and
this, as we shall see, forms part of the basis for his pessimistic
Weltanschauung. Schopenhauer remarked that the sexual instinct, missing in childhood, darkens life in later years:

> This instinct annuls that carefree, joyous and innocent
> nature . . . for it carries unrest and melancholia into our
> consciousness, accidents, worry and distress.

We are accustomed to trace the guilt feeling that is closely
connected with anxiety to the evil wishes which issue from the
oedipus complex and are directed toward parents and siblings.
These guilt feelings are intensified by the threats with which the
authority—the parents—opposes masturbation. Such a threatening attitude may be assumed in the case of Schopenhauer's stern
father. The youth apparently did not have his fantasies under
control. Incidentally, even at the age of sixteen the father had to

reproach him with his bad posture. With the secrecy and avidity common to those years, Schopenhauer devoured a great amount of poetry and novels, obviously with a bad conscience. "You are now fifteen years old," his mother once wrote him, "you have read and studied the best of the German and French and some of the English poets. Yet outside of your classroom work, you have not read a single book of prose, except a few novels, no history, nothing that you did not have to read in order to pass Herr Runge's courses . . . I would see you become anything rather than a so-called 'bel-esprit.' " Perhaps Arthur had read more novels than she thought, Moebius continues. "Schopenhauer told K. Baehr that at the age of fourteen, with the help of the key to his chest of drawers, he had gotten the novel *Faublas* out of his father's library. At night, sitting on his bed, he was buried in it, when his father entered unexpectedly, on the way to his wife's bedroom.—'Both caught in the act.'—Later, Schopenhauer often warned young people against reading novels. He must have felt the unfortunate results." The psychically significant struggle between sexual instinct and ego instinct may have played an important role in Schopenhauer's character formation and in his intellectual aims, both during puberty and in later years.[5]

The sexual abstinence for which he strove later in his life and from which he departed only periodically led in turn to an intensification or continuation of his anxiety, and that again found expression in the various already mentioned phobias: in strikingly exaggerated precautions against overrated dangers, particularly against disease and death. The subject of the fleetness and transitoriness of time and especially of death have always stimulated philosophers. Schopenhauer has realized it out of his own experience when he said:

Without doubt it is the knowledge of death, and with it the contemplation of life's suffering and distress which gives the strongest impulse for philosophic reflection and meta-

[5] It is interesting to note that he prided himself on a good memory during the first twelve years of his life. Why not later on? we must ask.

physic interpretation of the world [*The World as Will and Idea*, II].

And that is why Schopenhauer rightly says that death is the real musagete of philosophy.[6]

The exciting experiences of frequent travels could not pull this serious and brooding boy out of his dark moods. He remained introverted, and even at the age of twelve showed a burning love for scientific knowledge and a strong predilection for a scholarly career. After the death of his father he remained in a business career for two more years (Freud calls it "retrospective obedience"); then he could at last devote himself to science. He showed the noblest zeal and desire for knowledge, devoured countless volumes. Soon he had made up for lost time and laid a thorough foundation for philological and philosophical studies. In his twentieth and twenty-first years he began deliberately to occupy himself with those serious and profound subjects which he later treated in detail in the fourth volume of his major work. It is understandable that Schopenhauer who even in his youth had the bearing of a philosopher—"Youth paired with philosophy, always a paradox," says Moebius—was not very successful with the female sex, for instance, his sister's friends. As Moebius puts it, "He just wasn't their dish." Schopenhauer himself said: "In my youth the neglect I experienced in a society which favored the pedestrian, the commonplace and trivial, made me doubt my own worth." If we summarize Schopenhauer's state of mind at that time, we can understand the answer he gave Wieland when the latter advised him not to study only philosophy because it was not a sound and solid branch of learning: "Life is a doubtful business. I have resolved to spend it in reflecting upon it" (April, 1811).

We must not imagine, though, that Schopenhauer's outward life at that time was very different from that of other students.

---

[6] "Death is really the inspiring genius, the musagete of philosophy. That is why Socrates calls it the ξανατου μελετη. If it were not for death, people would hardly philosophize." (*Ueber den Tod und sein Verhaeltnis zur Unzerstoerbarkeit unseres Wesens an sich*, II, p. 542.)

His financial independence,[7] the achievement of his intellectual goals, the stimulating life in Weimar seem to have made him more sociable. His pessimism and depressive moods which had persisted since childhood were temporarily lifted with the help of various diversions, such as sport and social gatherings. We shall find one other period in his life which broke the seclusion that was his destiny, around the age of thirty when his major work was completed and he journeyed to Italy. At that time he wrote these triumphant verses:

> From long cherished and deeply felt pain
> It wound its way up from my inmost heart.
> I have long struggled to hold it fast:
> Yet I know that I have succeeded at last.
> You may behave from now on as you will:
> You can never endanger the life of my work.
> You can delay it; destroy it, never:
> Posterity will build me a monument!

It is a sign of his intellectual ambitiousness that a climax in his studies, in the progress of his work, can bring him close to joy of life. For years he had been chained to the counting house against his will. Now that he could plunge wholeheartedly into the great field of the sciences, a golden age had dawned. His interest and his diligence were admirable. He had excellent teachers and advisors to help him; his extraordinary gift for languages proved useful to him; and it can be assumed that even at that time his ideal was to be at home in every branch of knowledge so that he might one day serve the queen of all sciences. His interest in the natural sciences, probably including hygiene (which may have stemmed from his hypochondria), made him turn for a while toward medicine. It was the advice of his teacher and adviser, Professor G. E. Schulze, which gave the decisive direction to these general all-embracing studies which occupied Schopenhauer at that time. He encouraged him to become a philosopher

---

[7] At twenty-one his mother gave him his father's inheritance in full. This must have seemed to him sufficient for a comfortable income for life. This material independence which coincided with the independence from his mother must have increased his self-confidence.

and urged him to concentrate in the beginning exclusively on
Plato and Kant. In Berlin Schopenhauer threw himself into
philosophy with renewed zeal and began to withdraw socially.
He renounced the thought of establishing a home, having wife
and children, and lived for one goal only: to complete his work.
His thesis *On the Fourfold Root of the Principle of Sufficient
Reason* moved one critic to conclude that it was the young philosopher's intention to "make ethics the basis of all philosophy."
But Schopenhauer's plans were far more ambitious and his main,
his life's work began to take shape within him. It was to be a
philosophy not scientifically constructed but created through an
intuitive view of the world, a work of art rather than a work of
science. Schopenhauer has often described the joy of feeling
something great and precious grow inside him as akin to that of
a proud young mother. Thus he clearly showed to all those who
still believe that a philosopher figures out and constructs the
basic teachings of his system, that a philosophic structure can
develop just as unconsciously as a daydream or a work of art. This
is best proven by the fact that the youthful concept of his main
work—he himself called it his life's work—remained the definitive one and that all his subsequent working and thinking ad-
hered rigidly to this concept and served only to develop, elaborate, confirm and justify the basic principles. His young manhood
was the only truly creative period of his life, when he bore the
intellectual offspring that was worthy of him. He devoted the
rest of his life to protect, nurture and defend it. Quiet and leisure
were the fertile soil for the creation of this child and its defense
for decades. Let us picture Schopenhauer in his study, surrounded by the works of Plato and Kant, a bust of Socrates and
a picture of Goethe, and it strikes us that even at that time he
preferred his poodle to human friends. There may have been
occasional discussions among colleagues, and at such occasions
Schopenhauer behaved with brusque self-confidence. But in general he avoided all social, familial or organizational ties, allegedly because he considered them inconvenient and disagree-

able, but probably for the deeper, unconscious reasons of his asocial nature, his resistance to any association. He conditioned himself for permanent bachelordom. Even though he remained a bachelor—it has often been stressed that the unmarried state is a peculiarity of philosophers, cf. especially Nietzsche in his treatise *The Meaning of Ascetic Ideals*[8]—it may be pertinent to make a few remarks about Schopenhauer's love life, refuting both the widely held opinion that he never had anything to do with women, and Lombroso's unjustified and irresponsible assertion of the greatest sexual excesses. In contrast to his own statement that his overly powerful sexual instinct was a demon which never gave him rest until he was advanced in years, we know with certainty only of a few passing love affairs; he did not enter any of these without toying, theoretically at least, with the idea of marriage. He confided a great deal in his letters to his sister, and from her diary we know that his mistress in Dresden became pregnant. It is said, incidentally, that he behaved in an honest and straightforward manner. "Tender bounds tied him to Miss Medon, a member of the court theatre in Berlin . . . that he remembered her thirty years later with a considerable legacy speaks for the depth of his affection" (Damm).

Love and the thought of marriage were on Schopenhauer's mind when he was in Venice. For years, Italy had been the dazzling goal of his wishful dreams, and when he journeyed there after completing his work, he was hungry for life and probably also for love. The love affairs he engaged in in Italy, Moebius sums up as follows: "Aside from purely sexual affairs, Schopenhauer became involved in a relationship with a lady of society which might have culminated in marriage." And Adele writes: "His beloved is rich, she is even a lady of quality." Gwinner says: "We know of his inner struggles, of his fight against such temptation from casual notes he made in the English language. The general content of these notes, however, is such that it would

---

[8] Schopenhauer mentions, in comparing himself with them, that all true philosophers have been unmarried, such as Cartesius, Leibnitz, Malebranche, Spinoza and Kant. Socrates' suffering is well known; and Aristotle was a courtier.

not be proper to divulge it." Schopenhauer himself revealed how despite his aversion against a permanent union with that woman —or perhaps because of it—his sensuality, often ungratified, easily inundated his imagination so that he was hardly able to enter into a spiritual relationship with any woman. He wrote his sister that she was the only woman he had ever loved without sensuality.

This is not the place to go into the details of the psychology of bachelors. Much of what has been said here shows that Schopenhauer was utterly unsuited for marriage. He knew quite well that "man's fate is determined by nature: work by day, rest by night, and very little leisure; and man's happiness: wife and child who are his comfort in life and death." But he continued with this self-consolation:

> When an abnormal talent creates great intellectual needs which bring with them the possibility of deep intellectual satisfaction, then unrestricted leisure becomes the prime condition for happiness, and the ordinary human happiness with wife and child has to be voluntarily sacrificed to it.
>
> [In another passage he said:] Most men are enticed by a pretty face; for nature induces them to take a wife by showing a woman suddenly from her most attractive side, concealing the many drawbacks that go with it, such as the endless expenses, worries about children, obstinacy, caprice, growing old and ugly after a few years, deceit, attacks of hysteria, taking lovers and cuckolding their husbands, in short, the very devil. Marriage may be called a debt which is incurred in youth and paid in old age . . . Most men spend their days to earn free leisure for their wives. The philosopher needs this leisure for himself. The married man carries the full burden of life, the bachelor only half of it.

The unconscious but real motives are the rejection of sexuality and the anxiety connected with it. The bad example of his parents' marriage, among other reasons, combined with his innate asocial attitude and his need for solitude to keep him from ever getting married. It is not likely that Schopenhauer had any insight into these inhibitions. Rather he tried to find secondary intellectual reasons for them, i.e., he rationalized them. He all too clearly betrays fear of being deceived, fear of being weakened physically, financial sacrifices, etc. The decision could only be negative if we consider his sensitivity, his intellectualism, his sense of independence, his resolve to live frugally, without working, on his meager income, and, last but not least, his disparaging view of the female sex—even though that last is partly a secondary feature. The hated and despised image of his mother, or at least the ambivalent attitude of the son toward her, must surely have played a decisive role. Another feature which points in the same direction was his peculiar attitude toward women and his fellow men.

A trained psychoanalyst who knows about the generally bisexual anlage in all individuals, will assume that there was a rather strong homosexual component in Schopenhauer. This is evidenced in his resistance to a union with a woman, to a poor opinion of the female sex, and his disparagement of the sexual act (cf. Lindner and Frauenstaedt, 1863, pp. 393, 394). He refrained completely from intercourse with men and thus has to be classed as what Freud calls *"ideell"* homosexual. As proof for this assumption, the following important facts have to be considered. Schopenhauer found the body of a woman ugly, that of a youth most beautiful.

In *Parerga und Paralipomena,* Vol. II, "On Women" he wrote:

> Only the male intellect befogged by its sexual urge could regard as beautiful the undersized, narrow-shouldered, broad-hipped, short-legged sex. Its only beauty lies in this urge. It would be more to the point to call this sex not the fair but the unesthetic sex.

In *Metaphysik der Geschlechtsliebe* he speaks of youths "who really represent the highest human beauty."[9]

[9] If we feel justified in taking this statement as an indication for unconscious homosexual tendencies, we are not overlooking the fact that aesthetes have often decided the question of an objective beauty ideal in favor of the male sex.

In a letter to Frauenstaedt, containing a critique of his book *Aesthetische Fragen,* he wrote:

> A perfect woman is more beautiful than a perfect man,—quae qualis, quanta! Here you have given an extremely naive confession of your sexual urge . . . Wait until you have reached my age, and see what you will then think of these short-legged, long-torsoed, narrow-shouldered, broad-hipped, teat-bedecked creatures; even their faces are as nothing compared to those of the most handsome youths, and their eyes are listless.

B. Friedlaender, in *Die Renaissance des Eros Uranos,* referring to this passage, rightly said:

> In my opinion, anyone who judges like Schopenhauer is, so to speak, an aesthetic homosexual. Other utterances about women, about their psyche and intellect, breathe the same spirit . . . and this demonstrates a psychically homosexual tendency, if one can call it that. For it is obvious that somebody who thinks and feels like that must prefer an intimate relationship with a youth to that with a woman. [Friedlaender even conjectures that] the hostility to life, the refined peevishness, in short the pessimism of the great thinker, might it not have had its deepest roots in an uranic predisposition that remained ungratified? . . . Only the uninitiated could cite the temporary, purely sensual relationships with women as counterargument.

As complementary arguments we may cite Schopenhauer's aversion to bearded males and his remarks about the obligation to conceal the genitals (which will be quoted later). He objected to beards as ugly and bestial. In *Parerga und Paralipomena* he says:

> As an external symptom of the increasingly prevalent coarseness you see the beard, its concomitant—the long beard, this badge of sex worn right in the face, which clearly says that the masculinity that is shared with the animals is preferred to humanity . . . In all highly civilized ages and countries beards were shaved off, out of the opposite and correct feeling . . . All hairiness is bestial. A clean-shaven face is the mark of higher civilization.

Schopenhauer belonged to the not rarely occurring type of men who are comparatively reserved sexually. This reserve together with some other minor traits shows repressed homosexual tendencies. That Schopenhauer derisively rejected in advance the homosexuality which might be ascribed to him by his opponents cannot be considered a valid counterargument against this assumption. In an appendix to his *Metaphysics of Sexual Love* he devoted a special section to pederasty. He interpreted it teleologically as a frequent phenomenon of old age and early youth through which nature aims to forestall the propagation of degenerate offspring. At the end he justifies the writing of that section with this ironical statement: he "wanted to do the professors of philosophy a favor by providing them with an opportunity to slander me by saying I championed pederasty and recommended it."

We may further point to Schopenhauer's own statement about the development of his main work in which he saw himself in a feminine motherly role, "pregnant" with his work as a mother with child. "I look at it, and I say, like a mother: 'I am blessed with the fruit of my own being'" (*Neue Paralipomena*). This picture corresponds to the assumption of passive homosexuality which we often see develop as a consequence of excessive love for the feared father. In Schopenhauer's case this unconscious homosexuality may have been intensified by his rejection of women (i.e., the mother). But whereas other people sublimate their repressed homosexuality in feelings of friendship and social relationships, we find that during long periods of his life Schopenhauer rejected even such relationships with his surroundings which in a wider sense stem from the libido. Only in his old age he was surrounded by a small circle of intellectual followers. All his life he shunned all organized groups. His misanthropy was expressed with no less violence and exaggeration than his misogyny. This shows that Schopenhauer was always inhibited in transferring his libido to other people. We find only a few exceptions in passing friendships during his boyhood and youth.[10] Without a friend, without a wife, without social links, aloof, without any impulse to give to or to receive from the rest of mankind, he went his lonely way, a deeply unhappy man in this respect, shrouded in his pride and in his contempt for humanity, a contempt which stemmed from resentment and served as consolation in his solitude.

After an eleven-month sojourn in Italy the alarming news of a financial crisis which threatened the family fortunes reached him in Milan. His mother had lost the greater part of her and her daughter's money. He immediately wrote to his sister that he would be willing to share with her and his mother the little that remained to him. They never availed themselves of this offer. He nevertheless decided to apply for a position as *Privatdozent* (unsalaried lecturer who receives only his students' fees). His pronounced instinct for property, his efficiency in business and his obstinacy succeeded in preserving his own property intact. But the consequence of this epistolary conflict was an estrangement between brother and sister which lasted for ten years. His position as *Dozent* ended in failure. His opponent Hegel was at the zenith of his fame and Schopenhauer behaved with his customary rudeness. This experience provided him with what were for him justified reasons for depression and distrustful pessimism. Another adequate reason was that his life's work remained without recognition for decades. The years following this interrupted Italian journey Schopenhauer moved his domicile from city to city. In 1825 he returned to Berlin. In 1833 the cholera drove him away and he settled for good in Frankfurt am Main. There he ended his days, a familiar figure in the town, a world-famous celebrity, visited by many.

In general Schopenhaur had a sound physical constitution, was a good sleeper and hearty eater, vigorous and active into old age. Once, at the age of thirty-five, he had a protracted illness about which nothing definite is known. He often complained

10 Cf. a dream of the forty-two-year-old Schopenhauer about "his bosom friend and constant playmate," Gottfried Jaenisch, who had died at the age of ten (*Neue Paralipomena*).

about it and blamed on it his early gray hair and his weak nerves (neurasthenia). The nature of this illness gave rise to a scientific controversy between Ivan Bloch and Wilhelm Ebstein. Bloch sees in Schopenhauer's secret notes and in a few other facts proof that it was a severe syphilis in the tertiary stage (the primary stage would have been in 1813).[11] Ebstein, however, denies the cogency of this proof. He believes that the illness involved is the one described in one of Schopenhauer's letters to one of his oldest friends, Osann: hemorrhoids with fistula, gout and a nervous condition. There were no further aftereffects later in his life, and he died at the age of seventy-two after a short illness following a heart attack.

Like many other personalities, Schopenhauer became a popular figure through portraits of him as an old man. His serious, furrowed face with tufts of white hair on both sides of the powerful, domed skull belongs to the most striking pictures of famous Germans. He was a familiar figure in the streets of Frankfurt, striding along stormily on his frequent walks, in his old-fashioned clothes, talking to himself or uttering inarticulate sounds, stamping the ground with his stick, his poodle always at his side. There, he lived as a stranger to a greater extent than he had in his other places of residence. He ate at a restaurant, usually alone at a table, and hardly ever struck up a conversation with people around him—another sign of his misanthropy. But once a conversation appealed to him, he would sit up far into the night and enjoyed to philosophize. Many of his contemporaries extol his serious discourses, free from obscenity and banality. Even on those occasions he liked to be didactic. With deep psychological insight Gwinner reflects on the strange feeling "of listening to somebody speak about A equals A with an expression on his face as if he were talking to his beloved about love." Just as we see eccentric and pedantic traits in his relationships with others,

---

[11] Bloch finds in the venereal disease "one of the sources of Schopenhauer's ascetic philosophy and his pessimism."—We subscribe to this opinion, even in the event that he did not really have syphilis; he quite obviously suffered from fear of syphilis. Cf. Schopenhauer's own statement: "Venereal disease is a very useful curb which keeps the sexual instinct from gaining excessive power over mankind."

we find the same if we follow him to his home. In the morning he is intent on preserving an "optimum" of intellectual concentration: he must not be disturbed, not even his housekeeper is allowed near him. His room is soberly furnished except for a gilded statue of Buddha enthroned on a marble console. Portraits of Kant, Shakespeare, Descartes and Goethe hung on the walls—next to pictures of dogs! The poodle he owned for the fourteen years of his life in Frankfurt had two names: a secular one and another, more esoteric one for private occasions; he called him Atma, the World-Soul.

Summing up Schopenhauer's character we have to admit that Fichte's criticism of the *Parerga* which he wrote in 1850, unjust as it was in all other respects, was not far wrong in its characterization of the nature of Schopenhauer's personality. Fichte said that Schopenhauer had to be considered as a pathological psychological problem, "a riddle which could only be solved by personal acquaintance." It is strange how divergent the descriptions of Schopenhauer's character are. The reason for this may be that his works make an entirely different impression from the details of his biography, especially if the less public utterances of his letters and private notes are taken into consideration.

We shall see that the fundamental principles he advocated in his writings were by no means direct consequences of his own qualities, but rather reaction formations. Thus it becomes understandable that this champion of compassion is described as an obstinate, violent, distrustful man, quick to condemn; even by his pathographer, Moebius, who loved him personally. Von Sedlitz, who overestimated Schopenhauer's pathology, states that his detractors called his intellectual excesses fanatical self-praise, truly ugly moods, irreverent ambition, contempt for humanity, uncharitableness, brutality, and rabid propaganda against Western culture, civilization and religion.

In his pamphlet *Schopenhauer as Miseducator*, Graf Keyserling depicts the drawbacks of this "little man" who, to be sure, was a great mind. Keyserling calls him a decidedly practical man with the features of an enterprising businessman, a tough, strong man of action, ruthlessly living his own life; a rigid character, inflexible to a fantastic degree; riddled with contradictions, racked by passion, unharmonious, tormented, full of small, ugly traits, undistinguished, filled with resentment, repellent in his petty egotism and cynicism, deficient in his emotional life—a crippled soul. He did not succeed in conquering his odd individuality, his ideals remained forever beyond his grasp. This judgment may come from an unsympathetic individual; we have to record it nevertheless. But we must also remember that in a higher sense Schopenhauer was honest, true and unselfish; and that from his writings he emerges as a profound, inspired and brilliant thinker, a man with a noble view of life and of the world, an advocate of the idealistic demands on man, of everything that is spiritual and artistic. On the other hand, we have to reject those biased judgments which stress a particularly noble character or particular emotional depth in Schopenhauer. For he derived his strongest impulses, his main energy from that brutal, hard-hitting, violent disposition which he endeavored to overcome in his ethics.

There is a rift in the personality and in the work of this man who came from vigorous, active, practical forebears who defiantly had made their way in life, and who through a whim of fate had to content himself with sitting behind books and wielding a pen. Because I agree with it, I would like to cite here the opinion of the phrenologist Scheve after he had examined Schopenhauer's skull. He found the "organ responsible for the sense of action" most pronounced. According to this highly questionable theory, the sexual instinct was also strongly developed. Moebius, a follower of Gall, even believed that the skull showed a special instinct for destruction, similar to that which can be found in the skulls of murderers, though in Schopenhauer it became manifest only as unscrupulous and inconsiderate energy.

Schopenhauer once wrote in a secret note: "The guiding maxim of my life was to want as little as possible and to know as much as possible."

It would be interesting to speculate on the interconnection be-

tween violent temperament, suppressed aggression, cruelty, on
the one hand, and intellectual and artistic creativity on the
other. We would have to bring in the concept of sublimation.
But we must forego the further pursuit of the subject of creativity at this point.

AN INTERPRETATION OF
SCHOPENHAUER'S BASIC PHILOSOPHIC PROBLEMS

Before we proceed to apply the insights we have gained from
studying the biographical and characterological details to an
understanding of the origins of Schopenhauer's philosophy, we
have once more to define our task most clearly. We want to
avoid the impression that we intend to evaluate or to interpret
Schopenhauer's work in its entirety. We are going to consider
only the basic principles, the *Leitmotive* as it were, which aside
from the *Erkenntnistheorie* contain what is most objectively
valuable and lasting in his theory—and we believe we have good
reasons to do so. It is no coincidence that the few fundamental
pillars of his theory lend themselves most readily to psychological explanations since they are based upon the individual fate of
the psyche. Our survey will primarily attempt to give a psychological genesis of the basic thoughts of Schopenhauer's philosophy. This does not mean that we intend to judge and evaluate
his *Erkenntnistheorie*, his ethics and metaphysics, much less to
criticize them. It is not our task to probe the content of truth in a
philosophy, least of all that of a metaphysical system, but to answer the following question: why does a man solve precisely this
problem and in precisely this way? We want to explore the psychological hypothesis and the particular motives for philosophizing—and philosophizing in just such a manner. We want to practice individual psychology on a truly great man because his work
tempts us to do so and because, due to his fame, the details of his
life are known to us. That is our task. We do not claim to be
philosophers. We do not practice some general psychology—we
practice psychoanalysis.

The Theory of the Will

Schopenhauer's lasting contribution was the discovery of the will as "Thing in itself" (*Ding an sich*).[12] Man becomes conscious of his deepest nature by intuition. The will is "the inner, true and indestructible being of man . . . the only metaphysical and therefore indestructible part of man." Schopenhauer's will is not the conscious will, it is something new, it is an obscure, blind will, not guided by the intellect. Schopenhauer has broadened the concept of the will, the will in the usual sense is only one part of this new will. Schopenhauer's will is an urge, a sort of will to live, an instinct in the widest sense of the term. In Schopenhauer's system this will is not attributed only to conscious beings, it is manifest in nonhumans, even in the inorganic world. We shall see that the blindness of this will is one of the main arguments for Schopenhauer's pessimism. He sees the individual as an objectivation of this will. This will contains the urge to manifest itself in individuals, in species, and in ideas. This will is most evident in our passions, in our desires, and its most characteristic manifestation is in the "violent and dark urges," the sexual instinct. Schopenhauer quite rightly dealt extensively with sexuality, as he stressed in his introduction to *The Metaphysics of Sexual Love:*

> Instead of being astonished that for once a philosopher takes up this eternal subject of all poets, one should rather be astonished that something which plays such an important role throughout life should until now have been virtually disregarded by philosophers [*The World as Will and Idea,* II].

Schopenhauer considers the sexual instinct as the strongest and most concentrated manifestation of the will. This can be seen in several extremely characteristic passages, especially in the second volume of the main work, and in scattered outlined notes of a later period. But we find this view expressed even in his main work which was conceived in his youth:

---

[12] Concerning earlier, similar views by others, cf. Lindner and Frauenstaedt. (1863, pp. 251, 253).

It follows that the genitals are the real focus of the will, and consequently the opposite pole of the brain, that representative of perception and as such, of the other side of the world, the world as idea. The genitals are the life-preserving principle, ensuring time its eternal life. In this capacity they were revered by the Greeks in the phallus, by the Hindus in the lingam, which are thus symbols of the affirmation of the will. Knowledge on the other hand, makes possible the annulment of the will, redemption through freedom, conquest and annihilation of the world [*The World as Will and Idea*, I].

In later supplements to the main work, Schopenhauer enlarged upon the far-reaching importance of sexuality:

These observations explain why sexual desires have a different character than all other desires; it is not only the strongest, but specifically of a more powerful kind than all other desires. It is always tacitly presumed to be necessary and unavoidable and is not like other wishes a matter of tastes and moods. For it is the wish itself which determines the nature of the individual. In a conflict with this desire, no motive is so strong that it can be sure of victory. It is the main concern to such an extent that no other gratifications can compensate for the lack of its satisfaction: man and beast alike will risk any danger, any struggle for its sake . . . consistent with all this is the important part which sexual relations play in the world of man, where it is really the invisible center of all activity and all conduct, and despite all the veils that are thrown over it, it peeps through everywhere. It is the cause of war and the aim of peace, it is the foundation of seriousness and the aim of the joke, the inexhaustible source of wit, the key to all allusions and the meaning of all secret hints, of all unspoken proposals and of every stealthy glance, the daily fantasy and aspiration of youth and often of old age, the hourly thought of the unchaste and, against his will, the recurring dream of the chaste, the ever ready material for a joke, just because profound seriousness is at the bottom of it . . . And all this stresses the fact that the sexual instinct is the essence of the will to live, and thus the concentration of every act of the will; and that is why I have called the genitals the focus of the will. One can even say that man is the sexual instinct personified; for he comes into being by an act of copulation and his essential desire is for an act of copulation, and this instinct perpetuates and holds together his very being . . . Therefore the sexual instinct is the most perfect expression of the will to live, the most clearly manifest type: and both the origin of the individual from it, and its predominance over all other desires, are in complete harmony with this [*The World as Will and Idea*, II].

In the posthumous *Neue Paralipomena* which are so important for a greater understanding of his theory and his personality, we find the following passage:

If I am asked where can the most intimate knowledge be found of this inner nature of the world, that thing in itself, which I have called the will to live? or where does this nature become most clearly conscious? or where is the purest manifestation of its self?—then I have to point to the sensual pleasure in the act of copulation. There it is! That is the true nature, the real essence of all things, the aim and the purpose of all existence.

And similarly in *Parerga und Paralipomena:*

If in our view of the world we take the thing in itself, the will to live, as our point of departure, then we shall find its essence, its greatest concentration in the act of procreation: that is primary, that is the point of departure: it is the *punctum saliens* of the egg of the world and its main concern.

Schopenhauer was the first philosopher who recognized and stressed the general importance of sexuality. The motivation for this recognition can be found in his own constitution, in his own personality, in his own, previously mentioned, powerful sexual instinct. We have seen from his poem "O Sensual Pleasure, O Inferno," how much he suffered from it. This fact explains much in his nature as a reaction formation and sublimation, as a yearning to be liberated from this tormenting urge.

While we have found behind Schopenhauer's "irrational will" first of all his own vehement, impelling sexual instinct, we are well aware—and thus intend to forestall the objections of some readers—that Schopenhauer's will which he felt as an active, instinctual urge within himself, embraces more than just sexuality: every desire, every hope, every wish, every anxiety and every hatred. He sensed that dark unconscious which we feel to be behind every single act of our psyche, an energy which supports and carries everything but at the same time reaches beyond it. "Though we know what we want in any given moment, we never know completely what we want and why we want it," to quote the philosopher, Simmel. Schopenhauer's will is a dark, blind, and really unrecognizable ruling force behind our consciousness, behind our knowledge and our will—it is that which we psychoanalysts call the unconscious. At the end of this essay we will discuss the fact that Schopenhauer was the first to recognize the unconscious in the psychoanalytic sense, the unconscious which continuously drives and desires.

Confronted with the strong emphasis Schopenhauer put on this will in his life and in his work, the superficial observer must consider it a contradiction that the very man who discovered and admired this strong will to live, later on glorified the denial of this will (quietism). Such an objection has indeed been raised repeatedly by pupils and critics. Psychologically, however, it can easily be explained by the conflict within the human psyche, the struggle between the primal instincts and those inhibitions with which the ego of the civilized person opposes them. This opposition and repression is directed mostly against the sexual and the grossly egotistic instincts; consequently, the struggle is most manifest in these. At the same time, this struggle becomes the pattern for the whole attitude of a personality toward instinct and reaction and toward the outside world in general. The psychoanalyst, therefore, is least surprised if a person who shows strong instincts also shows strong tendencies to repress them.

As far as sex is concerned, only that man approaches Schopenhauer's ideal who renounces the ugly, objectionable sexual gratification which is the curse of mankind at the very root of life.

The gratification of the sexual instinct is objectionable as such because it constitutes the strongest affirmation of life [*Neue Paralipomena*].

In connection with this is the repellent and ugly impression which the sexual act and the genitals made on Schopenhauer:

. . . what the enamoured condition deludes us with is, as long as it is only a prospect and something in the future, a paradise of bliss; but once it is past and one looks back on it, it reveals itself as insignificant and unimportant, if not downright disgusting [*Neue Paralipomena*].

It follows that one ought to hide one's will just as one's genitals, although the two are the roots of our nature [*Parerga und Paralipomena*, II].

The act through which the will affirms itself and through which man comes into being is an act of which all are ashamed in their inmost heart, which they, therefore, carefully conceal; yes, if they are caught at it, they are frightened, as if they were caught in a crime. It is an act which, on somber reflection, one usually recalls with repugnance, in a more exalted mood even with abhorrence. . . . A strange sadness and remorse follow the performance of the act, which is most keenly felt after the first time, and generally is most clear the nobler the character of the person [*The World as Will and Idea*, II].

This aversion to sexuality, so characteristic for Schopenhauer who considered it as low and degrading, is clearly evident also in a passage that deals with dreams. Here dreams which are characteristic for himself are dealt with as general experiences. He starts with pollution dreams, and it is again characteristic for his personality that he mentions this type of dream so often:

It is known that nature avails itself of certain dreams for its own purpose, namely, to empty the overly full semen reservoirs. Of course, dreams of this sort produce slippery scenes. But there are other dreams which do the same, without having or achieving that aim. There is a difference, however, in that in dreams of the first sort the occasion and the fair one soon show themselves favorable to us, and thus nature achieves its aim. In the other sort of dream, ever new obstacles keep getting in the way of what we most desire; in vain we strive to overcome them, in the end we never reach our goal. What creates these obstacles and denies the fulfillment of our desire again and again is nothing but our own will; but it comes from a region which lies far beyond the imagining consciousness of our dreams, and thus appears as destiny.

Nothing can more graphically describe how Schopenhauer's attitude toward sexuality was inhibited by reason than this idea of will and counterwill in dreams. We know that Schopenhauer usually avoided sexual intercourse. This is probably the reason for his frequent pollution dreams. He certainly would not have lacked female companions if his aversion to sexuality and to women in general had not prompted him to avoid them.

Our observations of character development, especially medical observations have taught us that this contempt for and abhorrence of actual sexual pleasure is caused by negation and repression of what is felt to be sinful. This feeling is frequently intensified by education. It is not too far-fetched to assume that this conflict which may have had its beginning in guilt feelings about a youthful sin was intensified by the stern, rough father through a prohibition which degraded sexuality even more. Early knowledge of sexual intercourse of the parents often quite normally engenders contempt for women (the mother) and of sexuality in general. In Schopenhauer's case this attitude could never be rectified because of his hostility toward his mother which was quite evident even at that time. A person to whom at an early age sexuality seemed doubly polluted usually will generalize and objectivize his own experiences and consequently disparage women in general and be unable to enjoy sexuality naively and free of guilt.[13] He will find guilt everywhere.

Schopenhauer deduced the curse of the world from the object-

13 Every general judgment a man makes about women should be considered primarily as a symptom of his own psychosexual disposition; such judgments are of value biographically rather than as authoritative statements (Rosa Mayreder, 1913).

ionable nature of the procreative act (analogous to the original
sin of Christianity) and he was not content to explain the universal striving for sexual gratification and the follies of love with
the pleasures that sex offers in and for itself but conceived the
Metaphysics of Sexual Love and found it necessary to introduce,
wrongly, the teleological principle as a primary one. Schopenhauer had the peculiar need to look for a rationalistic motivation
because he felt that the naive, sensual enjoyment was not enough
motivation for erotic desire. It seems probable that according to
his own changing sexual impressions he did not find the enjoyment of love commensurate with the violence with which man
strives for it. It must have been a personal experience which left
an element of his erotic urge ungratified. This is not the only instance which leads to the assumption that Schopenhauer's sexual
enjoyment was poor and not fully satisfying. Since sexuality is
so often typical for the rest of the psychic life, we may see in this
also one of the roots of his generally unsatisfied enjoyment of
life, culminating in his pessimism. It is striking that he equated
pollution with gratification through coitus:

> As certainly as there is no specific and absolute difference
> between life and dream but only a formal and relative one,
> just as certainly there is no essential difference between pol-
> lution and coitus. Both provide a fleeting dream image and
> a discharge of semen [*Neue Paralipomena*].

Here we may also see a cause for Schopenhauer's rare and
passing relationships with women, and finally for his remaining
a bachelor. More pronounced than in others, we find in Schopenhauer a kind of division into positive and negative which provides, as it were, a skeleton for his entire system. He must have
had an unusually strong tendency to cut off the hydra head of
the sexual instinct which persistently recurred and produced
profuse fantasies, precisely at the moment when the urge was
strongest. Generally, when the sexual instinct urges toward
gratification, the individual is ready for it. Schopenhauer has the
strange impulse to suppress the sexual desire especially when it

becomes most urgent without a special object, that is, for somatic reasons or from fantasies:[14]

> During those days and hours, when the urge for sensual lust is strongest, not just a feeble longing that stems from emptiness and dullness, but a burning desire, a violent heat, at that very moment the highest powers of the spirit, the better consciousness, are ready for the greatest activity; though latent at that instant when the consciousness has surrendered to the desire and is filled with it, it only needs a powerful effort to reverse the direction and fill the consciousness with the activities of the highest intellectual powers in place of the tormenting, craving, desperate desire [*Neue Paralipomena*].

And now we are confronted with that psychological fact which turned the instinct-tormented Schopenhauer into the profound metaphysicist who was able to utter the enthusiastic words about the noble enjoyment of pure knowledge, free of the will; the fact that he was capable of denying the will, suppressing the instinct and escaping from anything earthy as few others. Even in his youth, in the period before 1815, his ideas were full of enthusiasm for a "better consciousness": we have something within us which goes far beyond sensuality, reason, intellect, beyond subject and object, and that is the common birthplace of genius and saint alike. Artistic, philosophic and ascetic redemption are here fused into an obscure unity. Later Schopenhauer clarified his theory and distinguished the basis for his ascetic ideal as a reaction against the violent will, the "denial of the will," from the "pure, will-less knowledge of ideas." Manifestations of the latter appear in philosophy and art and correspond rather to a sublimation of the instinct.

This interpretation is shared by no less a man than Nietzsche

14 Some people who habitually practice self-gratification continue the act to a high degree of excitement and then interrupt suddenly, either because they fear the loss of sexual substance or for other rationalizations of their guilt feelings. This masturbatio interrupta appears to be the model of the above-mentioned reversal of direction. According to a passage in *The World as Will and Idea*, II, Schopenhauer subscribed to the opinion that indulgence weakened while continence heightened all powers.

(in the third essay of his *Genealogy of Morals,* "The Meaning of
Ascetic Ideals"): He expresses this view in the most exemplary
fashion. The penetrating metapsychologist who has long since
outgrown his youthful enthusiasm for "Schopenhauer as Educator" raises the question: What does it mean if a true philosopher
subscribes to the ascetic ideal? A truly independent spirit like
Schopenhauer, "a man with a gaze of steel who has the courage
to be himself?" And he finds this answer: "He wants to free himself from torture." This torture is nothing else but the too de-
manding, ethically already rejected sexuality which, as Nietzsche
remarks, "was actually treated by Schopenhauer as his personal
enemy and which included its instrument, the woman, this 'in-
strumentum diaboli.' " The highest goal of this denial of the will
is, according to Schopenhauer, asceticism, a rejection and renunciation of the whole evil world full of sorrow, "the deliberate
breaking of the will by renouncing the pleasant and seeking the
unpleasant, a self-appointed life of atonement and self-chastisement to mortification." This ideal hovered before Schopenhauer
who longed for it intensely, and once, at the sight of a picture of
a Trappist monk, he described it with tears in his eyes as a matter of grace.[15] The uncompromising psychologist Nietzsche un-
covered the masochistic wish for suffering underneath this pes-

---

[15] A remark in *Neue Paralipomena* shows how conscious Schopenhauer, who
according to his own admission never reached the ideal of sainthood, was of the
discord and constant struggle and of the difficulty for man ever to reach this goal:
"It is an impossible and in itself contradictory demand of almost every philosopher, that man should achieve an inner unity of his nature, harmony within
himself. For inner discord is the very nature of man throughout his life. For he
can wholly represent only one thing; for all else he has the predisposition and
the indestructible potentiality. If he has committed himself to the one, then everything else stands ever ready in the form of predisposition and continuously demands to be converted from potentiality into reality: as long as he wishes to be
that one, he must continuously repress, overpower and kill. . . . Thus, once he
has committed himself to sainthood, then he has to kill the sensuous, lust-seeking
being within him all through his entire life, not just once and for all: for that
he will remain as long as he lives. . . . Thus it will be in all things with unending
modifications. Now the one, now the other will triumph within him: he is the
battlefield. Even though the one may constantly be victorious, the other is constantly fighting: for it lives as long as he lives: for as a human being he is the
potentiality of many antitheses."

simistic renunciation and dissected this tendency toward renunciation and sainthood.

> They think of themselves—of what concern is "the saint" to them! They think of what is most indispensable to themselves: freedom from coercion, disturbance, noise, freedom from business, duties, worries; clear-headedness . . . Peace in all sub-surface areas; all dogs well leashed. . . . We know what the three great catch-words of the ascetic ideal are: poverty, humility, chastity; and now let us take a close look at the lives of all great, productive, fertile minds—and we shall find all three qualities again and again—up to a certain point. But not at all, as is self-evident, as if these were "virtues" . . . [as if] they are the most necessary and natural conditions for their existence at its best, for their greatest productivity. And it is altogether possible that their predominant spirituality at first had to curb an unruly and irritable pride or a capricious sensuality.

In the knowledge of ideas (*Ideenerkenntnis*) our intellect has, according to Schopenhauer, turned away from the will, the will has withdrawn from consciousness, and thus all unrest, distress and torment are averted. He finds the purest serenity in the contemplation of ideas unhampered by the will. This is truly philosophic contemplation. And nowhere else is Schopenhauer's language so enthusiastic and rapturous as in the description of this will-less knowledge which finds its expression in the occupation with philosophy and art:

> What is the greatest pleasure that is possible for man?— The intuitive knowledge of truth. The correctness of the answer does not permit the slightest doubt [*Neue Paralipomena*].

Nietzsche vehemently contradicted this theory of pure disinterested knowledge in philosophy and in artistic pleasures and unmasked the much praised "disinterested contemplation" as a "non-concept and non-sense."

> From now on, my dear philosophers, let us beware of the dangerous old foolishness about a "pure, will-less, pain-less, time-less subject of knowledge"; let us beware of the traps

of such contradictory concepts as "pure reason," "absolute spirituality," "perception as such" . . . the more affects we allow to express themselves on a subject, the more complete will be our conception of this subject, our "objectivity." To eliminate the will altogether, to disengage the affects one and all,—even assuming that it were possible—, would it not mean to castrate the intellect?

We must add here that of course we, too, are of the opinion that a will-less perception is not possible—though in a different sense. Schopenhauer's idea that the will (the unconscious) could ever be silent and leave our thinking uninfluenced was completely mistaken. For this very reason his intuitively created philosophy (as he himself calls it) is such a beautiful example of the subjectivity of all philosophy. This method of working, to let the ideas rise up (Schopenhauer called it "contemplation of the world") brings out the individualistic element in its purest form. His error was that he endeavored to find objective truths by self-observation and by listening within himself. Let us compare this with Nietzsche's profound insight:

> We cannot help but count the greater part of conscious thinking among the instinctual processes . . . most conscious thoughts of a philosopher are secretely led by his instincts and forced into certain paths . . . beyond that are value appraisals, or to put it more clearly, physiological demands for the preservation of a certain way of life . . . a wish dear to their hearts is rendered abstract and carefully sifted and defended with reasons that are found for it afterwards.

In addition to the pleasure Schopenhauer found in the allegedly will-less knowledge, he could counteract his pessimism with the blissful and redeeming effect of art which exalts man above pain and boredom of his existence. Will-less and disinterested contemplation is also alleged to be the basis of aesthetic pleasures. These, like the pure philosophic perception, provide freedom from the will and redemption from the world. The tragic drama, in particular, leads to renunciation and denial of the will;[16] music most directly stirs the "better consciousness" and is furthest removed from everything empirical. Enjoyment of music was for Schopenhauer a palliative of the will. He loved music and could not praise it enough for cleansing the emotions. "Music washes away all that is impure, all that is petty, all that is bad, and elevates everyone to the highest level of the mind of which he is capable" (*Neue Paralipomena*). Let us remember here that others, e.g., Plato, Stendhal, Tolstoi, saw the fine arts as seducers. If Schopenhauer rejects the music of Wagner, which is generally considered sensuous,[17] it probably means that he avoided the seductive aspect of art. This aversion Nietzsche again recognized as a basis of Schopenhauer's aesthetics and this recognition in turn led him to the most penetrating interpretation of the whole system:

> Schopenhauer used for his purpose the Kantian view of aesthetic problems . . . "The beautiful," Kant says, "is that which pleases without interest." Without interest! Compare this with the definition another, a real "observer" and artist has made—Stendhal, who once called the beautiful "une promesse de bonheur."[18] He repudiates and eliminates that which Kant stresses as the sole point of the aesthetic state: le desinteressement . . . To return to Schopenhauer, his relation to the arts was much closer than Kant's, and yet he could not free himself from the spell of Kant's definition.

16 "In the tragic drama we see the noblest characters after long struggles and much suffering renounce forever the aims they had hitherto so vehemently pursued, and all life's pleasures, or even relinquish life willingly and joyfully, like 'The Steadfast Prince' of Calderon." Even as a youth Schopenhauer was so deeply stirred by Calderon's drama that he had to leave the usual social gathering at his mother's and seek solitude. Moebius conjectured from this that Schopenhauer had experienced renunciation at an early age "because even in his youth he was so deeply stirred by a drama in which the hero in a sudden outburst of noble feeling sacrifices himself and his own interests for his father."

17 He said Richard Wagner ought to give up music, he had more talent as a poet; and he, Schopenhauer, would remain faithful to Rossini and Mozart (Grisebach).

18 Cf., on the other hand, Stendhal's agreement with Schopenhauer's explanation of aesthetic feeling in another passage: "The soul, partly delivered from the vain wishes of this world, is in the mood to perceive exalted beauty." (Quotation according to Seillière.)

How was that possible? The facts are astonishing enough:
He interpreted the phrase "without interest" in the most
personal way, in accordance with what must have been
his most normal experience. Schopenhauer discusses few
subjects with as much assurance as the effect of aesthetic
contemplation: he states that, somewhat like lupuline and
camphor, it counteracts sexual "interestedness"; he never
wearied of extolling this escape from the "will" as the great
advantage and usefulness of the aesthetic state. Indeed, one
might be tempted to ask whether this basic conception of
"will and idea," the thought that a deliverance from the
"will" is possible only through the "idea," does not have its
origin in a generalization of his own sexual experiences.
[In every discussion of Schopenhauer's philosophy, incidentally, it should be kept in mind that it is the conception of a
twenty-six-year-old youth and is not only specifically Schopenhauer's own, but specifically his at that particular time
of his life.] Let us take, as an example, óne of the most ex-
pressive passages from the many he wrote in honor of the
aesthetic state (*The World as Will and Idea,* I) and let us
listen to the note of sorrow, happiness, gratitude, with which
such words are spoken: "This is the pain-free state which
Epicurus praised as the greatest gift of the Gods; we are in
that instant delivered from the will's base pressures, we celebrate the Sabbath after the convict labor of the will, the
wheel of Ixion stands still" . . . What vehemence in these
words! What images of torment and disgust! What near-
pathology in the comparison of time "that instant" against
the usual "wheel of Ixion," the "convict labor of the will,"
"the will's base pressures"!—Assuming that Schopenhauer
was a hundred times right in the light of his own personal
experience, what does it contribute to the insight into the
nature of beauty? Schopenhauer has described one effect of
beauty, the one that calms the will—but is it a generally
experienced one? Stendhal, as mentioned before, a no less
sensual but happier nature than Schopenhauer, emphasized
a different effect of beauty: "Beauty promises happiness."
He sees the crucial effect in the fact that beauty arouses the
will. And lastly, could we not raise the objection against
Schopenhauer that he is mistaken when he believes he follows Kant, that he understands Kant's definition of beauty
not at all in Kant's sense—that the beautiful pleases him because of his interest, the most personal, most powerful in-

terest of all, the interest of a tormented man who extricates himself from his torture.

Let us also quote a passage from *The Twilight of the Idols:*

Schopenhauer is a first-rate case for a psychologist: because of his maliciously brilliant attempt to cite in support of a nihilistic, total depreciation of life the exact counter-instance, the great self-affirmation of the "will to live." He has interpreted one after the other, art, heroism, genius, beauty, the great compassion, knowledge, the will for truth and the tragic drama, as phenomena of the "denial of the will" or "the need to deny the will." Next to Christianity, it is the greatest psychological forgery known to history.

So far we have followed along Schopenhauer's lines and have emphasized the great importance of the sexual instinct and its denial for the will. But there are other important factors which determined his solution of Kant's enigma of the "Thing in itself." Sex is not the only driving force of man, there is also the sum total of the instincts that serve the ego (self-preservation), the struggle to assert the personality. The will is not merely will for procreation, will for life, it is also will for power. In contrast to Fichte, Schelling and Hegel, who glorified the intellect and believed the world to be a product of conscious development, it was left to Schopenhauer to give to the instinctual life, to the unconscious, the will, the importance that was due it. But if we say that the will is also a striving for power, then we have to recognize that Schopenhauer who came from such strong-willed, passionate ancestors and who had to submit to his robust father, must have experienced this "will for power" quite intensively; and that the will was the symbol for the overly powerful father, the force that weighed so heavily on him in his youth, which he projected onto the cosmos. And so it happened that the so-called atheistic Schopenhauer, as Seillière correctly observed, made the will his God (God and devil), and so deified the paternal power. Only after his father's death could he begin to assert his own will in life; shortly thereafter he conceived his theory.

There is more to the denial of the will than we have hitherto

stated. All yielding, all renunciation, all humility are comprised
in it. We can understand why that scene of deepest humiliation
before the royal father in Calderon's *Steadfast Prince* made such
an impression on Schopenhauer. The obedience and humility of
the saint remained for him the ideal most worth striving for.

The fact that Schopenhauer's will takes shape even in inanimate matter, that the whole world has to be imagined permeated
by the will, this fact recalls the prereligious, prescientific, animistic views of primitive peoples. Schopenhauer, the mystic, can
thus explain the whole world from one point of view, just as those
primitives were able to do with their animistic views.[19] A naive,
infantile animism of inanimate matter we find in an anecdote
from Schopenhauer's early childhood which he himself related:
He threw a shoe into a receptacle of milk and fervently begged it
to jump out.

Summing up Schopenhauer's theory of the will, we have to
acknowledge that to enthrone the unconscious and the instinctual life into a position of such power is a brilliant intellectual
performance. We shall later return to a discussion of the application of this psychological insight to the development of philosophic systems.

Ethics

Nietzsche, who in his youth revered Schopenhauer almost as a
father, became the philosopher's most dangerous opponent. In
contrast to Schopenhauer, Nietzsche did not remain faithful to
the concepts of his youth but continued to develop and pene-
trated more and more deeply into an understanding of the human psyche. With his implacable criticism he pulled the ground
from under the feet of "the last metaphysician." Not only did he
dissect the "pure knowledge," not only did he tear "the saint"
down from his pedestal, he undermined with his psychological
criticism Schopenhauer's ethics of compassion which had found

---

[19] Schopenhauer's taste for magic, superstition, and other transcendental phenomena can be seen in the light of animism. Cf. Freud (1912/13).

so many fervent admirers, and with his intuitively psychological reasoning traced them back to their sources in the instincts.

There always have been Schopenhauer scholars and admirers who, inspired by the noble and tender ethics of compassion, and rendered uncritical by their own wishes, have seen in the philosopher a particularly kind and good man. Of course it is closer to popular views and psychologically easier to understand if a philosopher's life is in harmony with his theories, as seems to have been the case with Spinoza, Kant and Fichte; and it almost hurts to see that the man who taught compassion showed in his own life so little compassion, so little sympathy with the suffering of others. Psychoanalytic experience teaches us that compassion is a reaction formation to antisocial, cruel instinctual impulses; and that in general the civilized ego is a secondary structure superimposed on the instinctual ego; hence we expect that there must be various transitional stages between those individuals who preserve these primal instincts unchanged and give them free reign (criminals) and those who completely suppress their instincts and as a result show an altruistic character. Schopenhauer did not succeed in transforming his instincts into kindness and compassion. He showed impulses of malice, cruelty, spitefulness and envy, as well as joy in abusiveness and mockery to a high degree, and little love for mankind.

As previously mentioned, Schopenhauer's ancestors were of strikingly vehement, irascible temperament, driven to fervid activity. In the philosopher who had chosen an intellectual career, this nature could find direct expression only in a rude and uncomplying attitude, in abusiveness, maliciousness and aggression. We will not find these qualities in his work which idealizes compassion. But informal utterances in his everyday life and in his letters show a great deal of rudeness and grimly aggressive humor. He used expressions of abuse such as we do not usually hear from the lips of a cultured man.

He has been described as violent and dogmatic in discussions. Anybody who did not feel called upon or qualified to admire his mind found in him an unfriendly, spiteful, uncontrolled person.

He was capable of repeatedly throwing out by force a poor elderly woman because it did not suit him that she visited his landlady in his room. The woman sued him for compensation after a fall down the stairs had incapacitated her and she could no longer work. The proceedings lasted six years. In the end Schopenhauer had to pay a considerable sum to this "extremely crafty and malicious" person for the next twenty years. Not even her death assuaged his hatred. On her death certificate he wrote the following cruel bon mot: "Obit anus, abit onus." We could cite many passages from his letters bearing witness to his gruffness and unquenchable hatred (cf. Damm). In connection with the publication of his chief work, his publisher Brockhaus remarked not without justification: "I have to be very careful with this man, he is a real watch-dog." And he complained about Schopenhauer's unearthly rudeness and boorishness and his incredibly uncouth manners.

Once, when Schopenhauer was annoyed with his opponent, Professor Weisse, he wrote to Dr. Asher: "If you could somehow find an opportunity to rub it in and sprinkle pepper on the wound, I should be very pleased." He employed the strongest and most contemptuous terms when dealing with the philosophy professors (windbag, sophists), especially Hegel. He spoke of Hegel's sophistry, called his work a philosophic harlequinade, the most meaningless trash ever accepted by blockheads; described his theory as the most disgusting and senseless verbosity and said it reminded him of the rantings of the insane. Let us compare this coarse, cross-grained man, so prone to hatred, who on the other hand advocated the ethics of compassion, with the noble, reserved, gentle Nietzsche who said of himself: "I am not made for hatred and hostility"—and who in his ethics extolled the will for power, cruelty and unscrupulousness.

Only in a few isolated instances did Schopenhauer show compassion, as for instance in his youth when at the sight of the Bagno in Toulon he felt pity for the tortured. It may be that in his youth "his excitable temperament made him sensitive, even sentimental, before bitter experiences drove him to the opposite extreme and he became the most egotistic, occasionally even the most brutal of old eccentrics" (Seillière). One trait which is found most commonly as a reaction formation to cruelty toward people is most pronounced in Schopenhauer: a deep compassion for the sufferings of animals. All his life he was a bitter opponent of "the scientific torture of animals," vivisection. With words of burning indignation he branded the atrocity of a naturalist who starved two rabbits to death in an experiment. He even drew up proposals for protective laws. "Schopenhauer would have liked to see corporal punishment, which had been introduced in England for cruelty to animals, generously administered in Germany to protect the two- and four-legged fellow creatures from man" (Damm). Flogging of humans as protection for animals! This love of animals seems to be in contradiction to his frequently expressed misanthropy. Yet he not only learned to extol this quality from the Indians, he actually felt it deeply. He once stated openly: "I must frankly admit that the sight of any animal gives me immediate pleasure and warms my heart . . . whereas the sight of a human being almost always provokes repugnance" (*Neue Paralipomena*). Similarly, in an "Antistrophe to the 73rd Venetian Epigram," he said: "It does not surprise me that dogs are so often slandered by men, for all too often, alas, a dog puts mankind to shame" (*Parerga und Paralipomena,* II).

Schopenhauer's great love of dogs is well known,[20] especially of his poodle. He provided for him in his will. We have already mentioned that in his room pictures of animals hung side by side with the portraits of the great men he admired. As astute a psychologist as Schopenhauer could not quite fail to see the significance of reaction formation and sublimation. Once, while watching a young orang at a fair, he began to explain that even when he was young, it had struck him that the dog, this domesticated beast of prey, a descendant perhaps of jackal or wolf, had become the faithful, affectionate, docile, humanlike companion of man; and that the harmless, grass-eating sheep had not; and that something similar seems to hold true for men, in that those

---

[20] He said to Frauenstaedt: "I would not want to live if dogs did not exist."

who were originally wild, hard, with strong sensual inclinations and a passionate disposition aspire to the highest virtues; and that Plato had observed the strong propensity for evil in the best natures (Gwinner).

Schopenhauer's anxiety can most likely be explained to some extent as a repression of aggressive desires which in the form of anxiety are turned against the ego. It proves the original power of the instinctual anlage that despite these repressions and partial reaction formations it nevertheless permeates and colors his whole personality. Rarely has a person more intensively experienced the feeling of hatred within him, seen the cruel instincts in man more developed or felt them more and suffered more from them. Maybe only Nietzsche after him has similarly experienced and recognized the feelings of power, vengeance and cruelty. But unlike Schopenhauer, he did not repudiate them. Instead, he discovered in them man's primal strength and acknowledged them as the ideal of the healthy, nondecadent man. But like Nietzsche,[21] Schopenhauer frequently mentioned maliciousness in his ethics, when he discussed the mainsprings of human action:

The three mainsprings of human action:
a) Egotism which wills one's own well-being (is without limit);
b) Malice which wills another's pain (goes to extreme cruelty);
c) Compassion which wills another's well-being (goes even to nobility and magnanimity).

And more explicitly he wrote in the supplement to his ethics (*Parerga und Paralipomena*, II):

Allied to the boundless egoism in our nature there is in every human heart, to a greater or lesser degree, a store of hatred, anger, rancour and malice, like poison in a serpent's fangs waiting only for the opportunity to vent itself and to storm and rage like an unchained demon. If no good occa-

[21] "The aim of malice is not the suffering of others as such but our own gratification, such as a feeling of revenge or a more intense nervous excitement. Even teasing shows the pleasure we derive when we let others feel our power; it gives us a pleasurable feeling of superiority" (Nietzsche, *Menschliches allzu Menschliches*).

sion presents itself, it will use the smallest pretext, exaggerating it in fantasies.

Man is the only animal that causes pain to others for no purpose . . . No other animal ever torments just for the sake of tormenting; but man does just that, and this makes his character diabolical, which is far worse than beastly. In a general sense this feature has already been discussed; but it also is quite evident on a small scale, where everyone has occasion to observe it. For example, when two young dogs are playing, it is peaceful and charming to watch—and then a child of three or four will come along and intervene with whip or stick—it is almost unavoidable—and so will prove that even at that age it is *l'animal mechant par excellence*. Even the common aimless teasing and mischievous pranks stem from this source . . . Really, there is a wild beast in the heart of every man, waiting only for the opportunity to storm and rage, to hurt others and, if they should bar his way, to destroy them: this is the source of our eagerness for battle and for war . . . It is the will to live which grows more and more embittered by the constant sorrow of existence and seeks to alleviate its own torment by inflicting it on others. But in this way it develops gradually into its own true malice and cruelty . . .

Whereas Nietzsche's attitude toward this pleasure in cruelty was an affirmative one, though he himself repressed and sublimated it almost completely, Schopenhauer, who in his ethics extolled compassion as the human impulse *katexochen*, reacted with a defense which found expression in his ethics:

Nothing enrages our moral feeling so deeply as cruelty. We can condone every crime but cruelty. The reason for this is that cruelty is the exact opposite of compassion.

Schopenhauer set forth his ethics comparatively late, stimulated by an external cause. Yet perhaps his deepest feelings ring out in it. He made ethics the cornerstone of his whole philosophy. It is again a proof of the contradictions that reign in the human psyche where reaction formations so often represent the roots of character qualities, that a rough, implacable, envious, vengeful man like Schopenhauer who considered all other men as basically different and far beneath him, that precisely this

morose, lonely and selfish intellectual adopted from the Indians
the ethics of compassion and made them his own! He experienced
within himself impulses of compassion as a means of inhibiting
the evil instincts. He did not inquire what their source was but
considered them a primal ethical phenomenon. According to
him, it is a primary mainspring that comes by and from itself and
thus functions like an instinct. Compassion presupposes a pene-
tration to the essential unity of all living matter, called in Indian
philosophy "tat twam asi." This, too, is a primary act of knowledge without deduction or logical thought. We see here that
Schopenhauer lacked the desire to find the genealogy of morals,
in contrast to his antipode Nietzsche who had the urge to penetrate to the deepest roots of moral values in order to find an explanation.

It seems strange to see the youthful Nietzsche in the role
of Schopenhauer's grateful admiring pupil (in his enthusiastic
early work, *Schopenhauer as Educator*).[22] But here again Nietzsche was the opposite of Schopenhauer. He constantly endeavored to know and conquer his own self, while Schopenhauer
remained rigidly committed once and for all to his conception of
the cosmos. Nietzsche's self-analysis led him far beyond his
teacher and he never tired of his polemics against him, especially
in his "genealogy of morals." Both these personalities, so entirely
different in their lives and theories, offer perfect examples in one
respect: In each case their ethical system is in direct contrast to
their personality and conduct of life. Simmel said of Nietzsche:
"It has often been pointed out that Nietzsche's theories were in
contrast to his personality: this rugged, martial, occasionally bac-
chantic far-echoing call issued from a highly sensitive, quietly
introverted, mild and amiable nature." And Paulsen said of Schopenhauer, his ethics might be called his *catalogus desideratorum*.

Both Simmel and Volkelt emphasize that nowhere in his ethics
of compassion did Schopenhauer express such genuine, deep and
enthusiastic emotions based on personal experience as he did in

[22] With the exception of Schopenhauer (and Nietzsche in his youth) no philosopher has attributed such moral value to compassion.

his presentation of the "pure will-less knowledge." This leads them to conclude that the ethics of compassion are construed. We, on the other hand, attempt to show that this ethical system is an unconscious product which developed through the repression of his violently aggressive anlage and reaction formation; hence it is psychologically genuine and true. Those who object to this deduction may be answered in the sarcastic words of Nietzsche:

> How can anything develop from its opposite? Such as truth from error? or the wish for truth from the wish for deception? or altruistic action from self-interest? or the pure sun-clear contemplation of the sage from covetousness? Such an origin is impossible. He who dreams of it is a fool, if not worse. The things of highest value must have another origin, an origin of their very own, they cannot be derived from this transient, seductive, deceptive, trivial world, from this tangle of delusions and desires! Their foundations must lie in the womb of existence, in immortality, in the hidden God, in the "Thing in itself"—there and nowhere else must their foundations lie.

Whenever we find a sexual component (sadism) in conjunction with aggressive tendencies, we usually see also cruelty directed against the self, i.e., a masochistic attitude, such as Nietzsche recognized in the enervating ethics of compassion.

According to Schopenhauer, the exclusion of violent and egoistic motives is the criterion for the moral value of an action. But this stage of perfection alone does not satisfy him. It seems that very early in his life, at any rate as a young man, he saw before him a higher ideal: "He saw in the saint the judge of existence," said Nietzsche. Favored mortals, clear-sighted minds, reach this vision of their longing only in rare instances, actually only through a state of grace. They deaden their will and rise beyond justice to strict asceticism. The first step is sexual abstinence, followed by voluntary poverty, forgiveness for insults, fasting, chastisement and death as atonement. This is the masochistic-mystic picture Schopenhauer sketches of the saint. It goes far beyond the saint of the Christian religion. He especially admired those sudden radical conversions which Buddha exemplified for him. With words of moving beauty he related this myth to Karl Baehr (in April, 1856). Here we see again how Schopenhauer approached Indian mysticism: the saints enter Nirvana which again is an expression of wishes and longings such as we know to be the motives for all descriptions of paradise. This whole ideal of the saint, of renunciation, of drawing near the state of the fakir and the penitent, has to be viewed as an expression of fantasies of joy in pain, as of course masochism and sadism are closely interconnected. These tendencies toward self-punishment can derive their intensity only from deep feelings of guilt. From these guilt feelings springs the need for redemption.[23] Schopenhauer said of himself that in his seventeenth year he was suddenly overcome by the misery of life, just like Buddha in his youth.

It must be stressed as highly significant that these guilt feelings and redemption tendencies which underlie this transformation became so intensified right after his father's death! Joy in his own suffering is clearly discernible in the whole pessimistic presentation and philosophy of life, as "pleasure is experienced and sought in failure, pain, accident, ugliness, in arbitrary voluntary loss, in self-destruction, self-chastisement, self-sacrifice. All this is highly paradoxical. We are here confronted with a dichotomy of one who wants to be dichotomic, who finds pleasure in this suffering" (Nietzsche, *The Meaning of Ascetic Ideals*.) Simmel also put it very clearly when he said: "Revelling in one's own pain, sensual wallowing in every sorrow, the mania to make a great show of one's misfortunes for one's own self—this is what is always expressed in those formulae in which a pessimistic interpretation of the whole world is either the background or the foreground."

[23] "It is a trick of religions and metaphysics that they want to see man as evil and sinful by nature to make him suspicious of nature and thus make him bad in himself: thus he learns to think of himself as evil since he cannot throw off the mantle of nature. Gradually . . . he comes to feel that he is so oppressed by the weight of his sins that supernatural powers are needed to lift the burden: thus the need for redemption has entered upon the stage" (Nietzsche, *Menschliches allzu Menschliches*).

Pessimism

The popularity of Schopenhauer's philosophy is due primarily to his pessimistic *Weltanschauung*. Hardly anyone before him gave such pithy expression to his sufferings caused by the world, his disappointment in humanity, in love, in the value and content of life, in humanity's and the individual's capacity for development. The most important argument which Schopenhauer employed again and again in an attempt to rationalize the ill-humor the world provoked in him, is the already mentioned, blind, irrational, aimless will which can never be wholly satisfied and knows no resting point. Even more important perhaps than this metaphysical principle is the empirical impression of the contemplation of the world and of humanity, namely, man's incorrigibility in every respect: that there is far more displeasure than pleasure in life, that it is ruled by folly, malice and chance; that sexual love is a fraud, basically disgusting; that man is full of dissimulation and hypocrisy; all reality only sham, illusion, a figment of the mind; time, a disconsolately fleeting phantom; the best that can be hoped for, freedom from pain; only in spirituality, in turning away from life, can tranquility be found, as a sort of happiness. Schopenhauer said even of children, who in their innocence might reconcile one with everything:

> Children are like innocent delinquents, condemned not to death but to life, though they have not yet learned the content of the verdict.
> We are like the lambs that play in the meadow, even while the eye of the butcher selects this one and that one: for in our good days we do not know what disaster fate is preparing for us—disease, persecution, impoverishment, mutilation, blindness, madness, death . . .

And he repeatedly described his impression of mankind in words like these:

> To those who know mental and physical beauty, the sight and acquaintance of every new so-called human being offers nothing in ninety-nine cases out of a hundred, but a completely new, really original, never before imagined example

of a composite of ugliness, shallowness, meanness, perversity, stupidity and malice, in a word, repulsiveness and abomination.

[Life appeared to him to be] a constant struggle for the very existence, with the certainty of losing it in the end. And if want has been forced back, and a part of the field been won, then immediately a terrible emptiness and boredom set in, and the struggle against these is more tortuous still [Neue Paralipomena].

[He therefore concluded] that is far more truthful to say: the devil has created the world, than: God created the world [Neue Paralipomena].

That the source of these grossly pessimistic judgments lies in ill-humor is shown in the following passage which reveals full self-knowledge:

It may go so far that to many a person, especially in moments of hypochondriacal depression, the world may seem, from an aesthetic viewpoint like a collection of caricatures, from an intellectual viewpoint as an insane asylum, and from a moral viewpoint as a flophouse. If such a depression persists, the result is misanthropy [Preisschrift über die Grundlage der Moral].

Nowhere else can the strict subjectivity of a Weltanschauung be seen more clearly than in the optimistic or pessimistic attitude that the individual adopts toward the world. It becomes obvious that pessimism is not really a Weltanschauung but a mood —or to call it by its proper name, a depressive mood. Gwinner, who had known Schopenhauer personally, in his funeral oration used a psychologically profound metaphor. "Did he not go through his whole life hurt like a child that has been angered at play—lonely and misunderstood, true only to himself?" Even in his earliest years, at a time when the boy grew up in his well-to-do patrician home and could not have had any knowledge of the cold world outside, his mother said of him: "Even as a boy he brooded over the misery of mankind" (Gwinner). Perhaps with greater inner justification he could later say about his personal ill-humor as a youth:

In my seventeenth year, without any formal education, I was seized by the misery of life, as Buddha was in his youth when he discovered illness, old age, pain and death. The truth that spoke loudly and clearly from the world soon overpowered the Jewish dogmas with which I too had been indoctrinated, and to me the result was that this world could not possibly be the creation of an all-benevolent providence but rather that of a devil who called creatures into being in order to gloat over their torment. All data pointed in that direction, and the belief that it was so won the upper hand [*Neue Paralipomena*].

Let us cite another characteristic passage which is the more cogent if we consider that victims of melancholia show the deepest depression in the mornings, the least in the evenings. The analogous manifestation which Schopenhauer described we also encounter in neurotic and depressed persons as a flight from unsatisfying and tormenting reality into the state of sleep which these people occasionally attempt to extend unduly. Schopenhauer formulated this undoubtedly personal experience as follows:

Whatever one may say, the happiest moment of a happy person is the moment of falling asleep, the unhappiest moment of the unhappy man is the moment of awakening [*The World as Will and Idea*, II].[24]

No student of Schopenhauer can fail to notice how precociously early this seriousmindedness and depression set in. Moebius even asserted that Schopenhauer was "pathological from the beginning" and thought it already an indication of illness "that in his youth he posed the question about the value of life." It is quite pertinent when Moebius says: "It was not the recognition of the evil in this world that made of him the philosopher of pessimism. He looked for evil and described it because he needed verification for his hostile attitude toward the world." "Schopenhauer sought an explanation for his melan-

24 Cf. Hebbel's Diaries: "Last night upon going to bed, my dear wife put it very neatly when she remarked: When we are young we are happy to get up, when we are old we are happy to go to bed."

cholia, for his fear of life, and he found his pessimism," the kernel of his philosophy. According to Moebius, the innate feelings of dyscolia are later justified by his theories. We shall see later on that Schopenhauer's peculiar temperament has to be understood not so much as innate but rather as very early acquired or at least pathologically intensified by early impressions.

Furthermore, we have to bear in mind that those qualities of Schopenhauer which his mother so ruthlessly described, such as his arrogant and irritable nature, his conceit, his animosity and unfriendliness, his insistence on knowing everything better—that these qualities are bound to give offense and thereby again lead to an intensification of his ill-humor. And inasmuch as his demands on mankind were so excessive that they could never be satisfied, his vanity and sensitivity must have been all the more hurt and degraded. In fact, we have reports of his social failures, especially with young girls who laughed at the morose, aloof young philosopher who most certainly must have been inconsiderate and made them feel his intellectual superiority. Schopenhauer consoled himself about these failures in his familiar manner which controlled his entire thinking: by increasing the distance between himself and his fellow men.

> In my youth the neglect I experienced socially and the preference that was given to the trivial, the ordinary and the commonplace, made me doubt myself. Until at the age of twenty-six I read Helvetius and realized that homogeneity bound those together and heterogeneity set me apart . . . [Neue Paralipomena].

All too easily he offended his fellow men in all sorts of circumstances and took revenge by reproaching them with malice and lack of affection. Ambivalent in his feelings, he was not capable of pure love; hatred became all too easily mixed in with it. He had no alternative but to lead a solitary life. In this connection Paulsen remarked: "He saw that he could not live with his fellow men; not in harmony because he was too arrogant and irritable; not in disharmony because he lacked cold-blooded superiority; consequently he decided to live apart from them."

In notes that were not intended for publication Schopenhauer made this tragic confession:

> All my life I was terribly lonely and have often sighed deeply: Give me a human being! In vain! I remained lonely! But I can honestly say it was not my fault; I turned no one away, I fled no one who would have been human in mind and heart. I have found nothing but miserable wretches, dull spirits, cold hearts and narrow minds; except Goethe, Fernow, possibly F. A. Wolf and a few others, all of them twenty-five to forty years older than I. Slowly the resentment of individuals had to make way for a quiet contempt of all mankind. At an early age I became conscious of the difference between me and my fellow men. But I thought: Get to know a hundred, and you will find your man; and later: In a thousand you will find him. Then: At last he must be found, even if it takes many thousands. But finally I had to realize that nature is far more miserly, and that I had to bear with dignity and patience Byron's "solitude of kings."

When we compare these words, spoken only for himself, with those that were meant for his readers, we will find that in his public utterances Schopenhauer never confessed to long for intimates, but rather that he proudly cited a need for solitude as a sign of greatness and profundity:

> That a man is of noble nature will be revealed primarily in this: that he finds no pleasure in others but prefers solitude more and more to their company.
> Truly great spirits, like eagles, build their aeries high up, in solitude.
> "He is not gregarious," is almost synonymous with "He is a man of noble qualities."
> For the more one has in himself, the less he has need of the external world, the less others can give him. That is why eminence of spirit leads to unsociability.

Schopenhauer's failures in the teaching profession, with colleagues, in social gatherings, with women, gave rise to secondary resentment and arrogance. He interpreted his failure with others as their fault and therefore became a misanthrope, a foe of sociability, of philosophy professors, and in particular of women.

It is easy to recognize in this behavior the mechanism of projection which serves to transform subjective disappointment into objective depreciation. Of course, those decades when he waited in vain for outward success, and the great disappointment this inflicted on his inordinate ambition, justify to a certain extent his doubts in the benevolence and justice of mankind. This is evidenced by the fact that in his old age, which was illuminated by the splendor of his belated success, his pessimism and misanthropy mellowed considerably. Nevertheless, those failures were undoubtedly caused to a large degree by his attitude toward people, and for this very reason his reaction was such a typical attempt at justification by drowning out his own share of responsibility.

Let us now look at the mechanism of resentment. It is a kind of "psychic self-poisoning" (Scheler). A person disappointed and dejected by lack of success, lack of recognition and feelings of imperfection, does not vent his feelings and impulses of revenge, anger and envy, but represses them into the unconscious, presumably also because other strong instincts were broken in life. For this mechanism presupposes a feeling of being powerless, of being unable to find revenge or compensation in any other way; an obscure feeling of being imperfect is involved. We then depreciate all those aims, powers and virtues which are unattainable for us. A falsification of values sets in, and this alleviates the displeasure we feel if we have to renounce something or are unable to attain something ("sour grapes"). This leads to a falsification of the outlook on the world. But not only the expression of one's outlook is changed, "that would still be conscious falsification"; gradually the judgment itself changes, i.e., the unconscious adopts a new set of values.

We have seen the same mechanism in action before: when we said the subjective pessimistic depression was justified by the evil and objectionable nature of the world. On the basis of numerous observations in other areas of intellectual activity, we may conclude that the formulation of a philosophic system consists to a great extent in such unconscious projections.

Schopenhauer saw another justification for his gloomy view of life in the transitoriness of time: Every moment exists only in so far as it extinguishes the preceding one, the father, and is in turn extinguished just as quickly. The present is nothing but transitoriness, nothing but decay. Time reveals the transience and nothingness of all things. "What is no more in the next moment, what immediately vanishes like a dream, that is never worthy of earnest endeavor."

No one was so oppressed by the fleeting nature of time as Schopenhauer. It prevented any feeling of happiness in him:

> In such a world where no stability of any kind, no constant state is possible, where everything is in eternal change and flux, where everything hastens and flies and maintains its equilibrium on the tightrope by incessantly walking and moving, in such a world happiness is not even conceivable [*Parerga und Paralipomena*, II].
>
> Time is the form by means of which that nothingness of things appears as transitoriness; for it makes all our joys and pleasures become as nothing in our hands so that we afterwards ask in amazement what has happened to it [*The World as Will and Idea*, II].
>
> You bewail the flight of time: it would not flee so incessantly if anything in it were worth holding [*Neue Paralipomena*].

Among Schopenhauer's papers was a translation of Milton's poem *To Time* which expresses longing for release from blind chance, death and time (*Neue Paralipomena*).

In marked contrast to the obstinate emphasis on the transitory nature of time is the philosopher's oft-repeated complaint about the insufferable boredom that fills the pain-free moments of life. We are inclined to trace this also to the depressed mood, for only one who is depressed or deeply disappointed in life, or lonely and not loving, can complain so bitterly about boredom, that is, about his discontent of unused time. That this feeling is often experienced by brilliant and creative men we know from their autobiographies. In men who live solely for their work, this feel-

ing of inner emptiness is aroused and intensified in periods when
productivity is halted.

Schopenhauer repeatedly emphasized that his philosophy was
gained by contemplation of the world. Next to the transitoriness
of time, the dreamlike quality of everything earthly made such
an impression on him that this feeling forced upon him the
second foundation pillar of his philosophic system: the world is
nothing but our idea. Though of course he continued eclectically
along the lines of Plato, Kant and the Indians, it is evident in all
his work that the most profound inner experience gave him material and food for his brilliant argument for phenomenalism.

As Volkelt aptly put it, in Schopenhauer, Kant's idealism of
thought slides instinctively into Indian dream idealism. He is
completely serious about this. Since the world is an idea, it has no
more existential validity than a dream. He .proclaimed this in
numerous passages in his works, shifting the emphasis between
affinity and essential unity of world and dream.

> My imagination often (especially in connection with mu-
> sic) plays with the thought that the lives of all men, includ-
> ing my own, are nothing but the dreams of an eternal spirit,
> dreams of good and evil, and that each death is an awaken-
> ing [*Neue Paralipomena*].
> Life is a night, filled by a long dream which often turns
> into an oppressive nightmare [*ibid.*].

Here Schopenhauer follows the views of Vedanta philosophy
and its teachings about the veil of Maja, which "shrouds the
eyes of mortals and lets them see a world of which it cannot be
said either that it exists or that it does not exist." As Volkelt further explains, Schopenhauer wanted to express by this how utterly futile and unstable, how similar to nonexistence the whole
existence is, and at the same time how meaningless and full of
anxiety. It becomes evident that inasmuch as the world for him
was mere idea, the metaphysical value of its existence is lowered.
The evaluation of the objective world in the theory of knowledge
is a metaphysical value judgment and a pessimistically metaphysical one at that. If we keep in mind that Schopenhauer suffered

greatly from the brutal violence of the will to live, the assumption suggests itself that his tendency to flee everything earthly contained a longing for redemption. It is significant that characteristically melancholic patients experience the world as strange, as a dream or an illusion. These patients apparently have the same wish for release from the unbearable world, issuing from their depression.

Paulsen wrote: "As always, Schopenhauer's theoretical idealism is conditioned by an idealism of a more practical nature. The insufficiency of reality as it is leads to the formation of the idea of a perfect world. This ideal world makes the real world seem valueless and then unreal. A world which does not deserve to exist cannot be the real world."

As a further source of Schopenhauer's pessimism we have to mention the anxiety that embittered his whole life and kept him always and everywhere alert and ready to expect disaster. Fear of all kinds of trouble, especially of the greatest of evils, death, overshadowed the entire life so that man is barred from a carefree, lighthearted enjoyment of it. The philosopher found consolation for this unbearable thought of personal death where mankind in general finds it—in the fantasy of eternal life. For him this took the form of the eternal, indestructible will which becomes objectivated temporarily in an individual as *principium individualationis*.

> We might perhaps grow frantic at the thought of the expiration of our brief life span if we had not deep in our heart the secret consciouness that the inexhaustible fountain of eternity belongs to us [*Parerga und Paralipomena,* II].

If we go further and look for the origin of these depressive anxiety feelings, then, as previously mentioned, we come upon the instincts. In Schopenhauer's case, the excessively powerful, probably sadistically tinged sexual instinct and its repression. The anxiety corresponds to an unsuccessful repression of lust and rage. However, the interconnection between sadomasochism and pessimism goes deeper. Pleasure in the pain of others and pleasure in one's own pain are entwined even in their extensions into the abstract, especially in the manifestation of pessimism. Simmel said:

> A sublime pleasure in cruelty lies in the destruction he visits upon generally accepted values, in the passion with which he brings into consciousness sorrows that might have remained unconscious or unacknowledged, in the appraisal of our existence which deserves nothing better than this life and this world. The generally pessimistic outlook is by no means only linked to subjective suffering, but very often to a certain pleasure in this suffering.

These correlations and their sources in the instincts, which Nietzsche revealed in a masterly fashion in *Beyond Good and Evil,* come very close to our psychoanalytic views.

What we have said about pessimism so far still does not lead us to the real origins of depression and pessimism which lie in infancy. We have mentioned the significance of constitutional inherited factors, such as instinctual and emotional anlage; of the possible existence of some actual defect in Schopenhauer's sexuality, such as perhaps too great excitability. But as followers of Freud we are accustomed to find the decisive causes for the shaping of a permanent character or personality form in the earliest psychosexual development. In Schopenhauer's psychosexual development we find abundant material for the justification of a pessimistic *Weltanschauung.*

The first family impression that met the boy's gaze showed him a youthful, cheerful and affectionate mother. This is attested to by Gwinner's remarks that the mother "had no other thought by night or day" but her Arthur. And "like all young mothers she was firmly convinced that there was no more beautiful, no cleverer or better child in God's wide world." It often happens that a mother's love for her first-born becomes exaggerated if, as was here the case, the marriage had brought disappointments. And then it may happen that the father's strictness, his punitive seriousness, and his high demands leave a disagreeable memory in the boy's mind. If we consider the father's violent temperament, his sometimes excessive roughness, we can easily understand that Schopenhauer must have suffered greatly from his irascibility, pedantry and strictness, even though he spoke of him in later years with enthusiastic gratitude. With a typical allusion to his pessimism, he himself remarked:

> As a youth I was always very melancholic, and once—I may have been eighteen years old—I thought to myself, though still so young: A God is said to have created this world? No! Rather a devil! Of course, by then I had had to suffer a great deal in growing up, through my father's strictness [Lindner and Frauenstaedt].

This passage is one of the most important proofs that the early pessimism of the boy has to be deduced from the violent and oppressive character of the father. Thus the probably most significant and earliest source of his pessimism is his relationship with the father, who must have appeared even more evil and unjust in the light of Schopenhauer's own hostile attitude (the oedipus complex). But the second decisive root of his permanently gloomy view of the world and of mankind lies—as is to be expected, because of the significance of the whole oedipus complex —in his strange relationship with the mother. The most striking factor in this relationship is the peculiar reversal of the mutual affection between mother and son into aversion and hostility, which in the course of the years grew to bitter hatred.

In a passage of the *Parerga und Paralipomena* Schopenhauer reveals his knowledge that in a marriage where the wife cannot love her husband, her instinctive mother love disappears:

> In man as in animals, mother love is purely instinctive and ceases when the children are no longer physically helpless. At this point another love is supposed to take its place, one that is based on habit and reason. But this love often fails to materialize, especially when the mother never loved the father.

When we remember that after the birth of his sister Adele (1797) the boy was sent away from home for two years, it is not difficult to assume that a jealousy was aroused in him for the lit-

tle competitor who had robbed him of his mother's love. Such
emotions can frequently be observed in children when a new
sibling is born.[25] It is very likely that this event was a decisive one
which made the boy turn away from the mother and lose his respect for her. This reversal is a striking counterpart to that which
took place in the relationship with his father. During his life the
father had appeared to the son as an evil tyrant, opposed to the
child's inclinations and desires. After his death he was revered[26]
with an exaggerated, we would say "reactive" —love which we
recognize as a compensation for infantile evil wishes toward the
father. The tendency and intensity of these secret infantile death
wishes became manifest in their first stage of repression in the
anxiety of the six-year-old boy (his parents might not return
from a walk) and cannot be explained merely by the difficult experience of the father's strictness, though they were certainly
strengthened and consciously justified by it. It must be assumed
that they derived sustenance from unconscious erotic sources
which have their origin mainly in jealous rivalry for the mother's
love (oedipus complex). We cannot dismiss the assumption that
Schopenhauer might at too early an age have witnessed sexual

[25] Here we have to add some information about Schopenhauer's sister. No
matter how much interest and even love she showed for her brother, no lasting
intimacy ever grew between them, despite the large and intimate correspondence.
Here again, Schopenhauer's aloofness and sensitivity isolated him. He must have
been very attached to her originally, for he once wrote her that aside from her
he had never loved any woman without sensuality. Adele Schopenhauer was an
unattractive girl who resembled her father. She had various talents, was well educated and intelligent, esteemed by Goethe. She too suffered from her mother's
egotism and took part in very unpleasant family scenes which "made her want to
throw herself out of the window to escape this misery." Her life was unhappy and
she was often melancholy and resigned. Despite various attempts at love, she remained unmarried. She had great understanding and deep affection for her
brother. In her interesting diaries she says: "A glimpse of what love could give
him, of what it could have made of him, a look into the past and into the future
destroyed my cheerfulness; longing and grief raged violently in my soul."

[26] Cf. the affectionate "dedication" in the second edition of Schopenhauer's
major work to the "Shades of my father" in which he apparently contradicts his
own earlier reports about his father's strictness: "Oh noble and worthy spirit, to
whom I owe everything I am and everything I achieve. Thy guiding care protected
and bore me through helpless childhood and thoughtless youth and into mature
manhood until this very day . . ."

intercourse between the parents.[27] We know from the psycho-analyses of children and adults that when the boy—as in this in-stance—encounters this for him unheard of experience which defiles the pure image of his mother ideal, he will show a typical reaction, consisting of mixed feelings toward both parents. Toward the mother, feelings of envy and revenge intensify the fantasies of her impurity and possible depravity (prostitution fantasies). Consequently he turns away in disappointment from the original ideal. Later, during puberty, these fantasies are re-activated under the pressure of a powerfully awakening object love. If now the early fantasies of the mother's depravity are even presumably or in the very smallest degree confirmed, then this pessimistic contemptuous opinion of her—which is typical for a certain stage in the child's development but is usually soon replaced by a normal emotional attitude toward mother and women—becomes, in a sense, fixated. After her husband's suicide (for which the son held her responsible) Schopenhauer's mother had intimate relations with other men so that the now grown-up and experienced son found adequate motives to provide an ac-tual basis and apparent justification for his still active infantile fantasies. Intensified by his boyhood experiences, this disappoint-ment in the unforgettable love ideal of the mother had its deep and enduring effect on Schopenhauer. His mother's behavior in which he saw a betrayal of himself, and all her later loveless and even hostile attitude grossly contradicted those early demonstra-tions of intense affection. Normally, these fantasies are soon re-pressed and somehow oriented toward life in a positive way. In Schopenhauer's case the deep disappointment in the secretly al-ways beloved mother became the second source for his pessimistic view of life, and especially for his hatred and contempt of all women. Many contemptuous remarks about womanhood in gen-eral are derived from experiences with his mother. For example, he stated that women's extravagance always calls for male guard-

27 This appears to be born out by the story which Schopenhauer confided to K. Baehr: that his father once caught him at the forbidden activity of reading a novel, when he entered unexpectedly to reach the mother's room. "Both caught in the act," as Schopenhauer put it.

ianship, because he believed that he was justified in reproaching
his mother with squandering his father's fortune:

> In most instances, such a woman will waste with her para-
> mour what the father of the children, thinking especially of
> the children, has toiled all his life to acquire. It makes no
> difference whether she marries or not . . . After the hus-
> band's death, the actual mother often turns into a step-
> mother . . . In general, a woman who did not love her hus-
> band will not love his children; that is, after the period of
> purely instinctive mother love, which cannot be morally
> accredited to her, is past [*Parerga und Paralipomena*, II].

We believe that we have established the probability that the
earliest and deepest roots of Schopenhauer's pessimism can be
found in the peculiar parent constellation which at times made
his father appear cruel and diabolic, his mother dissolute. It is
most likely that here too we may find the explanation for the
often stressed objectionableness of the sexual act in which—following the views of Christianity—Schopenhauer saw the primary
guilt of all mankind.

> Human existence by no means has the character of a gift
> but entirely that of a contracted debt. The demand for its
> payment appears in the form of the urgent needs, torment-
> ing desires and endless distress created by that existence. As
> a rule, one's whole life is employed in paying off this debt:
> but this only covers the interest. Repayment of the capital
> occurs through death. And when was this debt contracted?
> —at conception [*The World as Will and Idea*, II].
>
> Life presents itself as a task, a problem to be solved, and
> hence a constant struggle against distress. And so everyone
> tries to get by and through with it as best he can: he serves
> his time, as if life were forced labor to which he was sen-
> tenced. But who had contracted this debt?—He who begat
> him in an act of gratifying his lust [*ibid.*].

Many of Schopenhauer's traits, his depression, his bitterness
about life and love, his pessimistic *Weltanschauung* in particular, remind us strongly of Shakespeare's Hamlet—as Paulsen
pointed out. The deepest root of this resemblance, which is much
more far-reaching, becomes clear on the basis of Freud's interpre-

tation of the Hamlet problem: the same constellation of the oedipus complex. In both cases we see a youth's overemphasized tender love for a father whose premature passing away was allegedly
caused by the mother, and contempt for the adulterous mother.
In both cases the result is the same, a conviction of the badness of
the world and of mankind, philosophic brooding, especially on
the subject of death, and the sexual aversion toward all women
on the part of a son who was originally enamored of his mother
and later on deeply disappointed in her. It cannot be a mere coincidence that Schopenhauer himself, in speaking of the inner
resistance to the ruthless unearthing of scientific truth, quoted
as a simile the Oedipus myth:

> What makes the philosopher is the courage to leave no
> question unasked. He must be like Sophocles' Oedipus who,
> seeking enlightenment about his own horrible fate, con-
> tinues to question, although he already foresees that the an-
> swer will yield the utmost terror. Most people are like
> Jokaste, who begs Oedipus to cease his questioning. And
> they give in, and that is why philosophy is in the state in
> which it has always been [Letter to Goethe, November 11,
> 1815].[28]

This passage would seem to indicate that the Oedipus theme
was an important psychic experience for the young Schopenhauer. Freud pointed out that those men who know themselves
preferred and favored by their mothers show great self-confidence
and unshakable optimism, qualities which not infrequently
bring real success in their wake (Freud, 1900, p. 207).[29] Schopenhauer provides a counterpart to this observation. The abrupt rejection by the mother and her stinging, unkind criticism of him
during the decisive years of his development had to turn him
into a pessimist.

On the basis of this peculiar oedipus complex, Schopenhauer
showed other character traits and eccentricities. Aside from the

[28] In connection with the psychological content of this letter see Ferenczi (1912).
[29] Let us cite the example of Goethe. According to Moebius, his parents were
similar in temperament to Schopenhauer's; but he never lost the mother's tender
affection and he developed an optimistic outlook, pleasure in life and people.

external and internal causes mentioned above, the strongest motivation for his confirmed bachelordom was the linking of his inner fate to his mother. When this type of man feels disappointed by the mother, hatred and contempt for women develop in the place of the usual respect for a love ideal that recalls the beloved mother.[30] In his love life he separated sexuality from nobler psychic sensations by having recourse to prostitution. That Schopenhauer hardly ever experienced the higher spiritual love but like Mephistopheles saw only the coarse sensuousness ("aus einem Punkte zu kurieren"—*Faust*, I) must be considered another source of his depression and pessimism. This interpretation of sexual love as devoid of any positive, elevating, spiritual element is shared by the pessimistic Eduard von Hartmann. Rosa Mayreder in her *Critique of Femininity* very rightly emphasizes the interconnection between an ascetic-pessimistic *Weltanschauung* and nonerotic sexuality linked to intense intellectuality. This separation of sex and Eros which includes the particular disparagement of feminine sexuality, goes back to the ambivalent feelings toward the mother and is strengthened by premature experiences which render sexuality in general contemptible. The psychic attitude toward the father is responsible for character traits which become significant in later life. Even though Schopenhauer succeeded in transforming the hatred for his father after his death into respect, he displayed a spirit of revolt and opposition toward everything and everybody, especially toward professors of science and toward his predecessors. He turned against everything established, against almost every kind of authority. His attitude of intellectual superiority, for which his mother sharply censured him, also stemmed from his father complex. Paulsen said: "Opposition and contradiction—these are the elements he thrives on. If others find security by upholding accepted values, Schopenhauer finds his in contradiction. He

[30] As proof of the maternal source of Schopenhauer's misogyny we may cite his brusque rebuff of all attempts at rapprochement by women writers who were abhorrent to him in his inmost soul; condemnation of the modern "lady" and her favored position in society; that he never used any term but *Weiber*.

would feel contemptible if he caught himself thinking, judging, feeling as the rest of the world thinks, judges and feels."

The son's inner struggle between love and aversion, respect and mockery, is evident in Schopenhauer's peculiar behavior toward teachers and other persons of authority to whom he was deeply obligated. Even as a child he incurred a teacher's displeasure because he wrote a satirical poem. He wrote malicious, arrogantly critical, sarcastic comments about his professors in the margins of his lecture notebooks ("drivel," "Sophist," "blockhead"). Later he assailed philosophy professors in general, and Hegel in particular, with boundless scorn and mockery. Even the respect he had for Kant did not save the latter from defamation. The changes Kant made in the second edition of *Critique of Pure Reason,* Schopenhauer ascribed to "hypocrisy and fear of his fellow men." Goethe, who had gone out of his way to assist and recognize the young philosopher, fared no better. As a young man, Schopenhauer revered him like a God (cf. his letter to F. A. Wolf: "praised be his name in all eternity"), but in later years he called him an egotist and coarse fellow. Another indication for the decline of paternal authority is the fact that contrary to Kant, Schopenhauer as a boy became irreligious and never believed in God. The cause may account, in part at least, for his dislike of his native country and his native town, and for his occasional remarks about his nation, which he called the most stupid of all.

In this interpretation of Schopenhauer's pessimism we have emphasized the personal psychological roots of this complex, roots that derived sustenance from an area bordering on the pathological. We have implied a criticism of this pessimism which is almost forced upon the objective observer by Schopenhauer's gross exaggeration. It is well known that even the average person is temporarily inclined to skeptical, pessimistic, aphoristic wisdom, especially in moments of introspection, and that the adolescent, particularly during the period of puberty, may suffer depressions. At such times, or at a time when something has gone wrong, one is apt to become an adherent of a pessimistic philosopher. But mankind will never concede that only pain is positive, that pleasure is nothing but a relief from pain. Natural feeling cannot follow the philosopher when his personal experience obviously makes him go against commonly accepted ideas. Altruistic pleasure, shared pleasure, was alien to this man whom his inner fate isolated from everybody. He had to renounce companionship of the home, friendship and family—all relationships in which egoism has to recede. According to Volkelt, "nothing finds Schopenhauer's appreciation that means quiet contentment, intimacy, cheerful jest, joyful play." Or as Paulsen put it: "For these things Schopenhauer, one might say, is colorblind."

In utterances of his later years, especially in the famous *Aphorisms on the Wisdom of Life,* Schopenhauer tended toward a somewhat optimistic view of life. He wrote these dicta as "directions for a happy existence." "Indeed, every line of these aphorisms tells us that the true sage, the man to whom was allotted the greatest possible earthly happiness, the man we should all emulate in all decisions and inclinations—is Dr. Arthur Schopenhauer" (Seillière).[31] Here it is easy to see how much complacent self-contemplation (narcissism) is involved in philosophical formulations.

That he did not conceal this more optimistic view of life is proof that Schopenhauer maintained his characteristic veracity and sincerity. But it would be wrong to call his pessimism insincere, as Kuno Fischer did. The fact that his unconscious pleasure in pain did not go further than to express itself in a pessimistic interpretation of the world, that he did not go around in sackcloth and ashes, did not commit suicide—we cannot consider that a contradiction, it only shows us the boundaries of his submission. The martyr, the penitent, the suicide—in the final analysis they all do what they enjoy doing. Schopenhauer's pessimism was his painful pleasure; his abuse, his fault finding, his moralizing were his gratifications. (Cf. the quotation: "*Celà m'amuse d'être triste.*") Happiness for him meant to give his intellectual personality free rein, to be conscious of his inner worth. In this sense, maybe, Kuno Fischer could say that Scho-

[31] S. S. Rzewuski has made a study of Schopenhauer's optimism (Paris, 1911).

penhauer was one of the happiest of men. But part of this happiness stemmed from his ability to express his pessimism. "The greatest gifts of life were his: great intellectual power, a completely independent existence . . . full leisure to live for his genius and to develop his talents . . . the fulfillment of a high calling in a number of works whose immortality he felt and foresaw with unerring certainty, rugged good health in the last decades of his life . . . a ripe old age, brilliantly illuminated and warmed by the sunshine of fame . . . and finally a quick, gentle death." Yet we have to record many liabilities in this life: cheerful moods, the giving and receiving of love, working for others—but if he had had these, what would have become of his pessimism!

Nietzsche sees in pessimism and asceticism signs of "life's decline." Schopenhauer belonged to that minority of participants at the Lord's table who do not relish the food. Their contempt for what is offered is no proof that it is bad—it only reveals the psychophysical constitution of the participant.

CONCLUDING THOUGHTS

Now that we have applied the method of psychoanalysis to the appraisal of Schopenhauer's personality and to the basic features of his philosophy, we have come appreciably nearer to the goal we had set ourselves. We intended to use Schopenhauer as an example to show that every feature of the living personality—the characteristics of his individuality, his activity, his method of work, his eccentricities, etc.—that all these may be explained, not only by heredity and the influence of experience, but on the basis of the instinctual predispositions that are manifest in childhood and especially by the constellations of the family. We wanted to deduce the basic features of a philosophy from the unconscious of its creator and to reveal the mechanisms by means of which all the known components were fused into one unique philosophic system. We consider Schopenhauer a classic example for the proof of our theories. Due to a certain simplicity in his philosophizing, a closeness to psychic primitivity, the psychic roots of his philosophy appear more clearly visible than those of other metaphysicians. Many Schopenhauer students have been conscious of this. Paulsen said, "There is perhaps no other thinker in whom the connection between philosophy and personality is of such fundamental importance and at the same time so obvious." As Keyserling remarked in his critique, Schopenhauer, the philosopher, did not succeed in "overcoming the empirical with the idea," as did Hegel and others. "Schopenhauer's philosophy is really and truly a self-confession, but it is no great philosophy," is the final verdict of the temperamental Graf Keyserling.

Since our psychological method of investigation was largely gained from the experiences of clinical psychoanalysis and only individual phases were later applied to the psychology of creative artists, we cannot overlook the pathological components that are present in Schopenhauer's personality, if they help further our analysis. We have to admit that, unlike Schopenhauer, we do not see in genius a metaphysical marvel, but rather, like Nietzsche, consider it something human. But we want to use this opportunity to refute the accusation that we want to belittle greatness, make genius seem banal. On the contrary, we are only too conscious that we must stop short in deference before the creativity of genius.

Let us sumarize Schopenhauer's pathological features. No matter how much recognition was accorded him by great men in his youth, no matter how the prophesies of his greatness were fulfilled, and how he succeeded in asserting his will for intellectual power, his self-praise and self-confidence must be called immoderate.

"It is futile to look for contradictions in me: everything is completely harmonious, poured from one mold," he wrote to J. A. Becker (1854) regarding his philosophy which was considered full of inner contradictions by the majority of competent critics. Thus R. Haym concluded his review with the statement that his own hypotheses led Schopenhauer to pull everything out of joint, "and it is not going too far to assert that not one stone has been left on another." The existence of numerous contradictions in Schopenhauer's system is partly caused by the inner dichotomy of his nature and by the stubborn obstinacy with which he persisted in a statement once made, but partly also by the small regard he had of conscious mental thought processes against intuitive views.

At this point a few more quotations may be added as proof of this exaggerated self-confidence which bordered on megalomania. Schopenhauer once wrote to Frauenstaedt: "My philosophy will play a part in the world such as no other philosophy in ancient or modern times."

> Within the limits of human knowledge my philosophy is the real solution of the riddle of the world. In this sense it can be called a revelation. It is inspired by the spirit of truth; in fact, there are some paragraphs in the fourth volume which could be regarded as inspired by the Holy Ghost [Neue Paralipomena].
>
> Among men I almost always feel as Jesus of Nazareth felt when he summoned his disciples who were always asleep [Dresden, 1816].

Schopenhauer indeed regarded himself as the founder of a new doctrine of salvation and redemption, he saw himself as the Occidental Buddha, so to speak, as the future subject for a cult of images and relics, and in all seriousness he addressed his pupils and adherents as "apostles and evangelists" (Kuno Fischer).

In his youth Schopenhauer showed some inclination for sociability, but as he passed into manhood his withdrawal into himself assumed decidedly morbid forms. More and more of his utterances attempted to justify this unconscious urge with the immorality of the world and of men in a paranoid manner.

> In a world where five sixths at least are scoundrels, fools and blockheads, every one of the remaining sixth must find the basis for his life's system in seclusion, the more so the farther apart he is from the others. If one is not to be the sport of every rascal and the mockery of every fool, the first rule of life must be this: be reserved. What a man like that thinks and feels bears no resemblance to what those others think and feel [according to Seidlitz].

Such hypotrophic ego feeling is induced when love is withdrawn from the surrounding world, upon which it is normally directed, and turned toward the own ego. In a sense, one would call Schopenhauer's nature "autistic," so completely did he ignore the surrounding world in favor of his own inner being, so unswervingly did he hold fast to his dreams and brooding. Whenever he could not ignore the world or take away its reality by withdrawal of his libido (the world as idea), he reviled it or experienced it as hostile. When we discussed his pessimism, we pointed out that Schopenhauer's hostile relationship to the world (as to his mother) was adopted only secondarily, after he had wanted to embrace it with expectant affection and had been disappointed. Freud deduced this mechanism from the analysis of a highly intelligent paranoiac who also had outlined a cosmic philosophy, though an insane one.[32] Apart from his pessimism and the feeling that the world was hostile, Schopenhauer actually had delusions about being injured,[33] revealed most clearly in his attitude toward professors of philosophy (Paulsen). He regarded them in all seriousness as being in a conspiracy against him. He charged that his writings were not only ignored, but deliberately kept secret.

Schopenhauer's feelings of anxiety, which we have already discussed in detail, were decidedly morbid. His illness could be described as an anxiety neurosis. We have in mind not only his attacks of anxiety, his dreams, the phobias of his later years; his whole being was permeated by anxiety and expectancy of disaster—against which he took all kinds of precautions—caused by repressed sexuality and aggression.

The peculiar emotional condition which we find mentioned even in his youth recalls the picture of "constitutional depres-

---

[32] D. P. Schreber (1903).

[33] Persons whose hearing is seriously impaired are frequently found to be distrustful, sensitive and "paranoid." We should add here that Schopenhauer, like his father, was hard of hearing. This hereditary defect, as he said, dogged him throughout life, even in his youth. At thirty-five he was almost completely deaf in his right ear, at sixty-four the left ear began gradually to deteriorate. This fact, too, must have played a part in Schopenhauer's social isolation.

sion" given by descriptive psychiatry of the old school. An explanatory and genetic science will have to trace this back in each instance to its psychogenesis, as we shall do now. By comparison we will quote Kraepelin's description of these symptoms:

> Constitutional depression is characterized by marked chronic feelings of gloom in all life situations . . . The patients are especially receptive to the worries, toils and disappointments of life . . . Life, every activity, are burdens which they endure in dutiful self-denial in a routine way without the compensation of enjoyment. The patients' entire conduct of life is considerably influenced by their suffering. They are indecisive, slow, inhibited by their melancholy outlook on life. Every impulse of lightheartedness or daring is stifled by the dread of responsibility, the fear of the most remote possibilities. Not infrequently, they develop whims and characteristics which are in some relation to their depression and serve as protective measures; by these means the patient seeks to extricate himself from his inner difficulties . . . In a number of cases the emotional life is dominated by a dejected, irritable, embittered mood. As a rule, this is accompanied by a heightened egocentricity. The patients are easily offended, sensitive, difficult to manage, distrustful, given to nagging, quarrelsome and discontent. They are rebellious against authority, dogmatic, claiming to know everything better. In some patients spasmodic irascibility is particularly prominent . . . Some patients are highly talented, often with pronounced artistic and literary inclinations . . . Some are able to perform competent and even important work in the intellectual field.

The profound difference, which we cannot here elucidate further, and which was a fortunate conquest over the threatening fate of permanent illness, lies in Schopenhauer's brilliant talent and in his capacity for concentrated purposeful work, as contrasted with the easily collapsing, neurasthenic inadequacy of the patients.

If we attempt to explain the development of a philosopher and of his philosophic system, we shall see that Schopenhauer himself has paved the way for a psychological interpretation in our sense. We trace philosophic intellectual activity back to the in-

fantile curiosity and urge to ask questions which later are chan-
neled into a need for inquiry into origin and decay, the whence
and wherefore of existence. We must assume that an inquisitive
propensity of special intensity, branching off from sexual instincts, returns as a philosophic need for knowledge and that now
the intellectual processes are invested with pleasure.[34] It is disappointment in life that makes a man persist in these problems
and give thought preference over action. We mentioned before
that in his younger years, when life appeared to him to be "a
sorry business," Schopenhauer resolved to spend his life in con-
templating it.

> Only after we have become discontented and to a certain
> extent at odds with the world of reality, do we turn to the
> world of thought for satisfaction.
> Philosophic pondering is basically perplexed and
> troubled. Philosophy, like the overture to *Don Giovanni,*
> begins in a minor key.
> Only want can lift you above yourself, says Goethe. As
> long as we have what satisfies the will, or even what promises
> satisfaction, no brilliant production will result: for atten-
> tion is directed toward our own person. Only when wishes
> and hopes come to naught, when unalterable privation ap-
> pears and the will must remain unsatisfied, only then does
> one ask: what is the world? Those who have only trivial,
> weak, easily gratified wishes, will be satisfied and held fast
> and will never reach a state of contemplation. Only those
> who strive mightily must become either world conquerors or
> great adventurers, or perish; or else they can, especially if
> nothing whatsoever can satisfy their strivings, arrive at con-
> templation.

In pathology we find that people with a highly charged instinctual life have the tendency to brood about death and to turn
reactively from the sensual to the metaphysical. Thus, in our
experience, the sadist succumbs most easily to compulsive neurosis. In persons so disposed, anxiety and death become the main
topics, as necessary reactions to repressed wishes of death and

---

[34] Cf. Nietzsche: "I do not believe that an 'instinct for knowledge' is the father
of philosophy, but that another instinct, here as elsewhere, has availed itself of
knowledge and the lack of it merely as a tool."

vengeance directed against people of their environment. Analogous to these compulsive neurotics (of whom Freud said that they misuse their thinking) we find in Schopenhauer, with his repressed violent instinctual life, his philosophic system, including his ethics, as a reaction and substitute.[35]

It may hold true for most speculative philosophers that, like compulsive neurotics, they prefer to brood over metaphysical matters, such as death and the beyond, because their thinking was originally filled with sensual fantasies. The energy of the sexual impulse was displaced from the objectionable content of the fantasies onto the act of thinking as such, erotizing the thinking, so to speak. Other psychic pecularities of compulsive neurotics manifest in Schopenhauer are excessive doubting and indecisiveness, and a superstition that is doubly striking in the light of his erudition and skepticism. Not only did he believe in the apparitions of second sight and spiritualism, he defended mankind's ineradicable bent to believe in omens, their bibliomancy, card reading, etc. His life insurance premium was for him "a sacrifice, offered publicly by everyone on the altar of evil demons." The following experiences, which Schopenhauer claimed to be warnings of an impending fate, prove the significant relationship between superstition and the subject of death, which Freud discovered in compulsive neurotics. The dream appears to hint at Schopenhauer's (previously conjectured) homosexual tendencies, while the vision would prove the repressed wish for the death of the parents.

In order to serve truth in every form unto death, I record that in the New Year's night between 1830 and 1831 I had the following dream which points to my death in this present year. From my sixth until my tenth year I had a bosom friend and constant playmate who was exactly my age; his

35 To point out the contrast between the need to live fully and the need for philosophic knowledge of the world, let me quote a passage from the novel "Sanin" by Artzibaschew, who favors full living: "My life—that means my emotions and experiences, good or bad. As to what lies behind their limits, I spit on it, no matter what hypothesis we might put forward; it will always remain just a hypothesis, and to build one's life on such a foundation would be folly. Whoever needs to do so may spend his life worrying about that, but I intend to live it."

name was Gottfried Jaenisch, and he died while I was in France, in my tenth year. During the last thirty years I very rarely thought of him. In that said night I came to a country that was unknown to me. A group of men stood in a field, among them a grown-up, tall slender man who somehow or other was introduced to me as that very Gottfried Jaenisch, and he bade me welcome.

(It was to a great extent this dream which induced me to leave Berlin at the outbreak of the cholera in 1831. It may have contained a hypothetic truth, a warning, i.e., had I remained, I would have died of the cholera.)

Immediately after my arrival in Frankfurt, I had a perfectly clear apparition: It was (I believe) my parents; and it indicated that I now would survive my mother who was then still living; my father, who was already dead, carried a light in his hand [*Neue Paralipomena*].

Concerning these dreams, Frauenstaedt remarked: "Just as Schopenhauer saw in magic effects the omnipotence of the will, he saw 'our omniscience' in premonitions, in fratricidal dreams, in visions that reveal the future." Another peculiar feature of compulsive thinking is a belief in the magical power to influence other people; this belief is based upon the feeling that thought is omnipotent. In Schopenhauer's fundamental philosophy we find to a certain extent this need to turn thoughts into force. The whole powerful, objective world is nothing but a product of our thoughts: The world is my Idea. That the world is also Will (the unconscious)—the title of the main work comprises both these concepts—points to the previously mentioned projection of Schopenhauer's dichotomy of conscious and unconscious onto his philosophic system which surveys the whole world through these bifocals. "As the philosopher himself is of a dual nature, he will survey the world from the point of view of this duality: as Will and Idea. He will find and point out this great contrast everywhere: in theoretical philosophy it is the contrast between the thing in itself and the appearance, in metaphysics between body and will, in aesthetics between idea and individual, in practical philosophy between egotistical assertion of the will and super-individualistic denial of the will" (Paulsen).

So we come ever closer to our goal, i.e., showing that what the philosopher regards as objective truth, as the definitive solution of the world's riddle, represents primarily nothing but individualistic compulsive thought processes and their projection and shows that his own particular affects force him into a set direction. Schopenhauer shows what Rosa Mayreder called "the two most peculiar qualities which most strongly bind man's intellectual life to its substrata: the dependency of all thought on one's own particular innate disposition, and the tendency to consider the results of one's own thoughts as objective truth."

In a similar sense Paulsen said: "I do not believe that there is any case better suited than that of Schopenhauer to study the influence which emotions have on thought."

We are not disseminating a new wisdom. People of insight have long since acknowledged that all philosophic contemplation is subjective. Zola said about art that it is an image of the world, viewed through a temperament. And philosophy, according to Simmel, is a temperament, viewed through an image of the world. Goethe very aptly compared philosophers to physicians, who prohibit or prescribe something for us, depending on whether they themselves like it or dislike it. "One person is borne to be a stoic, and therefore embraces stoicism; the same holds true for the Epicurean. Kant's strict moderation called for a philosophy that was in keeping with this innate quality. By virtue of his inclinations, every individual has a right to principles that would not deny him as an individual. Here and nowhere else the origin of all philosophy can most likely be found" (Falk, Biedermann).

According to the radical Nietzsche, who saw in thoughts only "a certain relation of the instincts to one another," and in reason and its laws nothing more than a "grammatical prejudice," this holds true even for moral principles:

There are those moral systems which are intended to justify their originator in the eyes of others; then there are those systems which are to calm him and make him be at peace with himself; with others, the originator proposes to

humiliate and crucify himself; there are those systems which
are meant to be a revenge; some behind which the originator
wants to hide; those that are to exalt him and soar high into
the far beyond; this system serves its originator to forget,
that one to make others forget him or something about him;
by his system of morals Kant gives us to understand that
"what is worthy of respect in me is that I can obey—and you
shall not be different from me!"—In short, moral systems are
nothing but a sign language of the affects [*Beyond Good and
Evil*].

Until now we have not attempted to explain how something
that has been seen in the mind—and, of course, one can really
properly look only into one's own mind—is unconsciously
grasped and made into thoughts and words and finds form and
validity in metaphysics or religion. Freud has expressed this brilliant thought: ". . . that a large portion of the mythological conception of the world which reaches far into the most modern
religions, *is nothing but psychology projected to the outer world.*
The dim perception (the endo-psychic perception, as it were) of
psychic factors and relations of the unconscious was taken as a
model in the construction of a *transcendental reality,* which is
destined to be changed again by science into *psychology of the
unconscious.* . . .We venture to explain in this way the myths
of paradise and the fall of man, of God, of good and evil, of immortality and the like—that is, to transform *metaphysics* into
meta-psychology" (Freud, 1904).

Such unconscious projections of endopsychic perceptions obviously play a part in all generalizations, in all statements about
one's own self and about mankind; it is not possible for man to
think in any other way than an anthropomorphic one. Incidentally, here too we are reminded of the symptom formation of paranoiacs which Freud explained by means of this "outward projection of inner (suppressed) perceptions." We have to take the
liberty to point to these analogies in pathology, for it was in
pathology that psychoanalysis could first study those mechanisms
clearly and thoroughly. Psychoanalysis has skillfully illuminated
those unsuccessful philosophic systems and cosmogenies of para-

phrenics who are preoccupied completely with themselves. These systems are but a caricature of the systems developed from similar complexes and with the aid of analogous mechanisms by serious and prominent philosophers. In the systems of patients it can be clearly shown that the objects of these withdrawals and later projections onto the outer world are fantasies of a sexual nature which appear as more or less unrecognizable intellectualizations of the most trivial physical and psychic events.

Schopenhauer's work, therefore, is essentially an image—be it positive or negative—of his own inmost nature. His metaphysics are the greatly enlarged image of his innermost being. "I have," said Schopenhauer, "reversed the dictum which pronounced man a microcosm. I have proven the world to be a macoranthropos."

All philosophy is ultimately self-contemplation. In the system of a philosopher his own features are mirrored with the same complacency with which Narcissus contemplated his own reflection upon the water, or with which a father loves himself anew in the reflection of his features in his children. As Sedlitz said, Schopenhauer was "enraptured by his major work to the point of fanaticism. It was the only thing in the world which he truly loved and wherein he loved his own self." No other philosopher makes it so glaringly obvious that "the Alpha and Omega of his philosophy, the center toward which everything within him gravitates, on which even the most remote prospect reflects its light, is the person of Arthur Schopenhauer" (Keyserling).

Up to now we have shown how the unconscious, which is so clearly manifest in Schopenhauer's personality and especially in his pathological features, also led, in the form of projection, to the formulation of his philosophic system. The psychological genius recognized the active unconscious—which was extraordinarily effective within him—not only in himself (endopsychically) but also in various phenomena of life, though, of course, only in a fragmentary way.

As we could show by numerous examples, the dream made the deepest impression on him. The dream emerges as an important problem in the foundation of his doctrine. He believed he had found its solution in his essay "On Second Sight and Related Problems." The intuitive faculty of the genius seemed to him almost identical with the "dream organ" which, as he believed, made it possible to prophesy the future.

Certain of Schopenhauer's observations, which characteristically take the dream life as their point of origin, read as if the philosopher had had a clear awareness of an unconscious life. We only have to discount the metaphysical consequences he drew from them:

> There is something beyond consciousness, which sometimes, however, breaks in on it, like a moonbeam on a cloudy night. And we realize that the course of our life takes us neither nearer to it, nor further away from it, that the old man is as close to it as the child, and we find out that our life has no parallaxis to it, no more than the world's orbit has to to the fixed stars [*Neue Paralipomena*].

> When we awaken from a dream that affects us deeply, what convinces us of its nothingness is not so much the fact that it vanishes; it is rather the discovery of another reality which lies hidden beyond the one that stirs us and which now comes to the fore. All of us have a pervasive foreboding or presentiment that another reality, a completely different one, lies behind the one in which we live . . . [*ibid.*].

> Consciousness is merely the surface of our mind; all we know is the surface of the mind, just as we know only the surface of the earth, not its core.

These and similar passages, and also his interest in magic, clairvoyance, table turning, etc., disclose a clear presentiment of the powerful influence of an unconscious psychic life.

Quite early Schopenhauer became interested in psychic abnormalities. It is reported that he often visited the Charité (the mental hospital) where the melancholics in particular aroused his curiosity. In his polemics against Fichte he pointed out the relationship between genius and insanity. Most surprising is his attempt at an explanation of insanity. This attempt clearly expresses the theory of the repression of painful ideas into the unconscious as the cause of psychoneuroses and many other mental illnesses,[36] and shows most striking analogies with the theories of Freud.

In the first volume of his major work (paragraph 36) Schopenhauer discussed the relation between genius and madness and said of men of genius: "Finally, they are given to monologues,[37] and in general may show several weaknesses which actually approach madness." He emphasized that a damaged memory has an essential feature of madness, in the following sense:

. . . that the thread of memory is broken, the consecutive connection destroyed, and no evenly connected recollection of the past possible . . . there are gaps in their recollection which they fill with fiction. . . . In their memory fact and fiction become more and more mixed . . . the influence of this fictitious past then prevents the use of the correctly perceived present. . . . That violent mental suffering, unexpected horrible experiences often cause madness, I explain to myself as follows. All such suffering is, as an actual occurrence, always limited to the present, therefore only transitory and as such not excessively grave. It only becomes unbearably great in so far as it turns into lasting pain; but as such it is again only thought and therefore lies in the memory; when such sorrow, such painful knowledge or memory is so tormenting that it becomes absolutely unbearable so that the individual would succumb to it—then nature, in this distress, takes recourse in madness as a final means to save life: it is as if such a terribly tortured mind severed the threads of memory and filled the gaps with fantasy, thus fleeing the mental pain that exceeds its strength and taking refuge in madness. . . . A weak analogy to this transition from pain to madness is this: we frequently try to scare away a painful memory which suddenly assails us, as if mechanically, by means of some loud remark or by a movement, to divert ourselves from it, to distract ourselves by force.

[36] Rank (1911) was the first to point out that this conception of Schopenhauer's was in accord with the psychoanalytic one. Hinrichson (1911) drew parallels between Schopenhauer and Freud. In the text above, reference is made to Juliusburger's pertinent comments (1912).

[37] The fact that Schopenhauer frequently held loud monologues while walking in the street leads us to assume that he made these observations on himself.

We quoted this passage at such length because of its significance. It clearly shows Schopenhauer's understanding of the repression of painful ideas from consciousness and its importance
for the origin of psychic disturbances. He also understood the
determinant significance of wishful thinking which under certain circumstances may lead to the individual's flight into illness.
The commentary on this passage in Chapter 32 of the second
volume contains an excellent formulation of the theory of repression and even takes into consideration Freud's concept of
"ill-fated repression."

> The explanation of the origin of madness given in the text
> will become more intelligible if we bear in mind how re-
> luctant we are to think of things which hurt our interest, our
> pride or our wishes, how much determination it takes for
> us to present such things to our own intellect for close and
> serious examination; how easily, on the other hand, we leap
> away again or steal away from them; how completely of their
> own accord pleasant matters come to our mind, and if chased
> away constantly recur again so that we dwell upon them by
> the hour. This resistance of the will to let what is repugnant
> to it come under the scrutiny of the intellect, this is the point
> where madness can break in upon the mind. For every new
> adverse incident must be assimilated by the intellect, i.e., re-
> ceive a place in the system of truths related to our will and
> its interest, even at the price of displacing something that
> would be more gratifying. As soon as this is done, the pain
> diminishes; but the process itself is often very painful and
> usually occurs slowly and against much resistance. Yet health
> of mind can only prevail as long as this process is each time
> properly completed. If, on the other hand, in any one par-
> ticular case the resistance and opposition of the will to the
> acceptance of a knowledge reaches such a degree that the
> process cannot be completely carried through; if thus certain
> events or changes are kept from the intellect because the will
> cannot bear to face them; if then the resultant gap is filled
> at random—then madness ensues. For the intellect has re-
> nounced its nature in order to please the will; now the in-
> dividual imagines something that does not exist. But the
> resulting madness now becomes the Lethe of unbearable

suffering; it was the last resort of tortured nature, i.e., of the will . . .

In accordance with this account, the origin of madness can be regarded as a violent 'rejection from the mind' of some matter. But this is only possible by means of 'taking into one's head' something else. The opposite process is rarer, that 'taking into one's head' comes first, and 'rejection from the mind' follows. It occurs in those instances where a person keeps constantly before his mind the occasion which brought on his madness and cannot rid himself of it. For example, in those cases where madness was caused by love, in erotomania, the victim constantly broods about the occasion; or when madness resulted from fright about a sudden horrible experience. Such patients cling almost convulsively to thoughts they have seized so that no other thought can arise, least of all an opposite one. In both processes, however, the essential aspect of madness remains the same, namely, the impossibility of a uniformly coherent recollection which is the basis of our healthy, rational reflection. This contrast in origin, which has here been described, might perhaps, if judiciously applied, provide an incisive principle of classification for cases of actual insanity.

I have only considered the psychic origin of madness, i.e., madness brought on by external, objective happenings. More often, though, it has purely somatic causes . . . In most cases both causes of madness would influence each other, particularly the somatic will influence the psychic . . . I have presented the psychic genesis of madness as it can be brought on by a great misfortune in what to all appearances is a healthy mind. In a person who is somatically strongly predisposed to madness, a very much slighter calamity will suffice to induce it. . . . If there is a marked somatic predisposition, as soon as this has reached maturity, no special occasion is required. It is possible that madness which has arisen from purely psychic causes may, through the forced reversal of thought process which produced it, induce some kind of paralysis or other deterioration of parts of the brain; such injury, if not corrected quickly, will become permanent. For this reason, madness is curable only in the beginning but not after considerable time has elapsed.

To what extent Schopenhauer was a forerunner of the Freudian theory of the unconscious and other psychoanalytic insights, is shown by Juliusburger who points out Schopenhauer's recognition of the fundamental importance of sexuality for the origin of psychic disturbances as well as for the committing of crimes.

Inasmuch as there is the closest relationship between the unconscious and the instinctual elements in man, the enormous significance of sexuality must have been obvious for Schopenhauer in whom it was, as we know, strongly developed and in a peculiar way. We have already quoted some words of his which acknowledge this importance for the human psyche in the widest sense. That Schopenhauer wrote *The Metaphysics of Sexual Love* is another proof. It is no coincidence that he thought and brooded about this subject. It rather seems to confirm that this may have been in his earliest childhood the subject of his first investigation. Not every one, however, feels the need for a metaphysical interpretation of sexuality. In keeping with our previous statements, it may have been astonishment, wonder, suffering and dissatisfaction that led him to look for the reasons behind it all. Schopenhauer himself described his philosophic production as an unconscious process and attributed to the results achieved in such a way the greatest possible truth content. Though he occasionally asserted (in his *Cogita*): "All the thoughts that I have recorded arose from external occasions, usually from intuitive impressions, and have been objectively written down," there are a number of confessions which contradict this statement and prove without a doubt the subjective, intuitive method of his productivity. In addition to the previously quoted remarks about the unconscious instinctual force in his creativity, reference may here be made to one of the most significant passages:

> In my hands, or rather in my mind, a work begins to grow . . . it grows, slowly and gradually it takes on shape, like a child in the womb; I do not know what came first into existence and what last. . . . I become aware of a limb, of a vessel, of one part after the other, i.e., I write it down, unconcerned as to how it will fit into the whole: for I know that all of it has sprung from one source. . . . I who sit here and

who am known by my friends, I do not comprehend the origin of the work, just as the mother does not comprehend that of the child in her womb [*Neue Paralipomena*].

What guarantees the genuineness and immortality of my philosophems is the fact that it was not I who made them; they created themselves; they grew in me without my assistance in moment when all will in me lay in deep slumber, as it were, and the intellect was entirely without a master, leisurely active, ready to perceive the contemplation of the actual world. . . . Together with the will all individuality vanished and was annulled: therefore my individual self was not involved, it was contemplation as such, pure and simple, i.e., purely objective contemplation or the objective world per se which settled down into pure conception per se [*ibid.*].

Schopenhauer does not want to admit more than what Nietzsche expressed in the words: "*Es denkt in mir*" ("It thinks within me"). What escaped him is that there can be no thinking without feeling and willing. Moebius aptly remarked: "Schopenhauer, in his attempt to continue along Kant's lines, let himself be tempted to speak of knowing, imagining and thinking as something separate from the act of willing. Actually, thinking or imagining cannot be conceived without willing." Fundamentally, however, Schopenhauer's teaching was right in that the will does everything, and his theory, in contrast to all preceding ones, leads directly to the insight that our conscious life is but a segment of what is for us the great unconscious.

> In our inner experiences we always reach the point quickly where consciousness ends, whence the path leads to what is for us unconscious, backward as well as forward. Instinct predominates over all individual reason, the hand that guides us is in the dark. Such knowledge shines through all of Schopenhauer's writings [Moebius].

It is evident that these words are in complete agreement with Freud's theory of the unconscious. We see in these references to the psychology of the unconscious which we find so often in Schopenhauer, a justification for our work. The most important justification—which we have long since pointed out—is the fact that

Schopenhauer represents one of the most striking illustrations of the correctness of psychoanalytic discoveries—to a greater extent, of course, than he himself could consciously express.

In taking leave of Schopenhauer's towering figure, let us once more pay our most profound respect to this discoverer of "the will," the driving unconscious force; the man who preached kindness and compassion; who glorified genius, art, and everything spiritual, truth, sincerity; who recognized only the inner values of man and conceded no other superiority save that of mind and character. Much as we must admire all these noble features, greatly indebted as we are to Schopenhauer as "educator," we shall tear ourselves away from the gloomy and all too personal dark sides of his philosophy and long to conquer it. Nietzsche, originally his greatest admirer and later his freest conqueror, shows that it is possible to conquer him through psychological knowledge and insight into the most personal, subjective conditions of philosophizing in general.

It has gradually become clear that every philosophy so far has been the self-confession of its originator and a sort of involuntary memoirs. Philosophy always creates the world in its own image, it cannot do otherwise. Philosophy is that tyrannical instinct itself, the intellectual will for power, for the "creation of the world, the causa prima" (Nietzsche).

In its subjectivity lies the limitation in all philosophic truth which Nietzsche recognized—a limitation that must lead to resignation because no system can be able to explain the enigmatic nature of the world and of life. A system can only provide an answer for one particular type of man and his metaphysical needs. In this sense we can speak of a hopelessness in all philosophy. As Nietzsche said:

When the origins of religion, art and ethics will be described in such a way that they can be completely explained without taking recourse in any assumption of metaphysical interference either at their inception or in their course, then even the most profound interest in the purely theoretical problem of the "thing in itself" and in the "phenomenon" will cease. . . . We shall then, with complete calm, leave to physiology and the history of the development of organisms and ideas the question as to how it is possible that our image of the world [*Weltbild*] could differ so markedly from the nature of the world as it is revealed.

Should somebody now, disappointed that Schopenhauer was "not healthy enough to be a philosopher" (Riehl), desire to seek his soul's salvation elsewhere, let him be warned. Even Nietzsche to whom we have given so much space here as Schopenhauer's critic and as the proponent of psychology—even Nietzsche does not appear qualified to be made the judge of existence. He who would venture forth to seek a man who is healthy enough to be a philosopher would fare as did that messenger of an ailing king who went to search for the shirt of a happy man to restore his master's health. For when he at last found a happy man, a shepherd, the shepherd did not own a shirt. The man who would be healthy enough to be a philosopher simply does not become a philosopher!

3

Psychoanalytic Comments About the Personality of Goethe*

IN contrast to some authors, especially to Theilhaber—though he does not belong to the psychoanalytic school—I think I should at once define my point of view. I refuse to adopt an attitude of professional superiority and to explain how Goethe could have been different, or how he could have behaved differently. On the contrary, in profound admiration of Goethe's genius we must admit that we owe his existence, his work, and his personality to an optimal set of circumstances. "Goethe," says Brandes, "guarded his self-development with an instinct that was wisdom."

Despite the deep grief it has brought us, this twentieth century is a wonderful age with its new spirit, its striving for truth and its love for facts; these trends are especially manifest in psychology. Psychoanalysis is both a natural science and a method for experimental research. Goethe, towering spirit and universal talent that he was, would have accepted psychoanalysis without prejudice. Did he not remark: "The most harmful prejudice is the banning of any form of scientific investigation."

This essay, of course, cannot do justice to the whole personality of Goethe; it can only discuss certain aspects and the problems they raise. It intends to appraise the importance of Goethe's father, to solve the riddles of Goethe's love life, and to say something about the poet's inner development.

There is no need to speak about Goethe's mother. Her forthright, cheerful nature, her soul, receptive to everything beautiful and good, her delightful letters—all this is well known to every educated person. I only want to quote one observation of Freud about the mother-son relationship: ". . . he who has been the

* First published in *Imago,* Vol. 18, 1932.

undisputed darling of the mother retains throughout life that victorious feeling, that confidence in ultimate success which not seldom brings actual success with it."

I

Life's serious conduct.

—GOETHE

From its beginnings, psychoanalysis has emphasized the decisive importance of the father for the fate of the individual. Strangely enough, Goethe's biographers have by-passed his father—as Rudolph Glaser stresses—"because of a peculiar prejudice." The poet himself has not always done the figure of his father complete justice; and it was Merck's judgment in particular that put the aging, ailing man, grown taciturn through deep disappointment, in the wrong light.

Besides many contemporary reports, Glaser drew from a hitherto concealed source, namely, Kaspar Goethe's own account of his Italian journey which had Vienna as its point of preparation and departure. This diary dates from his thirtieth year, but he was busy with its elaboration and completion till he was fifty-eight so that his children were brought into intimate contact with it.

From this diary Goethe's father emerges as an enlightened man of the world with high moral principles, open-minded, intent on self-education, widely interested in art, natural science, history, theater, etc. With amazement we gain the conviction that the far greater individual, the genius that was his son, was, after all foreshadowed in the personality of his father. The elder Goethe was already ahead of his time; he had an inquiring mind, was full of ideas, collected specimens for his natural science cabinet and brought home samples of marble, just as his son was to do later on. The father was especially interested in inscriptions and showed some skill in poetic translations from ancient languages.

If we realize that the Italian journey was the climax of the father's life and that he cherished its memories to the end of his days—only then can we understand that the same goal hovered before his son's eyes for many years, until he finally reached it. And, strangely enough, Italy meant for the father too—an adventure of love. The diary mentions a love affair this solemn gentleman experienced in Milan, and a collection of love letters, written in the style of the period, gives us more details. It did not go beyond words and outbursts of emotion. Kasper Goethe, the "habitual moralist," was too easily intimidated, his infatuation was, as he stressed several times, a "pure one"; he withdrew, not unlike his famous son who so often was to take flight in later years. He begs forgiveness for "the weakness he has shown in love."

Though Goethe the son often felt oppressed by his father's persistent pedantry and unbending sternness, and sometimes even rebelled against it, "the relationship between father and son was confident and friendly, while due respect was shown." The son felt the gentle soul behind the stern exterior. For the father Goethe collected Wolfgang's early verses, had them bound and presented them to him, and the father encouraged him. The father preserved the son's first drawings, recognized his talents, urged perseverance, and occasionally criticized the neglect of these talents. The father's schedule of studies could not have been more comprehensive. There was scarcely a field of knowledge that he ignored. When the poet puts his father's inheritance into the words "life's serious conduct,"—originally it was "serious features"—we know now how all inclusive this is: it implies character, the ideal of education and culture, the aim of universality. The father's upbringing pointed the way to that recording of experience which the son's genius made so peculiarly his own that he could call his literary work a "great confession."

Goethe's so characteristic propensity for self-education was the consequence of an inner voice, the echo of his father.

If we see his father's influence in this light, we must trace back to this same source the restraining force which again and again recalled Goethe from his amorous wanderings and his restlessness to his own true self and his nobler ideals. "The earnestness with which I looked at myself and the world from an early age was revealed in my behavior . . . ," wrote Goethe in *Poetry and Truth*.

Many other resemblances could be pointed out: father and son shared the predilection for collecting. The father collected maps, old firearms, Venetian glass, cups and goblets, ivory, bronzes, specimens of natural history, and Frankfurtiana. Anybody who has visited the Goethehaus in Frankfurt will remember the pedantic tidiness with which his collections were arranged. He was especially fond of studying and showing his copperplate engravings. "I have to own things," said Goethe, "to be able to evaluate them properly. Only when I own a thing can I judge it calmly and objectively, free of the illusions that are generated by desire. That is why I love possession, not for the sake of the thing possessed, but for the sense of comprehension it gives me which makes me happier and more serene."[1]

The didactic element took early and permanent hold of Goethe's nature. He shed no tears at the death of his little brother Hermann Jakob. When his mother asked the defiant lad whether

[1] In both father and son these traits are reaction formations to the anal instinct, a universal human drive of varying degree, and therefore of varying influence on the manifestations of character.

In this connection Ernest Jones notes: productivity and pleasure in creating; fondness of the graphic and plastic arts; refinement in artistic taste and discrimination; love of orderliness verging on pedantry; proclivity for collecting; striving for thoroughness and perfection; skill in handling concrete objects, etc.—all traits which we find in Goethe. He could draw, paint, and model in clay. "Everything asymmetrical, the slightest blot or wrong line was unbearable for him."

On the other hand, we know that pregenital anality is, so to speak, the counterpole of overt genitality. It is precisely the anal instinct whence stem the ascetic strivings, the rejection of the unclean, even in the moral sphere. Sexual activity depends in no small degree on the overcoming of the anal instinct. Especially the fear of infection, of which more will be said later, has its origin partly in the anal phase of development. Such persons often spend at least some periods of their life in sexual abstinence.

In Leipzig and later on in Frankfurt, Goethe suffered from severe digestive disturbances (obstipation). The familiar quotation from *Goetz von Berlichingen* and Mephisto's song in *Faust* in which "Floh" rhymes with "Popo" also recall the anal. Finally, a profound remark of Goethe's may be cited: "Hatred is like an illness, the *Miserere*, where you discharge by way of the mouth what ought to go out from behind."

Goethe's poetic productivity was by no means always easy flowing. English critics have pointed out that he completed only a comparatively small number of masterpieces; that he rewrote and experimented again and again. There are three versions of *Goetz; Iphigenie* was rewritten five times.

he had not loved his brother, he ran into his room and, from under the bed, pulled out a pile of paper, all filled with lessons and stories. He told her he had done all that to instruct his brother. (According to Bettina Brentano's report, this story was told by Frau Rath.) Wolfgang was ten years old at the time! Schoolmasterly, quite in his father's vein, was his attitude toward his sister Cornelia; and toward Maddalena Ricci in Rome. Before he fell in love with her, he taught her English! All his life Goethe remained eager to teach and be taught. Even toward Eckermann and Soret his attitude was didactic. The poet himself once said that his father had bequeathed upon him "didactic loquacity." *Wilhelm Meister's Lehrjahre* treats of the education of an individual; the *Wanderjahre* of the education of man as citizen in an ideal state.

To be sure, Kaspar Goethe was successful as a pedagogue with his son only. His daughter suffered too much from his severity and pedantry; presumably she missed the father's affection, while the son enjoyed at least the mother's tenderness in abundance besides getting more recognition from the father. Goethe's identification with his father also becomes obvious through his predilection to play the role of father, as Wilhelm Meister toward Mignon. Goethe had the desire to attract younger people who needed assistance, to help them and to teach them. Eckermann considered his relationship to Goethe that of pupil to master, son to father. Goethe was full of paternal feelings toward Fritz, the son of Frau von Stein. All the greater was the tragedy of Goethe's old age, to see his own son unhappy and a failure.

When we see how contradictory Goethe's personality was despite everything, how full of strife and suffering his life was, we must recognize that the one force which fought in him was the influence of his father's seriousness and severity.

> Two souls, alas, dwell in my heart . . .
> One, in crude sensuality, cleaves
> To the earth with clinging organs.
> The other yearns to soar aloft
> To the purer air and the broader view.
>
> *Faust*

Goethe's preference for friendship with men of high intelligence and culture is evident all through his life. At first he is the younger one, the pupil, so that Behrisch, Herder, Lavater, Merck, and others who befriended and stimulated him must be regarded as successors of his father, continuing and complementing his education.

The unconscious influence of father on son can often be seen quite plainly in the realm of belief in God. In general, the relation to a personal God receives its basic coloring from the relation to the father. I was able to demonstrate, in the instance of another poet (Dauthendey), that he exchanged his Deism—quite involuntarily—for Pantheism at the very moment he broke with his father and turned away from him. Goethe's towering personality that encompassed all humanity could never be understood in such a simple way. A harmonizing tendency moderates every characteristic, every one-sidedness. And yet, even with Goethe the impression remains that his faith was influenced partly by the strong father personality, overwhelmingly experienced in childhood, partly by his own conquest of the father, against whom a strong rivalry was often manifest. This influence also comes to light in his poetic outpourings.

> Could I but be replete
> With Thee, Eternal One—
> Alas, this deep torment
> How it endures on earth.

These verses reveal a wholly feminine-passive feeling and humble longing. The poem *Ganymed* is a glorification of becoming one with the universe; the poem *Prometheus*—open revolt, rebellion against Titans. Most characteristic seems to me Goethe's reply to his friend Jakobi, when the latter persisted in his efforts to convert him to one faith:

> For my part, if I consider the manifold tendencies of my nature, I cannot be satisfied with one single mode of thought. As a poet and an artist, I am a polytheist; as a natu-

ral scientist, I am a pantheist. I am as decidedly one as I am the other. And if I need a God for my own person, as a moral being, this, too, has been taken care of. The celestial and terrestial matters are so vast a realm that only the organs of all beings together are able to grasp it.

In comparison with the father's Protestantism, we find a turning away, a less deistic faith, a more diffuse and impersonal pantheistic religion of nature, a sort of victory over the paternal. Nevertheless, all his life Goethe remained religious in a wider sense of the word. The father had been tolerant toward his son. The son says of him proudly: "Though more old-fashioned in his religion, he did not take offense at my views and speculations."

This brings to mind the highly original altar the boy once erected, rather pagan, put together from products of nature for a God of nature, to offer sacrificial fires. "The God who was closely connected with nature. . . . He seemed to him the real God . . . The boy could not bestow a definite shape on this deity . . ." (Poetry and Truth).

Perhaps we may trace the uncertainty, the conflict, and the withdrawal of a personal God to the ambivalent relationship with his father. Perhaps a certain longing for the mother was interwoven with the feeling for nature. These relationships are complicated by the fact that to Goethe nature represented something divine: the religious feeling flowed together with the feeling for nature. It was for him a "pure, deep, innate and familiar perception to see God in nature and nature in God." Faust's confession of faith is that of a pantheist, too.

Goethe was, of course, particularly conversant with both these words, nature and God; and in both the content kept changing. "Neither the philosopher nor the theologian is able to arrive at a satisfactory idea about Goethe's God and Goethe's nature" (Chamberlain).

In summing up, I may repeat that we rate the effect of the father's influence on the development of Goethe's character extremely high; higher even, we might say, than Goethe himself rated it. For this influence, as we understand it, was largely unconscious for the son. Here a slight theoretical digression may be permitted, to indicate how we conceive of this paternal influence, and to clarify the psychic mechanism.

Taking neuroses as the point of departure, psychoanalysis in its beginnings was primarily concerned with the repression from consciousness of unacceptable impulses. Later on it directed its attention to the moral and aesthetic tendencies and their origins which furnished the impulse for repression. Prominent here is a process we call "identification," which plays an essential role. At a certain stage of development the boy identifies himself with his father, sets himself on equal terms with the father, incorporates him into his personality, and makes the father's ideals his own. This is an unconscious process. It goes without saying that an analogous influence is exerted by the mother.

The ego of the child changes according to these identifications. The child shapes for itself an ego ideal which it follows in the future and strives to achieve. Teachers, older friends, and other persons who inspire respect, continue this role of the father. Their commands and prohibitions, like those of the father, now exercise, by means of the conscience, a censorship of morals and taste. The voices of these authorities have become an inner voice, the voice of conscience. The discord between the claims of conscience and the actual achievements is experienced as a feeling of guilt. Our early identifications form our character.

Identification is not imitation, voluntary imitation, but an unconscious, compulsory process. It is especially the less loved parent, the parent who is feared, who has a strong influence.

In his later years, Goethe's father may be regarded as an eccentric. His choleric temperament, his touchiness and quarrelsomeness isolated him, his strictness and pedantry at times estranged his children. In his old age he became silent, dull and petty. But his cultural ideal, his restless striving for continuous development and enrichment of the personality, his methodical instruction, his guidance in evaluating and recording experiences, all this had set a pattern. In his son his severity and seriousness resulted in moral strictness toward himself and a tendency to guilt feelings. According to the son, though, Kaspar Goethe's achievements were not due to innate endowments but "to incredible industry, perseverance and repetition." Nevertheless, Kaspar Goethe would seem to have been the trunk of the tree which, in his son, branched out and blossomed under the rays of genius.

The parents were so different in age and in their attitudes toward life that many a discordance, many a conflict in the son's heart may be explained by it. One biographer says of Goethe: In character, in imagination, in ethics, everywhere Goethe perceives paradoxes that arrest his attention. Thus the opposing extremes in his origins, contributed to corresponding contradictions in his temperament and thereby influenced the outcome of many of the situations in Goethe's life.

We shall also find a peculiar discordance in his love life, the riddles of which we now propose to solve.

II

> *Man is born twice; the first*
> *time by his mother, a second*
> *time by his beloved.*
>
> —PROVERB

Goethe's rich and varied love life exhibits such peculiarities and puzzles that it has been exhaustively discussed in literature, notably by Wilhelm Bode. Otto Rank devoted a chapter of his book, *The Incest Motive in Poetry and Legend,* to Goethe's love for his sister. Brunold Springer, in his monograph *Der Schlüssel zu Goethes Liebesleben* (*The Key to Goethe's Love Life*), has adopted a similar point of view. The fundamental importance of Otto Rank's work must be stressed: it reveals the two most important complexes in Goethe's psychic life and poetic creativity— the revolt against his father, and the love for his sister. Proof is given by the evidence of motives and choice of subjects, but that would lead us too far afield.

Freud himself, in "A Childhood Recollection from *Dichtung*

und Wahrheit," emphasized the fraternal jealousy of the child Goethe. I have taken up the problem of the two contrasting types of womanhood, as represented by Frau von Stein and Christiane Vulpius, and have taken into consideration the change that occurred in Goethe during his stay in Rome, exemplified by the *Roman Elegies (Römische Elegien).*[2]

Goethe loved often and at every stage of his life; he has given us the most beautiful love poems and letters. Again and again he was capable of the ecstasy of love; he himself attributed recurring puberty to men of genius. Moebius has estimated a periodicity of seven years for Goethe, and Kretschmer, too, believes that various love phases can be explained in this way.

At the age of seventy-three Goethe once complained: "I feel poorly, for I am not in love with anyone, and no one is in love with me." And a year later, through Herzog Karl August, he asked for the hand of the nineteen-year-old Ulrike Levetzov in marriage. The fruits of this hopeless love were the *Marienbader Elegien,* one of the most stirring and most perfect of Goethe's poems.

Goethe never was a saint and especially in the early Weimar years there may very well have been fleeting debauches with girls of the lowest classes. But with girls of a higher social strata, with Käthchen, Lotte, Friederike, and Lili, the relationship follows a peculiarly typical course: a violent, stormy infatuation, then a period of irresolution and inner torment, and finally flight from the beloved, usually followed by self-reproaches.

According to Bode, Goethe was very reserved. We know of no permanent liaison prior to his Italian journey. Up to that time his psychic life often suggests that of a man who misses sexual satisfaction. Compared to contemporary writers he was especially reserved in his expression, never reveling in erotic descriptions. He had the inclination as well as the capacity to suppress his in-

---

2 In this connection, cf. a work by Reik who deals with the question why Goethe left Friederike, and one by the Swiss, Sarasin, about Goethe's *Mignon.* Another book, which achieved some unpleasant notoriety, Theilhaber's *Goethe, Sexus und Eros,* does not belong to the psychoanalytic school; along with quite a bit that is objectionable and in poor taste, it contains much that is accurate.

stinct; he suppressed it to a remarkable degree in the eleven years of his relationship with Frau von Stein. All the more sensational, of course, was the publication of his *Römische Elegien* with its more than frank description of Southern passion.

After these allusions you must permit me to talk about Goethe's development since childhood in some detail; for the affective impressions of our childhood have an intense aftereffect on our whole life.

The mother, so much younger, gayer, and livelier, drew the son to her; the serious, strict, and pedantic father became an object of rebellion, aversion, anxiety, and guilt feeling. There is a scene in *Poetry and Truth,* in which the children, kept from falling asleep by anxiety, are seeking out the servants; they are frightened back by the father who is difficult to recognize because he wears his dressing gown inside out. For many years little Wolfgang suffered from anxiety dreams. He had a bell of his own to calm him.

Thus the father became the representative of intimidations and prohibitions. The difference in temperament between father and mother had its share in fostering the "oedipal situation" which is natural in the early years. The psychoanalyst considers it most likely that the boy was harried by something like castration fears.

The great love he felt for his mother helps to explain his jealousy of the brother. This is how Freud explains the naughtiness with which Wolfgang one day threw a great deal of crockery out of the window, egged on by the Ochsenstein brothers who lived across the street. Supported by analogous cases from his analytic practice, Freud conjectures that it was not mere chance that this behavior coincided with the mother's going to the christening of a newborn son. The poet's love for his sister Cornelia was complete and unconcealed; it decisively influenced not only the choice and treatment of many poetic themes, but his actual love life. "Even when she lay in the cradle he loved her tenderly, brought everything to her, and wanted to feed her by himself" (Witkowski).

In Charlotte von Stein we also see an image, a reflection of the sister, and in his love for her, probably the deepest love of Goethe's life, a continuation of the attachment to his sister. It is by no means self-evident that the radiant, brilliant young poet was captivated for so long by this ailing woman, seven years his senior, who was neither magnanimous nor particularly understanding. Numerous utterances of Goethe prove that he suspected she awakened in him the image of his sister. He described his relation to her as the purest, finest and truest he had ever experienced for any woman except his sister. "If only my sister had a brother, as I have a sister in you," he said elsewhere. In one poem Goethe said to Frau von Stein: "Ah, in another existence, you have been my sister or my wife." And in a letter about her he wrote: "She has gradually inherited the place of mother, sister and mistress, and a bond has been formed like the bonds of nature."

The superlative feelings, the perfection of his love, the assertion that he found everything in her, show plainly an idealization and fantasy glorification with unconscious motives.

Goethe sacrificed almost twelve of his most fervent years to this woman who proved herself only to a small degree worthy of this touching devotion. In answer to the oft-repeated question as to the limits of this compelling attachment, it must be said that this prudish woman clearly never granted the ultimate. Every possible gradation of partial and inhibited, hasty and unhealthy relief exists in such relationships; but complete and uninhibited gratification Goethe never found with her.

This first decade in Weimar, full of varied official activities, was by no means productive and did not advance the development of the great poet. Only outlines and fragments mark this period. Nothing was completed except lyric poetry. Rightly it is Frau von Stein who is considered the work of this period—Frau von Stein who was so highly exalted through infantile reminiscence and unsatisfied desire. In the earlier Weimar years new plans still appear, such as *Iphigenie, Tasso, Wilhelm Meister;* but from 1780 until the flight to Italy the well of inspiration had gone dry.

The deep happiness of love which those years brought is evident in the letters to Frau von Stein; they mirror love's every facet and are a treasure of German letters.

But toward the end of this period despair seized the poet. "Rather death than the life of the past years," he wrote to Frau von Stein. And later to the Duke: "It was the main purpose of my journey (to Italy) to cure myself of the physical and moral ills which tormented me in Germany and rendered me useless in the end." Goethe later called this period "years of illness." Of course there were many other reasons for this weakening of his creative powers, such as his absorption in official duties. But it cannot be regarded as natural that in the prime of his manhood Goethe languished. Goethe started on his flight to Italy without even telling Frau von Stein. It was both flight and longing. A healthy instinct tore him free, the narcissism of the creative artist asserted itself once more. In a work entitled "On the Psychoanalysis of Travel," Winterstein made special reference to the interconnection between the urge to travel and eroticism, and he mentioned a significant symptomatic action of Goethe's: a few days before his flight he lost the ring off his finger which Frau von Stein had given him.

Flight from the beloved was always characteristic of Goethe's love life. Thus he fled from Käthchen, from Friederike, from Lili and Lotte, from Marianne von Willemer and others. The most obvious motive each time was of course the flight of the creative artist from disturbing obligation. Did not Goethe himself advise the creative person to be "highly egotistic." Our poet was concerned with his own growth and that of his work like no other. Yet more searching investigations, such as the one Reik has published, dealing with Goethe's flight from Friederike, have more to say and trace the succession of motives back to childhood events.

We stressed the tender attachment to the mother and the secondary one to the sister, the father as the source of prohibition and punishment, and the anxiety in the evening and in dreams. More needed details can be found only in other childhood observations. Here may lie the origin of the guilt feelings, the fear of consequences of forbidden actions, as well as the later fear of permanent ties. Again and again it comes to flight and abandonment. "And yet to seize hold is the most natural impulse in man. Do not children seize hold?" (*Werthers Leiden*). To be sure, what follows after the flight is the creative realization of the experience.

Added to this is Goethe's sense of purity. Goethe had a peculiar fondness for the word "purity." He said, for example: "The observation of nature needs a certain calm inner purity." Once, when he was to see some criminals, he suffered inner torments and wrote: "I flee from what is impure." He quickly put aside *Der Arme Heinrich*, because the description of disease in this morbid work "had such a powerful effect upon him that he feels contaminated by the mere contact with such a book." Kaspar Goethe's travel diary warns of the dangers of venereal disease. So do Goethe's letters to the Duke, and his *Römische Elegien*.

"May the idea of purity, which extends to the bite of food I put into my mouth, grow ever more shining within me!" he wrote elsewhere. Goethe had an insurmountable aversion against everything that was ugly, disgusting or diseased. When the Duke wanted to show him a human malformation, Goethe, the scientist, begged off: "His aversion against everything pathological seems to grow stronger with the years."

When his daughter-in-law fell from a horse and her face was disfigured, he did not want to see her before she had recovered: "He finds himself violently affected by defects and deformities." This also explains that Goethe finds caricatures repugnant.

We may recall the following verses:

> In our bosom's purity an effort surges
> Freely to give our self in gratitude
> to the higher, the purer, the unknown.

In old age, reason could let his microcosm—the goal of his longings—"revolve around a pure center. . . ."

To a certain extent physical and moral purity run parallel; their appraisal has one of its origins in the instincts, as has been previously stated (cf. footnote 1 above).

Particularly characteristic for the flight from the beloved was the strong guilt feeling that pursued the fugitive. In *Faust* where the crime against the girl is actually committed, it is committed with the help of the devil.

Stendhal—out of a different world—mockingly expressed his amazement "that Faust compacts with the devil to do what every one of us has done in his youth: to seduce a milliner." Goethe depicted the struggle between instinctual desires and the power of the inner conscience, just as once his own instincts had to struggle with external prohibitions. Years later, after Lotte Buff had been married to Kestner, Goethe was awakened by anxiety dreams which portrayed his guilt feelings, his need for punishment, and his father (symbolized by the Duke). He wrote:

> The other day I felt great anxiety in a dream about Lotte. The danger was pressing, there was no hope of success for any of my schemes. We were watched; everything depended on my speaking to the Duke. I stood by the window and thought of jumping down. It was two stories high: "you will just break a leg," I thought, "then you might just as well surrender."

So we see that despite the tendency to fall passionately in love, Goethe as a young man showed self-restraint and a sense of purity. Moral inhibitions, guilt feelings and the fear of disease were at work, but there undoubtedly also was the self-protection of the creative artist who puts imagination above reality and says: "Happiness is ever greater far from the beloved," or: "If I love you, what concern is that of yours."

Love does not exist for its own sake. Every love affair—from *Werther* to the *Marienbader Elegie*—led to creative work which offered freedom from conflict and psychic distress. In creative work the release from the love object is completed and, as it were, celebrated. And yet, it remains unlikely that a nature as strong as Goethe's should not long to taste fully of life and love.

We now turn to the second half of his life, separated from the first by the Italian journey. Our attention is drawn to a poetic work which is based on the records of this journey, even though it was only completed in Weimar, the *Römische Elegien*.

Although Goethe finished this work in the peacefully happy time with Christiane Vulpius and refers to her in it, there can be no doubt that its theme is his happiness of love in Rome. It sets a memorial to Faustina Antonii, née di Giovanni, the young widow whose actual existence can no longer be doubted since A. Carlotta has provided documentary proof. When Goethe met her she was already a mother, and stood under the guardianship of her uncle. Goethe spent nights with her that were replete with unrestrained enjoyment of love. "She takes delight in him, the free and vigorous stranger," Goethe wrote, "She shares the fire that is enkindled in his bosom." Eros had bestowed upon her the supreme gift "to awaken joy that slowly burned itself out as to ashes." For the first time he could give himself to sexual fulfillment without fear of infection. Plainly enough he says in the 18th Elegy: "It is wholly abominable to fear serpents on love's path, and poison under the roses of pleasure, when at the fairest moment of the joy of surrender, worry is whispering close to your ear."

This fear of disease was unnecessary with Faustina. "That is why Faustina is my happiness. She likes to share my bed and keeps faith with the faithful." And he continued: "What bliss! We exchange carefree kisses, breath and life we imbibe and infuse, full of trust." In another, incomplete poem which was withheld from publication, fear of disease appears as the greatest killer of joy; and mention is made of mercury as a remedy. To quote further:

> But we do not kiss all the time, there is sensible talk.
> When sleep overtakes her, I lie awake and reflect.
> Many a time in her arms I have written verses.
> The hexameter's measure softly my fingers count
> Tapping her back. She breathes in delightful slumber,
> And her breathing thrills me to my innermost heart.

When a man of forty in his elegiac recollection of Rome speaks with such enthusiasm about his enjoyment of love free from restrictions and free from the fear of infection, we have the right to assume that he had never before known such uninhibited passion. The elegies still contain words enough that have to ban guilt feelings: he states that he works during the day, at least: "though I am only half instructed, I am doubly blessed."

Only since he had seen and felt his beloved naked, does he fully understand marble. "When sleep overtakes her, I lie awake and reflect"—should this indicate that erotic gratification is after all something for which he has (or once had) to find an excuse? This would fit the introduction of Alexander, Caesar, Heinrich, and Frederick the Great—obviously father images—as men who would gladly give him half of their glory:

> Could I grant to each one this bed for a night.
> But Orcus holds them in his stern powers, poor creatures.

A slight satisfaction over the death of these fathers can be detected; a sort of victory for the rival son. Many a sternly ruled son cannot find free enjoyment of love until the death of his father.

The father rivalry shows through these ironic lines, but it finds its full satisfaction in deceiving the uncle guardian, "whom the dearest so often deceives, to possess me." No wonder that the lover once imagines to see the dreaded uncle in a scarecrow and flees:

> Now the old man's wish is fulfilled; the loose bird
> He scared off today, that robs both his garden and niece.

But the complete possession of a woman finally banishes any rivalry:

> Grant me, O Quirites, My happiness, and may each
> Be granted by God the first and the last of the world's
> blessings.

Paternal injunctions are most easily overcome away from home; in the outside world there need be no fear of censorship.

It was, apparently then, in Italy that Goethe encountered, for the first time, full gratification, without any feeling of anxiety or reproach; and it seems self-evident that upon his return to Weimar he seized the first opportunity to attract a suitable love object. The dictum, "Between sensual pleasure and peace of mind a man has only an uneasy choice," was presumably re-solved. At first he was disappointed and gloomy. But a few weeks after his arrival he was accosted by a simple girl who made arti-ficial flowers in a factory. She interceded for her brother who wanted Goethe's help in securing a position. She soon became his mistress and lived with him, despite the malicious small town gossip. She bore him a son, and, later, several other children who did not survive. He gave her his affectionate love and respect and regarded her as his wife. The actual wedding did not take place until eighteen years later. With her in mind he wrote these verses during his second Italian journey:

> Long did I seek for a wife, but I found only harlots.
> At last I caught you, harlot, and in you found a wife.

As soon as Goethe had gained full sexual freedom he was capable of marriage, though only with a love object of a lower social class. His attachment to higher love objects, such as his mother and sister, still influenced him. His marriage began as a purely erotic relationship which had to prove itself before he could permit the development of that higher affection which transformed this liaison with the simple girl into a quite happy marriage.

If we now look at the change the first Italian journey wrought in Goethe, we see the word "rebirth" leap out from his letters more than a dozen times, even in the first ones to his mother, then to the Duke, to Frau von Stein, and to his friends: "I am a new man, a different man, reborn." Of course, not only the wrenching away from Frau von Stein worked this transforma-tion but the finally realized fulfillment of the wish to experience Italy, like his father, and to taste freedom. We know how much a visit to Italy means to every cultured German. What must it have been for Goethe! The effect of Italy, her landscape, her magnificent art, the life of her people—that is a subject in itself which cannot be pursued here.[3]

The change in Goethe's love life has to be taken into consideration if we want to explain this continuous stream of *joi de vivre*: "In Rome I have found myself for the first time, for the first time in harmony with myself I became happy and reasonable." And in *Four Seasons* he wrote:

> Know'st thou the glorious effect of love
> that is satisfied at last?
> It binds together bodies in beauty, as it
> sets free the souls.

There was an upsurge of creative powers. *Egmont* and *Iphigenie* were completed in Rome, *Erwin* and *Claudine* were completely recast. The *Roman Elegies* were sketched out and later written for Christiane. Many of the Venetian Epigrams were meant for her. She hovered behind *Alexis und Dora*. Considerable progress was made with *Tasso,* to be finished later at Christiane's side. After an interval of twelve years, *Faust* was again taken up.

Not only the poet Goethe went to Italy, but also the art critic and scientist; and here too we see that great strides have been made since the early beginnings: Goethe outlined the *Farbenlehre (Theory of Color)* and wrote his essay on *Die Metamorphose der Pflanze (The Metamorphosis of Plants)*. And he decided to take on the management of the theater in Weimar.

Then there is another striking fact. Upon his return from Italy Goethe was cool toward all social and political movements of the idealists, the patriots and the religiously inclined (Bode). In support of our theory about this disenchantment, let me cite a case that was reported by Oskar Pfister: he tells about a man

[3] Cf. Schopenhauer in a letter from Italy: "I found that here everything that comes directly from the hands of nature, heaven and earth, plants and trees, animals and human faces, is exactly as it ought to be; in our country, it is such that one can barely put up with it."

who pursued his philanthropic ventures only as long as he exercised restraint in his sexual satisfaction. As soon as he gave rein to his sexual functions, he lived for his more immediate interests.

One more point on psychosexual parallelism: Goethe, who had hitherto only composed single poems, occasional poems, now with the *Elegies* wrote his first cycle; a great number of these was to follow. Gundolf draws attention to another fact: "Erotic mysticism no longer interested him . . . Now, when he loved, he no longer wanted spiritual exaltation, but immediate, pagan and physical gratification."

Goethe now used the word "infinite" less, and the word "clarity" more. He grew from genius to sage and self-contained Olympian.

Goethe's love did not wane; it outlived Christiane's youth and beauty and was expressed in words of gratitude and affection to the last. Yet at times Goethe must have suffered from her limitations, for in later years Christiane lost her charm and drank somewhat beyond her thirst. Gundolf remarks: "Goethe paid heavily for founding a life-time relationship on the needs of a passing phase of his life." Goethe once said to Count Reinhard: "First of all I must tell you that my wife never read a line of what I have written. The realm of the mind does not exist for her, she is made for housework. There she relieves me of all worries, that is her domain. But she likes finery, and company, and loves to go to the theater."

This remark may be contradictory to others. But it is obvious that Goethe could not find everything in Christiane. In the choice of this woman we see a consequence of his one-time inability to unite in one object physical and spiritual love. And in his long delay in legitimizing the union with his faithful partner, the mother who had borne him five children and who suffered from the contempt and malice of the small town, we see another proof of his dread of lasting commitments. What later bound him to her was partly habit. Goethe himself once wrote: "It is worth special contemplation that habit can completely take the place of passion; it needs a comfortable presence more than a charming one; then it is invincible. It takes a great deal to break the habit of a relationship; it endures, despite all annoyances; discontent, anger, vexation are powerless against it; it even survives contempt and hatred." In 1810 Goethe wrote a poem, *Das Tagebuch* (*The Diary*), which because of its intimate contents is not included in the general editions of his works. From this poem we learn that even after twelve years of marriage Goethe was unable to deceive Christiane. With drastic humor and self-irony *The Diary* describes his failure with a willing waitress. While the girl, a virgin, lies sleeping by his side, the man, aggrieved at his weakness, thinks of his beloved at home, and these fantasies bring excitement. Here is again proof of the limitations of his sexuality through psychic inhibitions.[4]

Summing up, we may say that the *Roman Elegies* with their elated mood, their feelings of victory and liberation, force us to assume that Goethe found fulfillment for the first time with Faustina and then with Christiane; in other words, not until the

[4] We can comprise these inhibitions under the name of "castration fear," for which there is much remarkable data in Goethe; but this can be appreciated better by those versed in psychoanalysis. The elegy *Amyntas* speaks a peculiar language. This elegy, under a delicate disguise, refers to Christiane. At the sight of an ivy-covered apple tree the poet is reminded of feelings which conceive of the passionate love of a woman as weakening, sapping a man's body and soul. Though recognizing the justice of these feelings, he does not have the heart to loosen the closely entwined ivy from the tree which bears scarcely any fruit:

> She takes away my nourishment; what I needed, she enjoys,
> And so she saps my marrow, saps my soul.
> Yes, it is treachery; she wheedles from me my life and my goods,
> Coaxes from me my striving strength and my hope. . . .
> Sweet is such squandering; oh, let me enjoy her beauty!
> Does he who entrusts himself to love, take counsel of his life?

When the nineteen-year-old Goethe returned home ill from Leipzig—whence "he had brought from home a certain hypochondriac tendency"—he did not, as he said, have too much to reproach himself with; nevertheless, there was an impression of weakness. Ever since his student days he had been afraid of not reaching old age. In those days he called himself a poor little fox who needed a rest. (*Note:* There is a play on words in German. A freshman is called a "fox.") For his first collection of poems he wrote a dedication in which he advised the lover to marry. Referring to his bad experiences, he calls himself a "fox who lost his tail." —In two passages Goethe treats copulation in a mystic, natural-philosophic way, comparing it to death; first in 1773 in the *Prometheus* fragments, later in the poem *Selige Sehnsucht* (*Blessed Longing*).

age of thirty-eight did he find complete satisfaction, that is, the capacity to focus his entire affective personality from time to time on purely physical love. The young Goethe must be considered fortunate in that he was able to endure congestions through intensive work and genuine sublimation. But of course, this was only possible within limits and for a certain period of time. His flight to Rome led to the change we have described.

To some extent Goethe himself was aware of this change and mentioned it. He called the psychic state of his youth a "loving condition" (meaning obviously "enamored"), and reproached himself with "having perhaps in my youth cherished my inner longings too much." But with progressing virility he "sought full and final satisfaction" instead. This step is of great importance in a man's life; it must be experienced, above all, as inner liberation.

There is a proverb: "Man is born twice; the first time by his mother, a second time by his beloved."

III

> There is not a line by Goethe
> which did not in some way con-
> tribute to his self-development,
> close or remote, direct or indi-
> rect, postive or negative.
> —GUNDOLF

We shall never be able to do justice to a creative person if we do not consider what psychoanalysis calls his narcissism. The term is taken from the ancient, mythological figure of Narcissus who fell in love with his own reflection in the water. Narcissism means a universal human quality, varying in degree, a kind of self-love, a concentrating on one's own personality, such as can best be observed in children. Narcissism is love of one's own person in the physical and spiritual sense, of the own personality, the ego and its products and powers. No artist would preserve his thoughts, his emotions, and his daydreams, if he did not love and value them as part of his self. The creative person lives for

his own self, he concentrates on his ego and his work; he himself
is always, secretly or openly, the center of his work. Thus, aware
or not aware, all production—and literary production most of
all—is self-portrayal, autobiography.

During the period of our development love and praise by our
surroundings teach us to love ourselves; make us vain. But there
are also affronts to narcissism, consequences of reproof and unfavorable comparisons. There is no reason to doubt Frau Rath's
story, as reported by Bettina: "From earliest youth, everyone's
eyes were fastened on him. Once somebody was standing at the
window with his mother when the boy came across the street
with several friends. They noticed that he was walking along
very gravely, and pointed out to him that his stiffly erect posture
distinguished him peculiarly from the other boys.—"That's the
beginning," he said, "later on I'll be distinguished in all kinds
of ways."

As his mother's darling, as favored pupil of the father who admired his talents, the young Goethe could give his narcissism full
rein. As a young, immature man, he was outwardly vain and
foppish. Self-confident even as a youth, he said of himself: "I
have never known a more presumptuous person than myself . . .
I never believed that there was anything to be achieved, I always
thought I already had it. Had somebody set a crown upon my
head, I would have thought it my due."

In his middle age we find an opposite reaction. Goethe shrouds
himself, becomes unpretentious. He wrote to Schiller: Out of a
certain realistic tic, out of his innermost being sprang his fault to
conceal from the eyes of the people his existence, his actions, and
his writings.

> I always like to travel incognito, I like to choose the more
> modest suit of clothes rather than the better one; when
> talking to strangers or acquaintances, I prefer the trivial
> topic and the less important expression (the less effective
> phrase), to behave more frivolous than I am, to put myself,
> as it were, between myself and my appearance.

At an advanced age [Kretschmer says of the old Goethe]
this trait [of self-complacency] contributes in a very refined,

subdued and stylized manner to the bearing of the connoisseur of living, the sage and the prince of poets; there is a slight suggestion of a solemn pose, of egotism and the role of handsome man; a bearing which comprises the youthful narcissism as well as the need to protect the oversensitive inner life, and which blends them into the total of a spiritualized personality.

We do not want to speak here of that part of narcissism which loves "what one represents," but of that which loves "what one is," the narcissism of the personality. What I have in mind is Goethe's active love for his ideal, his self-education, his life which in so many respects was consciously directed toward certain ideals that he himself called it a work of art.

This desire to point the pyramid of my existence, whose basis was given me and founded for me, as high as possible into the air, this desire outweighs everything else and permits hardly a moment's forgetfulness. I must not delay, I am quite on in years, and perhaps fate will break me in the middle and the tower of Babel will remain blunt and incomplete. People shall say at least that it was boldly planned; and if I live, my powers, by God's grace, shall reach the top [Goethe to Lavater, 1780].[5]

And in *Wilhelm Meister* he wrote: "To develop my own self, just as I am, that was obscurely my wish and my purpose since youth." Instead of "obscurely" we can also say "unconsciously."

As a writer, he says, he never asked: What does the great mass want, how could I serve the common good? Instead, "I have always tried to gain greater insight for myself, to make myself better, to enhance my own personality . . ." No matter if the poet lost, as long as the human being gained by it.

In other creative artists we find their work to be the sole object of narcissistic love; for Goethe, his personality was always the main object of all his strivings. His ego, his development, his self-formation, was his main work. We only have to see with

5 On this famous sentence Hohenstein based his book, *Goethe—Die Pyramide—Ein neuer Weg zu Goethe* (*Goethe—The Pyramid—A New Approach to Goethe*), a book which tries to present Goethe's plan of life and the connection between his personality and his work.

what energy he sought already in Strassbourg to make himself immune from his nervous weaknesses, his sensitivity to loud noises, his vertigo, etc. At parade he walked next to the drummer; he climbed the cathedral tower to the top; evenings he visited graveyards, and mornings anatomy classes—all in order to conquer his weaknesses. Is not this inner voice reminiscent of the constant admonitions of his pedagogically inclined father?

He was thorough and conscientious in his official duties. His versatility, his thirst for knowledge, his ambitions command our admiration. There is no event of the day, no work of art, no product of literature that found him uninterested, even in his advanced age. He made valuable contributions to natural science. A universality, still possible in those days, for which the father had sowed the germ, characterized his unique personality. He himself describes his life's work as "a collective being that bears the name of Goethe."

He felt his life to be permeated by "a mildly systematic plan." Even Goethe's grandfather had been narcissistic in this narrower sense. Too delicate for the smith's trade of his forebears, he had become a tailor. His aim was to reach the top of his profession; he educated himself by travelling, and wrote his name in the French fashion, with an accent on the "e": Goethé; the self-complacent man felt this addition necessary. Kaspar Goethe's narcissism, self-confident but sensitive, was of a nobler kind. He, too, strove toward self-improvement, attached some importance to cosmopolitanism and outward appearance, and did not neglect "what one has," material possessions, a home appropriate to his standing, and collections. He did not reach this goal for himself, he reached it only in his son. "It is a pious wish of every father," Goethe observed in *Poetry and Truth,* "to see realized in his son everything that he had missed; it is almost like living one's life over again, using to best advantage the experiences of the earlier existence."

Goethe's father retired comparatively early and could devote himself entirely to the education of his children. Goethe himself devoted the development of his personality and his work to the world! Thus the education of his son August may well have been stinted; Goethe reproached himself that August never had come to know the categorical imperative. If the children of men of genius do not succeed or turn out badly, it is not necessarily hereditary taint or exhaustion of germ plasma; the narcissism of the fathers should not be forgotten as an explanation.

The ideal of perfecting his personality lighted Goethe's way like a pillar of fire. As he grew older, this ideal became more and more conscious, his personality spread its wings more fully, his appearance became most imposing and towering. If we look at the impression of Goethe on his own people—indeed, on the civilized peoples of the whole globe—we will find that an intimate knowledge of his work is far rarer than the strong image of his personality. It is the image of a man who inspires reverence, a man mighty in the realm of the mind, whose face, whose figure, whose eyes above all, have become dear and sacred to mankind (E. Engel).

The people sense in him the embodiment of the people's soul, the ancestor of mankind; the figure of Goethe actually appears in dreams as the symbol of the father—and psychoanalysis deserves the credit for having established this fact.

A genius, a heroic personality like Goethe, represents for countless human beings the image of the father; they transfer upon it all the feelings of admiration, gratitude and respect with which they once paid homage to their real fathers.

4

Johann Peter Eckermann[*]

IF we are to turn to the classic soil of Weimar at the period of its flowering, it may not be inappropriate to begin with a well-known quotation from Schiller: "When kings build, carters are kept busy." But Johann Peter Eckermann, the man on whom our interest is centered, was no ordinary carter and cannot be disposed of by mass psychology. He could call himself Goethe's friend and collaborator. He belonged to that guild of men who despite the democratic progress of our time have not yet been organized. The friends and collaborators of great minds have no trade union. Perhaps that is why the relationship between disciple and master, voluntary collaborator and spiritual leader, is one of the finest of human relationships. An examination of the friendship between Eckermann and Goethe will give us a better insight into the nature and depth of such relationships in general.

The joint purpose of this collaboration was not—as is so often the case—some scientific theory or service to a political party, but first and foremost the completion of the royal pyramid of Goethe's works; and secondly the preparation of that book which, started on Eckermann's initiative, was to become world famous: *Conversations with Goethe in the Last Years of His Life* (*Gespräche mit Goethe in den letzten Jahren seines Lebens*), by J. P. Eckermann. Nietzsche called these conversations with Eckermann the best book in German; it is one of the most widely read; for many it is a breviary from which to cull words of wisdom in the evening hours or to renew one's joy in the figure of the great *homo universalis,* the cosmopolitan, the humanist. So skillfully has Eckermann captured the stature and the words of his great and beloved master that the reader seems to enter

* First published in *Psychoanalytische Bewegung,* Vol. 5, 1933.

Goethe's house and to see and hear him in person. It is the picture of Goethe the Olympian, an idealized portrait. But it is that image which represents for civilized people everywhere the prototype of humanity at its noblest, the image of a man who inspires reverence, a man mighty in the kingdom of the mind. The common people see in him the embodiment of the nation's soul, the ancestor of the race. The figure of Goethe actually appears in dreams as the symbol of the father.

Although the closest contemporaries, especially those well qualified to judge, like Chancellor Mueller, Riemer, Soret, and Ottilie von Goethe, vouched for the authenticity of the conversations, more exact research, particularly the comparison Professor Castle made with Goethe's diaries, raised many doubts and objections. One reproachful calculation pointed out that a thousand visits with Goethe yielded only two-hundred-and-fifty conversations. The stern critic Petersen even drew the conclusion that if we wanted to use the conversations for a biography of Goethe, we should give them the title *Poetry and Truth (Dichtung[1] und Wahrheit)*. The passionate, sarcastic, angry, the downcast and inaccessible Goethe is missing. Later it was possible to gain a somewhat higher vantage point. While it is true that a correct picture of Goethe can only be formed if the more realistic conversations published by others are included, resemblance is not the only aim of a portrait. Eckermann's artistic achievement is his presentation of Goethe in the majestic serenity of consummate, refined humanity. Eckermann's conversations are the most vital work in the vast literature about Goethe, about Goethe's legacy to posterity, handed down by his most faithful disciple.

Our great interest in the intermediary who conveyed to us this picture of Goethe with such remarkable reproductive talent is well justified. Eckermann's career was by no means straight and simple. He started as cowherd on a remote heath, far from any city, helped his mother in the fields, and accompanied the father when he went on peddling trips, heavily laden with his wares. To

[1] The German word *Dichtung* would, in this context, be better translated as "Fiction." (*Editor's Note.*)

rise from these beginnings to the role of collaborator and friend of the greatest poet of his time, that is a development which poses puzzles enough.

We have only scanty material about his childhood. But two autobiographical sketches, the introduction to and commentaries of the *Conversations,* newly discovered diaries, his letters, and the two-volume biography based on this material by Houben, give us many important clues for the accomplishment of our task.

Let us first see what Goethe himself had to say about Eckermann. He called him "a sensitive and quiet youth." In a letter to Zelter he rated his services "truly invaluable," spoke of him occasionally as an "industrious ant." He said that Eckermann gave him "important assistance," looked through his "hopelessly tied-up manuscripts with praiseworthy patience." "Eckermann," he wrote elsewhere, "understands best to extort literary productions from me; . . . it is mostly due to him that I continue with *Faust.*" But Eckermann was not only the driving force behind the second part of *Faust.* He also "extorted" the fourth part of *Dichtung und Wahrheit.*

In a letter to Carlyle, Goethe gave this appraisal of his helper:

> Eckermann's sensitive and lively—one might say passionate—feelings are of great value to me; I can reveal to him in confidence many things that are as yet unprinted, many that rest unused, for he possesses the fine gift of pronouncing a friendly opinion on what is set before him, like a modest reader, and yet he knows how to express clearly what is required by taste and emotions.

We know that the word "pure" was a favorite with Goethe. It is therefore especially significant that he used this word twice in a defense of Eckermann. Eckermann had paid a visit to Marianne von Willemer who found "something shy, reticent and puzzling" about him, whereupon Goethe replied: "The problematic in Eckermann is resolved when one realizes that he is a simple, *pure* soul who would like to live in *pure* harmony with himself and the world. But how few have achieved this! A nature such as his can only gradually reveal itself."

Soon the seventy-five-year-old Goethe addressed the thirty-two-year-old Eckermann as "my child," "my dear child." He had recognized Eckermann's unconditional devotion to him when he listened to his words as to the revelations of a deity, often to record them faithfully at home, to preserve them for posterity. Goethe gladly allowed Eckermann to involve him in animated talks, and in the course of such conversations he brought up from the treasury of his ever receptive mind opinions and words of wisdom which would otherwise have remained unsaid and unwritten.

Let me first give a brief outline of the external events in Eckermann's life. He was born in a little village between Lüneburg and Hamburg, late in the life of poor, honest parents. Two sons of his father's first wife had gone to sea. By the time he was ten, two older sisters were in service away from home. He may have been somewhat lonely with his elderly parents. But apparently he was spoiled by everybody, and his parents were ready to make sacrifices for him if he showed any talent.

He was delicate, and therefore "fit to become a tailor." But when he once sketched a horse which he copied from his father's tobacco pouch, he was to become a painter. It shows the cultural level of the people that they decided against painting because a sister told them that painters had to stand on high scaffoldings where it was easy to fall off; she obviously meant house painting. He was advised to eat charity meals in order to grow stronger. Still, he was too weak for a trade, and so the intellectual side predominated. The ideal that hovered before him all his life was a permanent official position, but he realized this dream for a brief period only.

Eckermann became increasingly conscious that there was a better, more interesting world. As a boy he had written poems, quite successfully imitating Koerner's martial verses. He dreamed of becoming a writer and studied to acquire the knowledge he deemed necessary for writing poetry. He developed a fondness for Schiller and a passion for Goethe, the universal master. At the age of twenty-six he became engaged to Hannchen

Bertram. But she had to remain his fiancée for thirteen years before he could marry her.

By that time he was completely under Goethe's spell. He had sent him a volume of insignificant poems and received a reply, albeit a cool one. Goethe fulfilled his dreams. Eckermann wandered to Weimar, ostensibly to ask for a recommendation to a publisher who might print some of his literary productions, but actually filled with longing to be near Goethe for a few moments. During this first visit to Goethe a destiny was shaped. Goethe was just then looking for a young assistant. The vigorous, resolute Schubarth was not available. The thirty-one-year-old Eckermann, almost feminine in his compliance, was easy to retain. Goethe embodied the goal of Eckermann's desires and fantasies. He was only too readily diverted from his own career. Goethe cautioned against undertaking major literary works and advised him to stick to the treatment of traditional themes. But there was an even greater need for his services in the arrangement of "a heap of big bundles of papers." Goethe drew him into conversations about future plans. Eckermann became absorbed in the *Theory of Colors*. He began to live his life for Goethe. As he wrote to his fiancée, who grew more and more impatient, Goethe was "his one and only happiness in Weimar."

He made a frugal living by giving lessons to young Englishmen. Poverty remained the background to his life. "My poverty is my misfortune," he wrote to Hannchen, "and the best years of my life are thus wasted." Such moods interrupted the feelings of happiness which pervaded his association with Goethe. Goethe had seen his work on the *Conversations* but had deferred publication.

At long last Eckermann was able to marry. One year later, his wife died in childbirth. He was left with a baby boy to rear and provide for.

Goethe died after nearly nine years of happy collaboration. A mental symbiosis came to an end. Eckermann was left "like a natural son who has been forgotten in the will."

He worked on the complete edition of Goethe's works in forty-four volumes. He was accepted at Court, became a *Hofrat* (Councillor). But the miserable three hundred Thalers he received from the Court reduced him to serfdom and chained him to Weimar which he would have liked to exchange for his beloved native soil with its freedom. For three years he was involved in an embittered, unjust court action with the publisher Brockhaus. He lived in want and debt. His only comfort was his son who showed talent as a painter.

Eckermann became one of the sights of Weimar. He lived only for nature and for his beloved animals. A visitor likened his serenity to that of the Vicar of Wakefield—a weary, embittered man, an odd character, until his selfless life came to an end.

Eckermann said about his first meeting with Goethe that he was speechless with happiness at the sight of him and could not gaze his fill. He was indescribably happy in Goethe's presence. Soon he had the satisfaction that Goethe obviously considered him part of the inner circle. Once Goethe, whose beauty he often stressed, appeared "young and serene, like the beginning of spring." Even in 1827 he wrote enthusiastically to Hannchen: "Now, as ever, Goethe is my only happiness here in Weimar . . . it is incredible how his mind remains fresh and young, his body beautiful despite his seventy-eight years."

When after his first unsuccessful attempt to flee Weimar, Eckermann received a friendly condescending letter from Goethe, he replied again "with sentiments of deepest love" and reported how very happy the letter had made him so that he had read it "God knows how many times between cornfields and villages."

Eckermann himself tried to interpret this peculiar relationship in his preface to the third volume of the *Conversations:*

> My relationship with him was of a peculiar kind and of a delicate nature. It was that of a pupil to his master, a son to his father, of one who craves education to one who possesses it in abundance . . . He was ever the same and ever different . . . At times he was like a smiling summer day, when every bird of the forest pours forth its songs of jubilation

from every bush and every hedge, when the cuckoo calls across the blue sky, and the brook murmurs through flowering meadows. At such a time it was a joy to listen to him; it was bliss to be near him, the heart swelled at his words . . .

When he emphasized the father-son relationship between Goethe and himself, Eckermann probably sounded the depth of this relationship. According to his autobiographical notes, he was particularly devoted to his own father, who in turn showed special preference for this late-born son.

As soon as I was big enough, I used to accompany father on his rounds and help him carry his bundles. I recall this as a very happy time (for I did not like to go to school) . . . During the day, when we walked across the bleak heath and I happened to lag a little bit behind, I became uneasy and would hurry to catch up with my old man, and would snuggle up to his arm, looking anxiously behind me . . . At night, I would lie next to him on the straw . . . and with a child's love would press very close to him and so fall peacefully asleep . . .

There is no doubt that in the aged Goethe, Eckermann found again a father whom he could help—an intellectually superior father, an ideal teacher and patron. The relationship to his own father, this deepest experience of his childhood, was repeated and provided the undercurrent of intoxicating happiness. To be taught, to be inspired, was a deep need; there is no trace of revolt. "The happiness I enjoy in my ever closer relationship with Goethe is so great that no one in the world could take his place— as indeed he has no equal," so Eckermann wrote to his fiancée. His love for Goethe competed with his love for her. When Goethe advised Eckermann *nolens volens* to accept a position as keeper of the Archives in Hannover so that he could get married, he confessed to his fiancée: "I was calmly happy in Goethe's love and in the hope of a happy life with you; but a melancholy feeling came upon me when I reflected that I should have to part from the glorious Goethe." And he never did.

A psychological-biographical study must not overlook the facts of heredity and constitution in its subjects. We have no information about the characteristics of Eckermann's relatives. His physical constitution on the other hand, was known to be delicate. As a young man he volunteered for a chasseur corps and took part in a military campaign. He survived it but fell seriously ill afterwards. All his life he remained susceptible to colds and frequently was ill, often when it was most inconvenient, as for instance before the journey to Italy with August Goethe. In Italy he suffered severely from the heat, in Rome he contracted cholera and was completely exhausted. Anxiety may have been partly responsible for his early return. Knowing that frequent illness may have a psychological basis, we are inclined to adopt this hypothesis in the case of Eckermann. Once ill, he did not always have the energy to pull himself out of it. There is a very characteristic passage in the *Conversations*. Eckermann complains to Goethe that he has been sleeping badly for weeks, has had uneasy dreams in which he quarreled and which left him exhausted even in daytime so that he lacks interest and strength for anything. Goethe calms him, diagnoses a slight sluggishness, and advises a few glasses of mineral water or a little salt. But Eckermann does nothing about it and continues to suffer. Goethe loses patience, he cannot refrain from smiling ironically and from deriding him. He compares Eckermann with the father of Tristram Shandy who for half a lifetime was annoyed by a creaking door but could not bring himself to get rid of this daily annoyance with the help of a few drops of oil. Eckermann's lack of energy for purging obviously irritates Goethe very much, for he paces up and down, mutters indignantly to himself, and from time to time utters unintelligible words.

Compared with the vigorous, narcissistic old Goethe with his capacity for work and pleasure, who advises radical self-help, the nervous, querulous Eckermann who persists in his suffering appears particularly weak.

On another occasion, when Goethe spoke about Italian ravines, Eckermann mentioned that such ravines frightened him. All his life he was afraid of draughts.[2]

2 Cf. Jones (1923).

Eckermann was no forceful personality. He never adopted a superior attitude, never showed any aggressive tendencies, only the most quiet resentment or resignation. In the letters of his youth he occasionally showed hatred or defiance. Later on these emotions were successfully repressed. Only in his old age, as unappreciated servant of the Prince, did he betray some revolutionary feelings.

As is often the case with people who, born in humble circumstances, had to scrape and bow, Eckermann was modest and subordinated himself, all the more so as he never overcame his shyness. Strained circumstances and dependency characterize his whole life, humbleness his personality.

He said of himself: "Lecturing is not my forte. I completely lack the gift for oratory. The presence of an audience hampers me so that I can rarely express my thoughts with any freedom or vigor!"

Half a year after his wife's death, more distraught than ever, he apologized to Ottilie von Goethe: "If only I could lose my shyness. It is the greatest torment of my life to think that my friends may misinterpret this shyness and turn away from me. It really is a morbid state. If I happen to stand at the window and see someone coming along the street who intends to visit me . . . I am always overcome by anxiety; if I look into the mirror I am pale as a ghost." It is the same when he has to pay a call. As soon as he enters, the pounding of his heart robs him of speech.

All authorities agree that Eckermann was a somewhat effeminate, wholly passive man who confronted life with too great a pliancy and was enslaved by the strong personality of Goethe. Until the end he kept a certain childlike naiveté.

Typical is a scene with Goethe's temperamental son whose enthusiasm for Schiller Eckermann opposed. August von Goethe squeezed Eckermann's arm: "Wouldn't it be fun if I were to break your arm some day, Doctor?" Later, quarreling about Schiller, August called Eckermann narrow-minded. When Eckermann found fault with Schiller, August said obstinately: "The early works of my father have plenty of faults, too." This behavior of August's has a general significance. The son sharply criticizes his father and finds pleasure in playing Schiller against Goethe. Here we see the ambivalence of the son toward his father which has so often been proven by psychoanalysis. Here is the root of the frequently observed fact that sons are not always the best "friends and collaborators" of their own fathers. The more energetic ones prefer to seek some other field of activity, only the weaker ones like to continue in their father's footsteps. In his usefulness for the father, the son by elective affinity may often be superior to the son by birth—especially if he is as tractable and passively feminine as Eckermann, whom Houben called the most defenseless of all of Goethe's friends.

It is hardly likely that this remained the only conflict with the wild and undisciplined August. Eckermann expressed his bitterness in one of his aphorisms: "The sons of heroes, it is said, are never-do-wells. Nature exhausts herself; she has reached a peak in the fathers and from now on goes downhill."

Goethe at once recognized Eckermann as a "good, straightforward, sensible man" and held him fast. We need not assume that the Mephistophelean element in Goethe consciously made game of him, as many authors think. Great personalities are usually "great takers," ready to enlist the help of everyone who might be useful to their work.

Goethe dissuaded Eckermann from undertaking overambitious poetic compositions. This led Auernheimer to the humorous remark: "It was one of Goethe's little appreciated services to German literature that he so nicely kept Eckermann from writing poetry." Yet Goethe did acknowledge one of Eckermann's ephemeral productions. He praised the poems about the King of Bavaria. Eckermann proudly wrote to his fiancée: "Goethe said I had the boldness of Lord Byron and his calm. Two great qualities."

Goethe always knew how to hold Eckermann, despite the latter's occasional reluctance. And Eckermann, who had come to use Goethe for his own purposes, renounced these almost completely and became the servant of a great personality in a great cause. A fundamentally insecure man, whose character was formed by a strong bond with his father in childhood, now enters another such relationship which becomes his destiny.

Neither Eckermann's productive capacity nor his energy appear to have been great enough to explain his rise in position. What seems to me of crucial importance is his belief in being chosen, a belief he developed unusually early. A late-born child, with brothers and sisters already grown up, is often spoiled and pampered. More is expected of him—and more is done for him. Favored by everyone, particularly by his father, he conceived the idea that God loved him particularly well and wished to make something worth while of him. In an autobiographical sketch he tells of this idea. "I do not know how this became established in my mind. Maybe it was due to the many attentions and distinctions heaped upon my humble self, maybe I derived it from the holy writ, where the humble are favored and elevated by God." One day, on his first visit to the big city of Hamburg, sitting somewhat apart from his father in a *Keller*, he felt uneasy and turned to God for a sign that He would elevate him to higher things. . . . "And suddenly," Eckermann continues, "while I was pursuing these thoughts, a stranger rose and accosted my father: 'Is this your boy, old man? I tell you, he will amount to something!' " In later years, Eckermann often drew strength from this incident.

In a nonmetaphysical sense, this divine calling is narcissism, self-love. A belief in himself has taken root, the ascent seems possible, thought it is not yet clear to what goal, to what height of intellectual success it might lead.

Eckermann early developed a strong sense of honor. Every time a visitor stressed that Hans Peter had to become a tailor because of his slight build, he was deeply unhappy. He was of course hurt and disappointed in his physical self-assurance, and so, as we can learn from his dreams, he all the more valued strong, healthy men. He admired Goethe's physique even in death, he admired the figures of a regiment of dragoons. He reported in detail one dream in which he exchanged his build with that of a handsome, vigorous swimmer; in another, Faust and Mephisto appear as young, good-looking men and make him happy by taking him between them for a promenade. On the other hand, his estimation of his intellectual products was narcissistic. He started early to write down his poems, later often recorded dreams in his diaries.

His ability to identify, to equate himself with another person, was developed to a remarkable degree. In a letter he once said about his behavior with his fiancée: "If you could only see us and observe how we have adopted each other's movements, laughter and speech." Identification leads him to write poems like Koerner, to attempt plays like those of Muellner and Grillparzer. His capacity for empathy with someone greater than himself was extraordinary. In this sense his reproductive talent was exceptional. In the *Conversations* he succeeded in depicting Goethe exactly as he was. Eckermann was original in his unoriginality.

We know that he went too far, identifying himself with Goethe to the point of ridicule. Heine mockingly called him "Goethe's parrot." Eckermann was capable of writing to Carlyle: "You are very much in our thoughts . . . We have not yet read . . ." He adopted Goethe's expressions and mannerisms, he called Molière a "pure" man, etc. Of course, in the *Conversations*, this identification of style and manner is an asset.

After a short period of enthusiasm for Schiller, Goethe became his inspiration, the ideal after which he patterned himself. He loved in Goethe what he himself wanted to be. He wanted to own Goethe. He wanted to be Goethe. Before knowing Goethe, he had studied his works carefully. "Wherever I went, whatever I did, Goethe was in my mind. He was present even in my dreams, his personality appeared to me in many delightful forms." Eckermann tried to acquire a portrait of Goethe. He sought a personal interview with Goethe—an endeavor that was not rare among young men of letters of that time. In his case, this meeting brought about the actual encounter with the ideal—an ideal that had been preformed through the father and now became transformed through the higher intellectual personality. A kind of repetition compulsion led him to a faithful attendance on this

new father, just as in the past he had attended his own father with
the pack on his back.

On December 19, 1821, a year and a half before his first visit
to Goethe, Eckermann had the following dream, which he described in a letter written from Goettingen to his fiancée in Hannover:

> All night long I dreamt I was with Goethe. I spoke to him
> at length. I embraced his knees, he wore heavy underwear;
> he said he could no longer keep warm without it. He was
> already very old, but he was very fond of me, he brought
> me a whole handful of pears from the pantry, he even peeled
> them for me. . . ; I was to eat them all, but I told him I
> would keep two for my Hannchen. [Goethe introduced his
> grandchildren. Then they discussed one of Goethe's verses.
> Eckermann corrected Goethe and asked him "whether he
> did not know his own poem better than that," and Goethe
> conceded that Eckermann was right. The dream continues:]
> Goethe wept over present-day poetry, he said that it weighed
> heavily upon his heart, he would soon have to depart; but
> that he had set his highest hopes in me and could now die
> more peacefully. I asked him what he thought of me; he
> answered that if I went about it in the right way, I could one
> day achieve as much fame as he himself, for my talent was
> no less than his. He left me in the dark as to how I ought to
> go about it; he said it would be dangerous to tell me that.
> Then the conversation turned to other things. There were
> other people present, the Grand Duke of Weimar and other
> dignitaries, but they remained in the great hall. I only saw
> them from afar, whenever a door opened. He spent most of
> the time with me in his study.

This dream shows how indispensable the interpretation of
dreams is for a psychological biography. The meeting with
Goethe and his acknowledgment of the dreamer's talent constitute pure wish fulfillment. The figure of Goethe in the dream
is a composite of detailed recollections of Eckermann's father
and his empathy with the beloved poet-hero who appears as a
kindly human being. This dream gives us important insight into
the unconscious of the young Eckermann. The aged father, now
dead, and the aged Goethe are fused into one: in the dream

Goethe, too, is near death. Eckermann himself clearly is present in the dream, a little would-be Goethe. He dreams, i.e., he wishes unconsciously to gain the same fame as Goethe, who may die peacefully now that a worthy successor has been found. Several things are clarified in this dream: Eckermann's narcissism, his love for the ideal, and the latter's connection with his once so beloved father. Untrained interpreters might be led to explain this as a prophetic dream because it shows actual details of Eckermann's later life: Goethe leaves him in the dark as to how he should go about becoming like him; in reality Goethe did parry all such probings. In the dream Goethe's visitor can see the Duke and other dignitaries "only from afar"; thus it was to remain throughout his life. Eckermann did not dream what fate was to bring him; he dreamt what he wished for—but not more than might be possible for him, the upstart, to achieve. That Goethe fetched pears from the pantry may be a repetition of a childhood scene. And that he wears heavy underwear because he is sensitive to cold, is probably a memory of his old father to whom the son, as a young boy, snuggled up closely at night. Incidentally, in the *Conversations,* Eckermann writes about the first meeting: "We sat together for a long time, in a quiet, affectionate atmosphere, I pressed his knees, I forgot to speak at the sight of him. . . ." Here, too, attention is paid to the legs.

The conceit in the dream, that Eckermann knows one of Goethe's poems better than the poet himself, and Goethe's acknowledgment that Eckermann's talent is equal to his own—these surely are unconscious wishes of the dreamer. To be sure, his own simple father was easier to surpass.

This dream permits us to surmise why Eckermann found in Goethe the man who from that moment on meant everything to him and caused him to forget himself. He identified his own interests completely with Goethe's. As long as he lived with him, Goethe had no place in his dreams, but during the first years after Goethe's death, when every day evoked strong memories, Eckermann often dreamt about him. He usually saw him as a living person, had all kinds of conversations with him and left him with the happy conviction that he was not dead. This, too, follows the usual pattern of dreams after the death of a close relative.

Eckermann recorded such a rather lengthy dream four years after Goethe's death. In this dream he asks Goethe: "You are not dead, are you?" Goethe answers: "Those foolish people who think that . . . why should I be dead? . . . I have been on a journey!" Eckermann then asks: "How do you like my *Conversations?*" Of course Goethe has read the book, and he praises it. He approves of the free use of Eckermann's notes. This spurs Eckermann to further such experiments, since the earlier ones have, so to speak, been sanctioned. Again, clearly, wish fulfillment, justification of his activities.

As so often, the purpose of these dreams was to resolve a psychic conflict. Eckermann's work owed its success to his artistic freedom, its credibility to the authenticity of every word. "His weak, unstable nature was worn down by the conflict between conscientiousness and artistic ambition as well as by the struggle for existence which at the same time demanded and paralyzed great physical exertion" (Petersen).

Another dream, which is discussed in the *Conversations* (March 12, 1828), is of the greatest importance for an understanding of Eckermann's nature. In the evening Goethe had expressed his opinion that the vigor of the sea and the sea air influenced people and made the inhabitants of islands and sea coasts in the temperate zone far more productive and energetic than those people who live in the interior of great continents. This had touched Eckermann personally. He dreamed of a happy, festive summer day on the seashore. Someone suggests to undress and swim across; Eckermann demurs: It's easy for you to talk, you are young and handsome and good swimmers. I am a poor swimmer and I am not well built so that I do not enjoy to appear before strangers on the beach but feel uncomfortable. Thereupon the handsomest of those present offers to exchange appearance with Eckermann, and he does so. Eckermann then proves himself a strong swimmer and mixes cheerfully with the people, unembarrassed in the happy knowledge of his handsome limbs. With uneasiness he remembers the youth who now represents his body, his former ego which he never enjoyed. He fears that the other will demand his pleasing form back. But the latter, too, has now increased in size and beauty, Eckermann watches with pleasure his back and thighs. In the end, the youth relieves Eckermann by saying he does not want to change back, he is quite satisfied with these limbs: the only important thing is to make something of oneself.

This dream reveals Eckermann's feelings of inferiority about his appearance and his inadequate strength, as well as his heightened sense for manly beauty and virility. In the dream the vain wish of his waking hours is fulfilled, he takes on the tall, handsome body, the active masculinity of another person. The comparison, the envy, the subsequent reassurance show a naive wish fulfillment as consolation for the dreamer. Many assume that this exchanging of his physique with someone else "certainly refers to Goethe." Scoptophilia and shame of nakedness are involved in this dream. We see that Eckermann is a visual type. This explains his appreciation of manly beauty, but also his shyness (which we know to be a function of offended consciousness due to one's imperfect exterior, be it a real or an imagined defect). All his life Eckermann was ugly and insignificant looking. We know that he could not often enough admire Goethe's beauty. Even when he looked at Goethe's dead body he "was amazed at the god-like magnificence of his limbs. The chest extremely powerful, broad and arched; the arms and legs full and gently muscular; the feet graceful and perfectly shaped . . . A perfect human being lay before me, and my delight . . . let me forget for a moment that the immortal spirit had left this mortal form."[3]

Eckermann, like Goethe, once wanted to become a painter; like Goethe, he had a talent for visual observation; in this respect there was a close resemblance between them. Eckermann was easily won for research on the *Theory of Color* and collaborated

---

[3] Actually, Goethe had short legs and a disproportionately long torso and was said to show a "slight indication of stuntedness" (Hans Wuertz, 1932).

with Goethe on it. Among his projected works (1834) he announced that he would publish "his new discoveries in the *Theory of Color*." He composed an enthusiastic poem about Stieler's portrait of Goethe. We know that he longed for a portrait even before he knew him.

Eckermann was a great daydreamer, a lonely walker. "I have lived a life of solitude from early youth," he wrote to Goethe, "solitude is my true element."

Eckermann the daydreamer had always had a compulsive hobby. He used to visualize people he liked in their absence so clearly that he could have sketched them. He did this once with the three women who were closest to him, the actresses Sylvester and Kladzig, and his Hannchen. "This phenomenon was often repeated. I have no other explanation for it, except that lasting impressions of my life involuntarily reappear before my mind." Goethe, the most lasting impression of his life, was of course available for conversations at any time. He was so faithfully observed and depicted that he actually seems to live in the *Conversations*.

People who have the ability to see objects, after these have been removed from observation, with the clarity of the senses, are called eidetics (E. R. Jaensch); the phenomenon is called *Anschauungsbilder*. It is interesting to note that Goethe had this ability (Kroh). He could, for instance, visualize plants at will before his mind's eye. As we know, a vision of himself confronted him as he rode away from Sesenheim.[4] In Eckermann and Goethe two eidetics found each other. This is obviously an inborn talent, a special visual gift.

Goethe was a visual type; he owed much to his power of observation and advocated the training of the eyes. The passive aspect of this visual quality—the feeling of being looked at—can evoke either pride or shame. On Frau Rath's authority, Bettina related Goethe's proud bearing as a boy. As a youth he was fond of fine clothes (uninhibited exhibitionism and narcissism). In Eckermann the predominant feeling was shame about his in-

4 Cf. Theodor Reik; also E. Menninger-Lerchenthal (1932).

ferior physique and clothing, e.g., in his student days in Goettingen (repressed exhibitionism and hurt narcissism). Here we can see one source of his self-consciousness.

In his autobiography *Poetry and Truth* (Part III, middle of Book 13), Goethe spoke of his need to transform monologues into dialogues:

> Accustomed as I was to spend much of my time, by preference, in company, I used to change even my solitary thinking into social conversation in the following way. Whenever I was alone, I would summon some person of my acquaintance in spirit. I would ask him to sit down and would pace up and down past him, would stop in front of him and discuss with him the matter that happened to be on my mind. He would occasionally reply or indicate his assent or dissent by some habitual gesture, such as everybody has. Then the speaker would continue, expound further what had appeared to please the guest, qualify what he had disapproved of or define it more clearly, may at the end even courteously cede a point . . . These "guests" . . . were usually persons who were receptive rather than communicative by nature, ready to take a dispassionate, unbiased interest in things within their ken; sometimes, though, I invoked contradictory spirits for these dialectic exercises.

The abstract process of thought is presented as something concrete through the discussion of several people. Goethe thus turned soliloquy into conversation, thinking into dialogue, in which he assigned to himself several roles. If we look at the nature of these discussions with an imaginary guest, we see that Goethe anticipated quite accurately Eckermann's presence. He was often to pace up and down in front of Eckermann, instructing, pondering, receiving approval and objections. Somebody who so exactly embodies a previously imagined person has to become as indispensable as Eckermann became for Goethe.

The third part of the *Conversations* with Goethe is based on a manuscript of Soret's; Eckermann had to rely on particularly propitious hours, when he was able to, so to speak, restore the long dead Goethe to life and to hear him speak, in other words, to create hallucinations. "The living Goethe was again present;

I again heard the characteristic, beloved sound of his voice. . . ." Before his eyes he saw Goethe in a circle of friends, joking and laughing and carrying on animated conversations, wearing his black frock coat with the medal; or he saw him in a carriage, riding beside him; or in the evening, in his white robe, sitting across from Eckermann at the table by soft candlelight. "There was between us the most intimate harmony. He stretched out his hand to me across the table, and I pressed it. Then I seized a glass of wine that stood next to me and without saying a word I drank to him, my eyes rested on his across the glass. Thus I was close to him again, as in life, and his words sounded as before."

Goethe, for his literary purposes, had created fictitious dialogues out of his own imagination. Eckermann used the same device, though he, of course, merely drew on his memory.

At this point the reader may well ask: What kind of a psychoanalyst is this who forgets to discuss the love life of his analysand? The answer is that Eckermann cannot be regarded as an erotic character. Women played no great part in his life. His eroticism lacked any aggressive feature. His thirteen-year-long engagement to Hannchen Bertram reveals loyalty, warmth of feeling, and a certain sentimentality. But later she was partly supplanted by Goethe and sacrificed to him. It was a long time before the marriage took place, and then only after Hannchen had repeatedly complained that Goethe had neither released her fiancé nor rewarded him materially. Eckermann never rebelled against the long engagement. Soon his beloved wife died, and he had to live for his little son.

In Weimar two actresses crossed his path. One of them, Sylvester, was not very important. The other one, Auguste Kladzig (1828–29) made a deeper impression on him. He owed her many happy hours and some poetic inspiration.[5] He liked to moralize to her, wanted to improve her. Again, dreams are recorded in his

[5] For Example, *First Visit:*

> Did you allow me to enter your room
> How charming, how intimate this visit
> I am too old to beg of you your love
> But I am young enough to offer mine.

diary, revealing many doubts and guilt feelings. Here is an example:

> All night long I dreamt of Auguste. I was in her room and had a violent argument with her mother, who had spoken ill of me . . . and had turned her daughter's heart against me. I paced the room in great excitement, scolded and wept. Auguste sat on a little footstool, she sided with me and sought to confirm my words. Upon leaving, I gave her my hand but she did not take it . . . which I took as a sign that I should stay . . . Later I saw her again; she was with another man, and I told Holdermann that this was not right. I saw her in danger, and from then on for hours the dream was a never-ending search and flight . . . Finally I was again alone with her, it was as if she had injured herself, my hand stroked the bared side above her heart and a part of her back. I found her body undamaged. I felt it was not her bosom but her face that was turned toward me, radiant and all herself. I asked her whether it was necessary to call Vogel [the doctor]. Then I saw myself downstairs, as if I had to flee from her . . ."

Both Hannchen and Auguste sometimes conflicted with his duties toward Goethe, but Goethe always remained victorious. Incidentally, he never deemed it necessary to receive the wife of his Dr. Eckermann. He only met her once at the house of his daughter-in-law, Ottilie.

No, Eckermann was not an erotic character. He was morally inhibited, devoid of any aggressiveness. He fulfilled himself not with women but in his dreams, in his poetry, in his Goethe, in short, in his ideal. It was the man-to-man, sublimated relationship with an exalted father image that provided the course of his life with a goal. His characteristics were a delicate constitution, shyness, and talents that can only be called mediocre. He was no hero. His life was turned inward rather than outward.

Eckermann served with joy, but he also suffered. He was an intellectual anvil, to use his Goethe's own words:

> Thou must rule and win
> Or serve and lose

Suffer or triumph
Be anvil or hammer.

J. P. Eckermann was a normal individual, though peculiar in his talents and peculiar in his development. Now we have to consider two strangely intriguing features of his personality which we would not expect to find in a man who is so perfectly adjusted socially. In fact, Eckermann remained all his life somewhat of an eccentric. Such solitary natures do not easily relinquish the right to go their own way. In this respect they are narcissistically self-satisfied, they have their own *Lebenslüge,* their own "wild duck." They are proud of it and do not even notice that people sometimes smile behind their backs. They devote a part of their time to their own special interests, through an unconscious impulse they become collectors or acquire expert knowledge in a small field with which they can then impress others. Our Eckermann shows two such peculiarities. He had a collection of bows and arrows, bows of a size that reached the ceiling. He loved birds, kept them in his room, partly in cages, partly free—a love that stems from his childhood and later became somewhat excessive. Goethe once added to the collection a bow which Bashkirs had brought him from their homeland, as a tribute to the world-famous man. Eckermann had learned archery on his military campaign in Brabant and brought equipment back with him. The Austrian Hermann Rollett, who visited the old Eckermann, saw the giant bows, some home-made, some foreign, which filled a whole wall. Eckermann demonstrated for him how to shoot with an Indian bow that came from South America, "and as he did so, his profile was sharply outlined." To oblige Eckermann, Goethe shot once, too, as he said "to please the foolish fellow." It is an amusing picture, the delicate little man with the profile of a bird of prey, shooting such a powerful bow! One cannot help but assume that the heroic attitude was supposed to provide a certain stature for the would-be-great and would-be-strong man. Some aspect of his repressed aggressive instinct may have found shelter there. Some mastering of anxiety may be involved, too. Were the bows to afford protection in dark nights? Eckermann's self-confidence was certainly strengthened by this specialized knowledge of bow production and of the materials used for it. In the third part of the *Conversations* he has full revenge on Goethe. Here it is he who lectures Goethe at length on archery and on a second topic: songbirds and their habits. Eckermann was an expert and breeder. His apartment was full of noisy bird cages, a few of the bigger feathered friends were always running around loose.

Eckermann loved his birds extravagantly. Sometimes in the spring he let them fly away. He raised a young falcon. His love for animals was revealed in other ways, too. He was fond of dogs. Once when he was putting on his shoes, he found a mouse in one of them, about to give birth. He considerately put on another pair.

A visitor relates that "the windows of both rooms were almost always kept open so that the birds would not lack fresh air, and the old gentleman, who was particularly sensitive to draughts, protected himself with double clothing and sat around in overcoat and cloak, with his hat on his head."

Despite the open windows, visitors detected a certain odor, as in a zoo. The floor was not always clean. Eckermann continued to make special studies. He had a nest in his room in order to measure the projectile power of the birds when they relieved themselves without fouling the nest. Newspapers were spread on the floor for protection.

This predilection for birds, their nests, their newly hatched young, dates from Eckermann's youth and was fostered by the peddling expeditions through the villages: "No matter how wearily I was trailing behind, the sight of a bird's nest could always revive me."

The giant bow in the dwarf's hands betrays quite clearly the wish of the little would-be-strong-man to be strong and impressive. The psychogenesis of the excessive interest in bird breeding is not so transparent. But we do know that a craving for power can be sublimated in animal breeding. Eckermann also was very fond of children. He encouraged all the boys of the neighborhood to bring him birds. To be a puppeteer, to be able to pull strings, in a small way at least, with birds and little boys—here he was able to achieve it. Along with this, anal interests are clearly involved, as well as a certain reactive kindness. Who could deny that a kind of motherliness finds an outlet in the breeding of animals?

Many found this peculiarity of Eckermann ridiculous. Even his fiancée wrote: "I could not help but laugh about your many birds. One bird is quite enough for me."

Eckermann, the heroic archer, and Eckermann, the eccentric who breeds birds in his apartment—seen in this light, he becomes a Spitzweg figure. Many a repressed impulse of a fettered man, living in a circumscribed circle, may thus have found compensation; it may have been motivated by the mastery over some childhood anxiety.

Though not a star of the first magnitude, though shining only with reflected light, Eckermann's memory gleams in the literary firmament. For he has, after all, lived and worked in the sense of Goethe:

Immer strebe zum Ganzen, und kannst du selber kein Ganzes Werden, als dienendes Glied, schliess an ein Ganzes dich an.
("Aim at the whole with all your strength! If you cannot attain it, Aim at becoming at least one of the parts of the whole!")

5

Samuel Johnson's Character*

I SHOULD like to show here once again that psychoanalysis is the best available method for interpreting and constructing coherent pictures of the development of a personality. I should like to prove it by a study of "the most unforgettable character I have met," the famous Englishman of the eighteenth century, Samuel Johnson. His biography by James Boswell is called the greatest among English biographies. When I arrived in London in 1938, Johnson was still the most widely quoted man. Boswell's biography of him was recommended reading in the same sense as the Bible and Shakespeare. Samuel Johnson (1709–1784) was a writer and a poet; among his publications were a dictionary, a drama, a novel, some biographies, and many essays. Yet it was not his works which survived him, it was rather his imposing personality, his oddities, his conversations full of wit, humor and knowledge of human nature. He was famous for his charity and religiousness. An immense literature was published on this exceptional man. Carlyle and Macaulay wrote essays on him.

If you hear the similes used by contemporaries and the titles given him by various writers, you will get a very striking impression. A mighty giant with a penetrating voice, Johnson was a popular person in the streets and taverns of London. He was compared with a tiger, a bear, and an old lion. His laugh was said to remind one of a rhinoceros and his mouth of that of Gargantua, his spirit of the far-reaching trunk of an elephant. He was called "the most national man of English letters," "the embodiment of the essential features of the English character," "an awfully majestic philosopher," and "a tremendous converser." He was especially famous as one of the most outstanding talkers and conversationalists. Carlyle acknowledged him as "the largest

* First published in *The Psychoanalytic Review*, Vol. 32, 1945.

soul that was in all England" and as the "ruler of the English nation for some time, not over them but in them." In Parliament Johnson was called "a pattern of morality." People saw in him "their magnified and glorified selves." In spite of his lifelong suffering from a compulsive neurosis, the distorting convulsions of his severe tic, and his attacks of depression, one biographer even declared: "Johnson embodies the healthiest instincts of the Anglo-Saxon race."

Some of these writers have pointed out that the problem of Johnson's character is still unsolved. Christopher Hollis wrote (1929): "Had Johnson lived at a later date, science would have been able, if not to cure his oddities, at least to name them."

A. C. Roberts (1935) remarked: "The explanation of Johnson's mind is still worth looking for, and the modern seeker after truth will not return from the voyage empty handed."

Two attempts have been made by doctors to explain his character, but they are disappointing. C. MacLaurin (1925) wrote a short and erroneous essay on Johnson and R. MacDonald Ladell published a paper in the *British Journal of Psychology* (1929) which deals with Johnson's neurosis. Ladell's diagnosis of anxiety hysteria entirely fails to understand the structure of his neurosis.

The proper psychoanalytic interpretation of such an original and effective personality would require a whole book. The concepts of our science can comprehend his character development. His compulsive neurosis complicated by depressions and tic is unusually transparent. His own psychological insight often anticipated psychoanalytic opinions. Incredibly enough, Johnson appreciated the importance of a child's dream. He led the interest of a young mother to the dreams of her small son, confessing that "the first corruption that entered my own heart was communicated by a dream." But Johnson never disclosed more about this dream.

Some of his sentences could have been written by Freud.

Children are always cruel. Pity is acquired and approved by the cultivation of reason. No man was naturally good, he is no more than a wolf. No man loves labor for itself. Abundant charity is an atonement of imaginary sins. It is affectation to pretend to feel the distress of others as much as they do themselves. Nothing is more common than to call our own condition the condition of life.

Johnson's pessimism reminds us of Freud's *Civilization and Its Discontents*. "Human life is everywhere in a state in which much is to be endured and little to be enjoyed . . . The cure of the greatest part of human miseries is not radical but palliative." Johnson belongs to the characters Freud has described as "the exceptions." He was infected with tuberculosis by his wet nurse and subsequently remained half-blind and hard of hearing, predestined to become introverted. These "exceptions" feel that early frustrations guarantee them the right to demand a reimbursement from fate and become pretentious.

Johnson accused his father of stinginess because he had hired the ill nurse, and never forgot that his kind mother "gave me coffee which she could ill afford to gratify my appetite when a boy." On all occasions he was entitled by her to preferential treatment.

After the early traumatic event, little Sam developed his oral instincts of voraciousness. "I never knew," says Boswell, "any man who relished good eating more than he did. When at the table he was totally absorbed in the business of the moment . . . his looks seemed riveted to his plate; nor would he, unless in very high company, say one word, or even pay the least attention to what was said by others, until he had satisfied his appetite which was so fierce and indulged with such intenseness that while in the act of eating, the veins of his forehead swelled and generally a strong perspiration was visible." Really an alimentary orgasm!

Johnson named the chair in the tavern "the throne of human felicity." He was a gourmet and boasted that he would be able to write a better cook book than had ever been written.

He showed a similar greed in drinking. Originally a wine drinker, he became in later years abstemious but consumed tea in abnormal quantities, sometimes twenty-five cups at a sitting.

Especially during the night he liked to have women provide him with this warm, sweet liquid. Johnson called himself "a hardened and shameless tea drinker who with tea amuses the evening, with tea solaces the midnight, and with tea welcomes the morning." It may be mentioned here that Johnson suffered from a severe insomnia which frequently occurs in connection with oral insatiability.

We may add here that Johnson was an omnivorous reader, a finger nail biter, and that his fighting talks were full of biting, sarcastic remarks. The violence of his youth appeared later in sublimated form in his discussions. "From a spirit of contradiction and a delight in showing his powers, he would often maintain the wrong side with equal warmth and ingenuity . . . when he perceived that his opponent gained ground, he had recourse to some sudden mode of robust sophistry." "There is no arguing with Johnson," somebody said, "for if his pistol misses fire, he knocks you down with the butt end of it." However, he could also be silent and never spoke till he was spoken to.

Envy and impatience also belong to the oral character traits. Johnson had a brother three years his junior, and Johnson's envy was exceptionally intense. "We are all envious by nature," he said, accusing himself. "Envy is almost the only vice which is practicable at all times and in every place."

Johnson was very impatient. The articles in his periodicals were usually written at the last moment, and he never read proofs. He confessed that he never read a poem to its end in spite of his predilection for poetry. His thirst for knowledge was insatiable and all-encompassing. His passionate mouth was—besides eating, drinking and kissing—eager to talk, to teach, to recite, to deride, to translate, to rhyme, to play with words and to invent new ones. We know from Brill's paper on "Poetry as an Oral Outlet" (1931) the importance of the oral instinct for writing and composing poetry.

Johnson's disposition for melancholia is well determined by traumatic events in his infancy, the narcissistic hurt of his childhood, and by the strength of his oral erotism. There was also an

inheritance of depressive tendencies from his father. His identification with the father and deferred obedience appear clearly in
the self-reproaches of his depressions: "I should not be idle,
should not eat so much, should not daydream in bed in the morning, I should get up earlier, should pray more!"

As predisposition for his compulsive neurosis and the tic we
find aggression and anality of the same high degree. We do not
yet know enough about the psychogenesis of tics, but it is certain
that the movements are meant to ward off or express hostile and
anal impulses, following the psychic pattern of the compulsive
neurosis. It is very interesting how Johnson's friend, Reynolds—
two hundred years ago—interpreted this tic: "My opinion is that
it proceeded from an habit which he had indulged himself in, of
accompanying his thoughts and certain untoward actions, and
those actions always appeared to me as if they were meant to
reprobate some part of his past conduct." In spite of the fact that
in Johnson's time cleanliness and personal hygiene were on a
lower level than they are today, we find in the description of his
appearance and his lodgings generally criticisms of his great
negligence and want of orderliness. He must have liked dirt. He
said he had no passion for clean linen, and his disinclination for
bathing he expressed in the sentence: "I hate immersion." Cook-
ing and chemical experiments were his hobbies; producing, writing and printing, his job. He compared "The Katharsis in the
Tragedy" of Aristotle with the process of purging.

When a lady, riding with him in a coach, complained that he
"smelled," Johnson answered: "Nay, madam, give me leave to
correct you; you smell, I stink." This is a proof of Johnson's word
pedantry and his compulsive word purism.

When Johnson got his pension, a younger friend impudently
remarked: "I hope you will now purge and live cleanly like a
gentleman."

Very striking contradictions appear in his relation to money.
He gave freely to persons in distress. He used only one third of
his royal pension of three hundred pounds a year for himself and

the rest for indigent people. Poverty and distress seemed to be the strongest of all recommendations to his favor. As a widower he took care of poor ladies and an old quack. His home was called "a retreat for the lame, the blind, the sad and the sorrowful." Yet the same Johnson could be avaricious and stingy in little things and showed an inclination to paltry saving.

We can find only one opinion about Johnson's aggressiveness: "There is a vigorous animal at the base of his mind," says a biographer. And such was the heat and irritability of his blood "that not only did he pare his nails to the quick but scraped the joints of his fingers with a penknife until they seemed quite red and raw."

As a boy he was stubborn, especially in relation to his father. As a student at Oxford, which he had to leave without a degree because of his miserable poverty, he played the cheerful and gregarious youth, but was, as he said, "mad and violent." His revolutionary mind opposed all authority. It is known that he cut down a man in rage, and he boasted of some others, who had kept quiet. He was a very good hater and held fast to his dogmatic antipathies against the Scotch, the Quakers, the American Colonists, against Swift, Rousseau, etc.

In his later years Johnson developed into a very kind, compassionate, religious and charitable man who was aggressive only in his social talk—the sole residue of his oral aggressiveness.

If an adult neurotic says that as a child he feared the ghosts of a murdered father, the psychoanalyst listens attentively. Johnson related this childhood memory: "When I was nine years old, having got the play of Hamlet in my hands reading it quietly in my father's kitchen, I kept on steadily enough; coming to the ghost scene; I suddenly hurried upstairs to the street door that I may see people about me." Like many other compulsive neurotics, Johnson in his boyhood passed through an irreligious period. He refused to read religious books, was reluctant to go to church, became a sort of "lax-talker" against religion and acquired mighty feelings of guilt because of his infidelity toward God, the Father. He subsequently became one of the most zealous and pious Christians. The constant fear of being damned in hell remained the deepest motive for his religiousness. Religion stayed with him all his life and was, as Baily has said, "the nightmare of his life," which he betrayed by ejaculatory prayers. There was much lip service, and "nothing inconsistent for him between pious talk and vicious practice."

Even as a boy Johnson was a moralist; all his writings are full of ethical and pedagogic ideas. Almost all the essays he published in his own periodicals deal with his own vices. (That may be the rule for all moralists!) The French have never understood Johnson, this insular and rude man who was not at all cosmopolitan. Taine criticized his essays as sermons, "the national food of the English people." The unbeliever Voltaire called him a "superstitious dog." Johnson remained only a local celebrity.

The typical compulsive neurosis which forced him to touch every lamppost on the street, to count his steps when he had to leave his room, and to start always with the right foot, also showed the familiar mechanism of "undoing" in a grotesque example. Johnson had once, as a boy, stubbornly and arrogantly refused to substitute for his father in a bookshop on the market. Fifty years later he felt compelled to go to this market and to stay there in contrition, bareheaded in the rain for a considerable time—a deferred obedience after fifty years! His "original sin," the thought of killing his father, appeared later in his preoccupation with the notion that "to say a man was sick was very near wishing him so." This is an example of the well-known "omnipotence of thoughts."

I shall deny myself a further discussion of Johnson's exceptional physical constitution,[1] the personalities of his parents who were about fifty years old when he was born, and his lifelong mother fixation which led him to marry a widow twice his age. The marriage was not a happy one; hers was "perpetual illness and perpetual opium," reports her doctor. There were always

1 The American novelist Thomas Wolfe, who was fed by mother's breasts for three and a half years, shows analogous constitution, mother fixation and lifelong habits.

quarrels. Mrs. Johnson liked to live in the country. Johnson was interested in prostitutes and eager to hear the stories of their lives. He once took a drunken, unconscious prostitute home, let her stay until she was cured, and tried to rescue her spiritually.

All his life he sought for a woman on whom he could be dependent, who would feed him and keep him. As a widower he found her in Mrs. Thrale, the young wife of a rich brewer, a gifted and literary ambitious lady. This relationship lasted for about twenty years.

Many of his essays deal with the difficulties of married life and the wretched existence of prostitutes. Johnson's sexuality might be characterized as ejaculatio praecox. He never developed to full genitality, and long periods of his life were without real sexual relations. He had a strong tendency for friendships with younger men. Among these were men of genius: the poet Goldsmith, the actor Garrick, the painter Reynolds, the politician Burke; and Boswell, his biographer.

I cannot refrain from mentioning the only dream of Johnson which Boswell recorded. This dream shows Johnson in a polemic contest with some other person. Johnson is mortified by dreaming that his opponent has the better of him and is victorious. The dream clearly represents a failure of Johnson, a dramatic expression of his nocturnal self-criticism, and a gratification of his superego. What shame for the ambitious talker who always fought for superiority and put his opponents to flight! But let us listen to Johnson's comment after he had awakened: "One may mark here," he said, "the effect of sleep in weakening the power of reflection . . . for had not my judgment failed me, I should have seen that the wit of this supposed antagonist by whose superiority I felt myself depressed, was as much furnished by me as that which I thought I had been uttering in my own characacter." What a tenacious narcissism! This compensating narcissism, a too obvious desire to instruct and improve, essentially characterizes Johnson. He was always convinced "that it was his to teach in this world and theirs to learn."

Freud has said: "It is easy for a barbarian to be (mentally) healthy." Exaggerating, we dare say: if Johnson had not repressed his archaic, very barbarian instincts, he would have bitten off the nipples of the breasts of his wet nurse, would have castrated and killed his father, blinded his brother and let him die of hunger, would have committed incest with his mother, slayed some of his enemies, and would have died from overeating; his corpse would have been found in very dirty underwear.

We now understand better the seemingly irreconcilable contrasts in his character. Johnson was violent and kind, gluttonous and abstemious, mean and generous, envious and charitable, insulting and conciliating. He was a believer and a cynic, partly hedonist and partly ascetic, a Tory and a friend of the poor, a Falstaff and a Puritan. In a certain sense he was the opposite of what he appeared to be. He never could achieve his ego ideal, to be a saint.

Johnson received full homage from his contemporaries, something that men of genius in general receive only from posterity. When he died, people behaved "like a bee swarm which had lost its queen." Had he really been "the embodiment of the essential features of the English character"? Is there such a thing at all as an unchangeable national character? Johnson represented the English character of his time and his class. The national character is not something given once and for all, it is always in the making, molding and being molded by the circumstances in which nations find themselves (M. Ginsberg).[2] Psychoanalysis has not yet taken up the problem of "national character," partly because no differences appear in the analyses of individual members of different nations, partly because such a problem could evidently be solved only in collaboration with other sciences, such as history, sociology, etc.

There is another challenge. Johnson's general attractiveness for men, women and children remains an unsolved problem. W. H. Craig, in his book *Dr. Johnson and the Fair Sex* (1895) explained this mysterious attractiveness with an "odic force or any

---

[2] Two analysts have written on English habits and peculiarities: A. Maeder (1912), and, more recently, Matté-Blanco (1941).

male magnetism," but he expressed the hope that "adepts in mental physiology should find out sounder and more practical ways to fill the gap left by all biographers." We analysts may try to fill this gap and answer the question. A jovial man with such a fatherly, imposing figure, kind and generous, bisexual and an ungratified neurotic too, with free-floating libido, enjoys general attractiveness. Psychoanalysis does not pretend to know the origin of special talents, but the intellectualism of the compulsive neurotic and the shrewdness produced by "the threat of instinctual drives," pointed out by Anna Freud (1936), are well known.

Returning for a moment to Johnson's pessimism, we find it mitigated by his enjoyment of the pleasures of life. "In his company," a witty observer remarked, "life was worth living, if only to hear the vigor and vitality with which he denied that it was worth living."

Johnson could be very cheerful for hours at a time and some spells of roars of laughter are reported, when he felt free of anxiety and guilt, when he forgot "the vanity of human wishes," a recurrent theme in his writings. An orthodox analyst would have the right to find reasons for this ambiguity in Johnson's oral destiny: that he was first starving at the breast of his tuberculous wet nurse and was then overfed by his mother. According to Abraham's classic character studies, the effect is the same whether the infant lacked gratification of the sucking period or was spoiled by excess of gratification. The lust to bite and an excessive ambivalence develop.

Some remarks may be allowed on the façade of neurotics which a strong ego builds up for self-assertion. We see such impressive façades, especially in compulsive neurotics who may represent on the one hand ideal philanthropy and on the other hatred and irascibility. Johnson's façade did not reveal a spotless ego ideal. As a glutton, a squabbler, a filthy and conceited fellow, he was not everywhere welcome in good society, but his façade won the people. They may have felt that he was a hero of inner fights and had overcome much suffering. His interest in human nature not only led him to become one of the foremost biographers, it also caused him to initiate a new kind of biography. He refused to write panegyrics, insisted on truth and the importance of the familiar and domestic picture of the subject, and knew how to value "the minute peculiarities." In this sense Johnson was the precursor of our psychoanalytic supplements of biographies, which have often more than a casual importance because they illustrate an instructive type of character.

Johnson, an individual with partly inborn and partly conditioned invincible instincts—oral and anal aggression—developed an extremely strict and aggressive superego. A lifelong fight between the instincts and the conscience was the consequence, a compulsive neurosis with tic and attacks of depression. But a strong ego was able to build up for the surrounding world the façade of a higher type of man, of a moralist, a man of letters and a conversationalist of erudite education.

Johnson's character verifies the psychoanalytic formula that character traits are either continuations of the original instincts, their sublimation, or reactions against them.

6

Boswell: The Biographer's Character*

INTEREST in the character of James Boswell has mounted rapidly in recent years. J. W. Krutch, who in 1944 published a biography of Samuel Johnson, describes Boswell's personality and asserts: "No doubt his [recently published] *Private Papers* will some day be used in an attempt to psychoanalyze their author."

In a similar vein, C. E. Vulliamy (1932) wrote in his book on Boswell: "The ultimate assessment of character—if such a thing is possible—lies outside the true province of biography, and would only be attempted by means of rigidly scientific analysis of mental components and of personal permutations." Vulliamy continues elegiacally: "biography used to be a vehicle for noble sentiment or profitable moralizing. The good biographer brought his work to a close with gentle harmonies or approval or with pious meditation. Now we are more accustomed to reviews of neuroses and complexes and all the rest of the psychological paraphernalia." Because he finds "the grapes too sour" for his limited knowledge of psychoanalysis, he predicts ironically: "Those who are not yet tired of playing at psychoanalysis will find in the history of Boswell most promising material for their pastime."

"This mind of Bozzy has never been analyzed or studied," said Percy Fitzgerald in 1912; but he used "analyze" in the general sense of the word. Growing respect for scientific characterology no longer allows the acceptance of a personal opinion about anybody as correct because the man who expressed it was a polyhistor. Macaulay, the famous historian, expressed an opinion of Boswell which hindered future generations from being objective.

* First published in *The Psychoanalytic Quarterly*, Vol. 17, 1948.

Macaulay's own character made him unable to understand Boswell's quite different nature. His judgment that ". . . logic, eloquence, wit, taste . . . were utterly wanting to Boswell . . . that he was a dunce, a parasite and a coxcomb," certainly does not do justice to Boswell. It is meaningless abuse to call Boswell ". . . a fool who could write the finest biography in English because he was a fool."

George Mallory, in his book, *Boswell, the Biographer* (1912), emphasized the importance of Boswell's relationship to his hard and dogmatic father who did not understand or appreciate his son. Mallory acknowledges Boswell's genuine interest in human character and his warm attachment and devotion to Johnson.

Vulliamy detects the feminine qualities of sensibility and responsiveness in Boswell and calls his attitude toward his father that of a "frightened child." He makes the assumption "that the story of Boswell, of this unfortunate man, is the story of one who was doomed by a nameless, incurable and persistent malady of the mind. If there is a moral here, it is a purely eugenic moral in favor of exogamous marriages." "It is important," Vulliamy asserts, "that Boswell was the first child of cousins-german, that one of his own children, Euphemia, was mentally deranged, and that his brother John, the second son of Lord Auchinleck, was taciturn to a degree bordering upon actual insanity." Louis Kronenberger, in his book *The Portable Johnson and Boswell* (1947), goes so far as to call Boswell "schizophrenic," a layman's diagnosis with which we are not at all impressed.

Boswell was, in fact, a very gifted, ambitious and learned man, who was for years happily married, a beloved member of society, and who wrote, in addition to remarkable books and essays, the greatest English biography, of his fatherly friend Johnson, whose friendship he ". . . had the honor and happiness of enjoying . . . for upwards of twenty years." Was this eminent biography Boswell's merit alone, owing to his special gifts, or was it the fortuitous result of a happy combination of external influences? One certainly could not have found a more exceptional subject than Johnson who, moreover, delighted in exercising in company his wisdom, originality and vivacity. Boswell wrote proudly to his friend Temple: "It will be without exception the most entertaining book you ever read."

Conscious of the enormous influence of Johnson on Boswell's technique, on his choice of material and the completeness of the biography, it is true that Boswell "thought after Johnson's pattern and said some sentences almost as Johnson would have said them" (Fitzgerald). Boswell became in the course of time so pervaded by Johnson's personality that he imitated him habitually, even copying his loose clothes and fidgety manner. Boswell, who was not always reliable in acknowledging quotations, must certainly have read Johnson's essay, "On the Dignity and Usefulness of Biography," published in *The Rambler* of October 13, 1740. We find that Boswell's biographical principles are indeed the same as Johnson's. "I, who was taught discrimination of characters by Johnson," asks the pupil, "should I have omitted his frailties?" "If I delineate him without reserve, I do what he himself recommended both by his precept and example." Boswell had resolved "to adopt and enlarge upon the excellent plan of Mr. Mason, in his memoirs of Gray," but he far surpassed that or indeed any other model.

Johnson's essay on biography had recommended the inclusion of domestic privacies and minute details of daily life. Johnson praised Sallust who wrote of Catilina that "his walk was now quick, and again slow." More knowledge of a man's real character may be gained "by a short conversation with one of his servants than from a formal narrative," said Johnson, condemning "uniform panegyrics."

In his instructive book *The Development of English Biography,* Harold Nicolson writes: "Johnson's observations, when collected together, constitute perhaps the best definition of biography as an art, which has yet been formulated." Johnson often pointed out that the interest of the biographer stems from identification with the subject. He said once to Boswell: "Nobody can write the life of a man but those who have eaten and drunk and lived in social intercourse with him." Johnson's first published biography was of his friend Savage with whom he had passed the poorest years of his life and whom he took to his heart in spite of his vices and weaknesses, all of which he described. Later he published his famous *The Lives of the Poets*. Bergen Evans in *Dr. Johnson as Biographer* notes Johnson's pre-eminence as a psychologist and biographer who seized essential facts and presented them vividly. His narrative and dramatic talents placed him among the foremost of biographers.

It seems justified to assume that the lion's share of the merit of Boswell's *Life of Johnson* belongs to the subject of the book, as author, teacher and innovator of a new kind of biography. If Boswell's originality is dubious, his merits as biographer are still less. Some interest that "posterity dedicates to him with printer's ink" seems a luxury. But his character remains an instructive and rewarding study even if he is no longer "one general paradox" (Fitzgerald).

A psychoanalytic interpretation of the character of Boswell, whom Krutch calls a "neurotic drunkard and victim of satyriasis," is restricted by the lack of almost any report about his childhood and his pious mother. Boswell, describing his feelings during one of his many depressions, said: "All the dreary ideas of my youth recurred upon me. I thought myself a boy and an unhappy discontented being . . . I lived at home in such bondage that I was not only afraid to stir from home without leave like a child, but scarcely opened my mouth in my father's presence" (Letter to Temple). To Rousseau, Boswell complained: "My education has in every way been such as to make me a slave of my father." He often regretted his "narrow upbringing." "His attitude toward his father was that of a frightened child, maintaining with some difficulty the proper level of respectful sentiment," said a biographer.

The father was a noted attorney and judge who on his elevation to the supreme court took the name Lord Auchinleck. He studied Anacreon and Horace, collected classic manuscripts and possessed a valuable library. He was conceited and sarcastic, as a young man very vain. James mockingly remembered his father's "red heels and stockings." His attitude toward his sons may be characterized by the fact that even in later years he called them idiots. James bore the brunt of violent attacks from his inflexible and domineering father whose great contempt he felt keenly. All this imbued the humiliated son with rebellion. In later years, the adult son still suffered from his father's unfeeling harshness toward him and his wife to such a degree that he was disturbed to find himself debating whether his father's death would not be "a desirable event" (*Private Papers*). The evocation of such parricidal impulses is inevitably accompanied by intense feelings of guilt and a partial retreat into passive submission to the father-judge. In contrast to the exaggerated male character of his father, James showed feminine qualities. He admitted himself "not to be of the iron race," but by temperament timid. He avoided dueling by apologizing. He felt "a transfusion of mind from Johnson," about whose readiness to fight he stated: ". . . he goes with his sword through your body in an instant." "There is a complete surrender," Vulliamy says of Boswell, "almost a womanly surrender." And Macaulay, with consistent vituperative exaggeration, states: "Boswell was always laying himself at the feet of some eminent man and begging to be spit upon or trampled upon."

Psychoanalysis has shown that a man's conscience originates in an identification with his parents, chiefly the father, which is favored by a good relationship between father and son. Older men in positions of authority, whom the son meets in later years, may contribute to this development. But where a father merits only his son's hatred, the healthy development of the son's masculine character is impaired. Boswell sought to repair his damaged masculine self-ideal by attaching himself to substitute fathers. Chief among these was Johnson. There was a succession of other great personalities, such as Hume, Rousseau, Voltaire and General Paoli, whom Boswell used as models, from whom he sought the acceptance of intimacy, acknowledgment, advice—also, of course, to boast of these acquaintances. More than he may have expected, he found later that Johnson "had done him infinite service, assisted him to obtain peace of mind, to become a real Christian." In contrast to the harsh, implacable father, Johnson had idealism tempered by humor and some cynicism, and was a famous writer who accepted Boswell, in the company of distinguished contemporaries, as an equal. As part of a process of identification, Boswell basked in the reflected splendor of the great, and with tablets in hand visited the celebrities of his time.

Characteristic of Boswell's superego was his conscious awareness of its weakness for which he sought help. A memorandum to himself reads: "Be like Johnson!" Another: "Seek to attain a fixed and consistent character, to have dignity . . . deserve to be Johnson's friend." Letters to his lifelong friend, the Reverend Temple, are full of good resolutions to attain a proper conduct of life, to make himself a man, to become steady and sensible. He wrote to Temple confessing his "dissolute conduct," but begging indulgence. "Admonish me, but forgive me!" But Boswell easily forgave himself. His conscience appeared to be more an adornment than an effective force. He could not acknowledge that renunciation is the essence of morality.[1]

Boswell was extremely vain and narcissistic, tended to be exhibitionistic and to parade in showy costumes. One may assume the inner conflict behind such overstress to have its origin in feelings of inferiority which motivate compensatory corrections. He had to prove to himself and others that he was the equal or superior of any man. He never desisted from calling himself Esquire. The early humiliating injury to his self-esteem by his father's sarcasm accounts in part for the son's compulsive need to correct an unconscious conviction of his worthlessness by various excesses to a degree that achieved results opposite from those intended.

Boswell's sexual promiscuity may be similarly interpreted both as hedonistic overindulgence and the desire to prove that he was

---

[1] "A moral man is one who reacts to temptation as soon as he feels it in his heart, without yielding to it. A man who alternately sins and then in his remorse erects high moral standards lays himself open to the reproach that he has made things too easy for himself. He has not achieved the essence of morality, renunciation, for the moral conduct of life is a practical human interest" (Freud, 1928c).

virile. Only during the first years of his relatively happy marriage to a poor cousin was this habit moderated. In his letters to Temple we find confessions (or boasts?) that "we drank a good deal until I was so intoxicated that instead of going home, I went in a low house . . . and like a brute as I was, I lay all night with her." In the same year he wrote: "I have got a (venereal) disease from which I suffer severely. It has been long of appearance and is a heavy one . . . I greatly fear that Mrs. X is infected; for I have been with her several times since my debauch."

Boswell's correspondence with Erskine shows him in early years as an expert libertine, siring an illegitimate child, eloping with an actress, indulging whims of becoming a military officer and an actor, justifying his father's criticism that he was a frivolous spendthrift. Wine, women and gambling brought James into association with other young men of fortune, a company which he did not like to abandon. However, he had an idealistic love for his wife, and when he lost her he lost his guardian angel. He never neglected his duties to his six children. Boswell had qualms about marrying, had to overcome much anxiety to do it, and did it with the significant reservation that he would "not . . . be bound to live with her longer than he really inclined; and whenever he tired of her domestic society, he should be at liberty to give it up."

It is well known that sexual promiscuity and whoring are often a defense against unconscious homosexual trends. Such a trend is inherent in a comment of Boswell about one of his mistresses: "My lively imagination often represents her former lovers in actual enjoyment of her." Boswell once gave a supper to friends in payment of a bet "that he would not catch the venereal disorder for three years." A gruesome note is recorded in the *Private Papers:* Boswell reads in Paris about his mother's death, rushes off to an Ambassador's dinner, and then, "as in a fever," to a bordello. He had to prove repeatedly to himself and others that he was not inferior, not "castrated." Once he wrote to Temple: "The death of Johnson will be like a limb amputated."

The same Boswell who was so sociable, cheerful, and humor-

ous, suffered often from depressions. Over a period of six years
he wrote anonymous essays under the title *The Hypochondriac,*
in which he dealt extensively with problems of hypochondriasis,
drinking, love, death. Here we find self-reproaches about the
wretched inertia of hypochondriacs including himself, beside all
the good intentions of a rational standard of conduct and of the
consistency and dignity he never achieved. His depressions were
severe. To Temple he wrote: "I have at bottom a melancholy
cast, which dissipation relieves by making me thoughtless and
therefore, an easier, tho' a more contemptible animal . . . I am
always apprehensive of it. I dread a return of this malady." "The
mere gratification of the senses" was, says Boswell, "during a
depression the only pleasure of existence." Inveterate drinking
he used as an excuse for sexual debauches. Boswell's cyclothymia
corresponded to different states of his conscience, which vacillated between severity and indifference. Boswell in later years
failed progressively in his legal, political and social ambitions,
and his escape through drinking increased in proportion.

"It is a very remarkable experience to observe morality . . .
functioning as a periodic phenomenon," says Freud. "Our moral
sense of guilt is the expression of the tension between the ego
and the conscience . . . The melancholic during periods of
health can, like anyone else, be more or less severe towards himself; but when he has a melancholic attack, his superego becomes
oversevere, abuses, humiliates and ill-treats his unfortunate ego."

That a very gifted man with good intentions finally fails in his
life and never achieves a lasting and genuine reputation does not
seem easily understandable. There was in Boswell a compulsion
to make a fool of himself and, by his buffooneries which appeared
at just the most unfavorable moments, to destroy the reputation
deserved by his accomplishments. For example, as a young man
he placed himself at the head of an uproarious mob which broke
his father's windows. Once, from the audience of the Drury Lane
Theatre, he took upon himself to imitate the lowing of a cow
so that the universal cry from the galleries was "encore the cow!"
His book, *Account of Corsica,* was a great success. But at a Shake-

speare anniversary in Stratford, Boswell appeared dressed as an
armed Corsican chief with a ribbon around his head imprinted
"Corsica Boswell." Moreover, he publicized the fact in the *London Magazine*. Just when he had the chance of winning the
esteem of the great Prime Minister Pitt, he made a fool of himself by composing a song about himself, six times repeated, ex-
hibiting his insolence and wantonness:

> So not a bent sixpence cares he
> Whether with him, or at him you laugh.

Was this behavior a demonstration against his father's overwhelming dignity? Was it a self-punishment for feelings of guilt?
Did he need spitefully to conform to his father's low opinion of
him?

After the deaths of his wife and of his mentor Johnson, the
demoniac component of Boswell's personality became more and
more visible in his downfall.

His ambivalence toward his father was occasionally betrayed
in his behavior toward the father-image Johnson. Mrs. Thrale
reproached him with "inclination to treachery." Macaulay expressed the opinion that Boswell published many anecdotes "as
never were published respecting persons whom one professed to
love and revere." Indeed, Boswell sometimes seemed to take peculiar delight in the absurdities of Johnson, who, it is true, could
humiliate him like a school boy, especially when irritated by
Boswell's obtrusive curiosity and provocative questions. But it
is owing to just this ambivalence that Boswell's biography is so
complete and amusing. Boswell's "animosities" were called by
Fitzgerald "the motor forces" of his observation and writing.
Some denudation belongs in every biography. Boswell said about
himself: "I impose nothing, I propose nothing, I expose."

There is no doubt that Boswell had special abilities for writing vivid biography. His habit of writing down and preserving
details of all events and impressions led him to instruct Temple
"to put his [Boswell's] letters in a book neatly." The wealth of
information in many diaries and private papers that are pre-

served regrettably includes nothing about his childhood. He well might not have liked to remember that unhappy time.

Boswell's boundless introspection and interest in his own character helped him to understand others: ". . . his knowledge of others began with himself." Each new person he met excited his curiosity. "I have ever delighted in that intellectual chemistry, which can separate good qualities from evil in the same person." The striking variations of his mood—periods of conceited elation alternating with depression and disillusionment—make his efforts to become clear about himself by writing down impressions and confessions seem like attempts at self-therapy. He lived, it is said, "a second life black on white."

"One would have expected," Fitzgerald rightly said, "that this gay young man would have followed someone of rank and influence; but no—he preferred the excellent Johnson." Johnson represented in many ways a contradiction, the opposite of the father who hated such types as Johnson and did not understand nor like bohemians. Johnson was the reverse of the pedantic, implacable and parsimonious father. Boswell sought a father, not cold and dignified, but one who would show warmth and commendation, would be admonishing but forgiving, would be a great and wise man like Socrates who liked young men. Johnson, distinguished by intellectual and moral greatness, was above all humorous. He had an Olympian gift for not taking the world's problems too seriously. He did not like to be alone with his compulsive thoughts. He especially liked "young dogs," and preferred wealthy young men who, unlike himself, had not had to go through the ordeal of poverty.

Vulliamy came to the conclusion that only a mentally ill personality could have achieved and failed to achieve what Boswell did; that all that is unaccountable in his behavior, all the variations and facets of his life are understandable if we admit "that the story of his life is the story of one who was doomed by a nameless, incurable and persistent malady of the mind." We feel justified in declaring that Boswell was neither neurotic nor psychotic; that his abnormality is best specified as psychopathic personality. This type is not a clear-cut one. It is characterized by intact intelligence, a defective superego—though not to a criminal degree—by self-destructive tendencies, social maladaptation, unpredictable behavior, intense narcissism, and a weak ego. This type is often very gifted, even brilliant and creative. Boswell's inclination to manic-depressive changes of mood is not a regular symptom of the psychopath, but an individual characteristic of his dubious conscience and makes visible the defect in his superego.

We avoid here problems of heredity, constitution, general environment in his era, and restrict ourselves to the influence on Boswell of his exceptional father. The psychoanalytic biographer "can never have access to such first-hand information as is available to the physician who is working with a patient" (Glover). The advantage over other biographers is based on the understanding of causal connections, unconscious psychological determinism and the effects of conflicts in family life.

Phyllis Greenacre has published a paper about the influence of a certain type of father on the development of psychopathies in the sons. Greenacre describes these fathers as usually respected and often prominent men whose very work or profession puts them in positions of conspicuous public trust and authority, as clergymen, judges, heads of schools, civic leaders. Such a father is often stern, obsessional, remote, preoccupied and fear-inspiring in relation to his children. He is highly narcissistic in his more than ordinary dependence on the approval and admiration of his contemporaries. But his relationship with his children is poor. To them he appears fearsome, awe-inspiring and something of a frightening demi-god, lacking in substance and vital warmth, too exalted and aloof to permit the son to imagine himself as ever being able remotely to approximate his eminence. A son's masculine self-esteem is injured by such a father's harshness. A common defense for the son is to retain his infantile sense of narcissistic omnipotence. The development of healthy love impulses is diluted or stunted. The son is forced into submission, and the hatred which is evoked in consequence makes the necesary identification with the father impossible. It is an influence that often fosters the development of homosexuality.

The influence on Boswell's character and ego of this type of father was not simply traumatic: this wound had to be healed. Curiosity about people was one of the consequences. Boswell developed from early years not only this interest, but an urge to record his observations of the people he met. His introspective self-revelation belongs here too. Another fortunate consequence was Boswell's search for kinder, better, more famous substitute fathers, which landed him finally with Johnson. With him he attained, as he said, "peace of mind." Johnson was fifty-four, Boswell twenty-three when they met. His identification with Johnson had great influence on young Boswell, even though in reality he never achieved a balance between idealism and cynicism. Boswell's extreme vanity and exhibitionistic behavior were compensations for the early lesion of his self-esteem. He had to attach himself to friends, inspire love and admiration to regain self-confidence. The ambition which "raged in his veins like a fever" had a similar compensatory value.

Boswell represents an instructive example of defective moral development and infirmity of purpose stemming from the impossibility of developing a lasting ego ideal by identification with the father. His ambivalence kept him from making use of his father as a model. Something unknown in himself kept him from doing what he knew he should. He talked and wrote much about morality but was often unable to do what theoretically he acknowledged. Moral weakness characterized him, and his feelings of guilt caused his depressions. It seems evident that the attacks he called "hypochondriacal" were manic-depressive.

This rebellious son vacillated for many years in the choice of vocation, resisted becoming a lawyer like his father, choosing first to become a military officer or an actor. But his literary gift prevailed, and his biographical genius left behind a masterpiece which makes its subject better known to us than any other man in history. This subject was a unique fatherly man, a many-sided spirit, an exceptional conversationalist and writer.

Deferred obedience to his father's wishes and practical considerations caused Boswell, in later years, to become a member of the Bar. But he failed dismally as a lawyer. He ended as a heavy drinker in a forlorn condition, "grievously aggravated by hypochondriasis."

7

Johannes Brahms and Women*

> *Indeed, what would become of
> all historical research and of all
> biographies if they were under-
> taken with too many scruples
> about giving offense.*
> —BRAHMS *to Clara Schumann*

IT is evident that the musician commands a language which enables him to express his inner self without revealing it to all the world. There is often a wide range of alternative possibilities in the interpretation of a musical composition. "If you cannot get any meaning out of it, put some meaning into it" (Goethe).

Among the great musicians we find reserved, taciturn personalities, creating in solitude. The musical language they employ is often derived from the traditions of the home, learned early in life; it is used because of some deep spiritual need, seeking to resolve internal conflicts and moods.

When we are told how emotionally stirred Brahms was while composing, how often he wept, how easily tears came to his eyes while he was playing, we become interested in his otherwise well-concealed inner life. We shall not neglect the professionally trained interpreters of his compositions, but we shall not forego other sources which will help us to understand his personality.

This essay does not seek to give musical instruction of any kind; it uses the special means of psychoanalysis to investigate the love life of a great artist, an investigation which has been much neglected by other biographers. It is our aim to examine in Brahms's bachelorhood a typical phenomenon and to make a contribution to the estimation of his personality. He himself

* First published in German in *Psychoanalytische Bewegung,* Vol. 5, 1933, and in English in *American Imago,* Vol. 6, 1949.

said that it was his life's misfortune not to have been married, not to have had children; he recognized this as the source of the grief that gnawed at him and made him appear so harsh and unjust whenever disappointment and envy rose in him. As to the causes, he deluded himself with rationalizations.

We prefer to call the fate of bachelordom and spinsterhood by the name of marriage inhibition, a phrase implying that to remain unmarried signifies an exceptional fate, the causes of which —apart from rare objective hindrances—are unconscious mental inhibitions which lose their effectiveness when brought into consciousness. Our object in taking the bachelorhood of Brahms as an example for the popularization of psychoanalytic knowledge is not to enlighten the inglorious herd of bachelors but to communicate general truths about great men who are by no means infrequently matrimonially inhibited.

We shall avoid the complicated subject of the connection between giving full rein to one's erotic instincts or sublimating them on the one hand, and artistic creativity on the other. We will just quote two artists on this subject. "We burn within," one poet said, speaking for many. It could be called making a virtue of necessity—a completely unconscious process, of course. Nietzsche certainly meant nothing else when in his fragmentary *Psychology of Art* he wrote: "Chastity is merely artistic economy. It is one and the same power that is exercised in artistic conception and in the sexual act. There is but one power."

Brahms came from a poor home and his youth was oppressed by untoward circumstances, but his later life ought to have been called a fortunate one. His musical genius attained early success, in good time he found abundant help from distinguished friends, he enjoyed good health and earned fame and money. Yet he was not "a happy man." He had the appearance of an obstinate person of melancholic temperament, and he called himself "a man apart." Even if he seemed to be otherwise in society, he wrote that he never felt inner cheerfulness. He also said that he was never—or hardly ever—satisfied with himself; that he was never in a quiet, peacefully happy mood but alternately joyous or gloomy. Brahms was often irritable, quarrelsome, harsh and bad-humored; he offended nearly everyone and rejected people who once had attracted him and whom he had invited to use the intimate *Du*.

"I always celebrate festive occasions," Brahms once said, "in a rather lonely way, alone in my room with a few dear ones, very quietly—for these few dear ones are dead or far away. How happy I am when I realize with my whole being how love fills the human breast." This may have been the resignation of advanced years; yet even at the age of thirty, Brahms had written: "I was made for the monastery—but I never found a suitable one."

We must not expect from Brahms many statements about himself, for he was an exceedingly uncommunicative person. Thus, Clara Schumann says in her diary: "We had once more spoken frankly with each other, as far as that is possible with him." And in another place: "I miss as always the exchange of sentiments." In 1880 she said to Kalbeck: "Would you believe it that during all those years of our long and intimate friendship, Johannes never spoke of what moved him. He is still an enigma to me, I would almost say he is as strange to me now as he was twenty-five years ago."

At this point we must put a question to the experts: Is the emotional life of this great musician expressed in his compositions and do we there, too, find this same sad state of mind?

"Only in his music did he say what moved him," said Max Kalbeck. And Richard Specht found Brahms, despite his shy reticence, "in his music and in the poems he chose, eloquent to the point of baring his soul. The poems he set to music all are confessions; his works are the eloquent diary of his existence, blessed in loneliness." Kalbeck once had a chance of listening to Brahms while he worked out a piece for piano: Brahms whined, moaned and cried aloud like a dog. Afterwards Kalbeck saw him furtively wipe his eyes with the back of his hand. He must have wept copiously, for tears still glistened in his beard.

When Julie Schumann, one of Clara's daughters, who was especially dear to him, married, Brahms seemed really distressed.

After the wedding he gave the mother a composition full of grief in words and music (Rhapsody for Alto, Male Chorus and Orchestra, Op. 53). He called it *his* wedding song. Clara wrote about it in her diary: "This piece can only be the manifestation of his own inward sorrow. If only once he would speak thus from the heart in words." Connoisseurs think they hear again and again in Brahms' works grief and unsatisfied longing. "In the stirring melodies of the Rhapsody, The Song of Destiny, the C-Minor Symphony, in the many tender movements of his chamber music, heavy with unwept tears, he seems to free himself, and his wounded heart is throbbing with unfulfilled longing."

Brahms' life was early filled with music. His father was a diligent musician who quickly recognized the uncommon musical talent of his Johannes. He took him to qualified teachers. We must imagine the boy, who showed the desire for knowledge in other fields as well, filled with musical ambition, inspired by his identification with the father but aspiring beyond him, already composing in his youth. The first impression he gave as he emerged into the the world was that of "a nature such as could develop with complete purity only in the utmost seclusion, pure as a diamond, soft as snow" (Joseph Joachim). Clara Schumann described him in her diary as far advanced in his education but very childlike in his emotions. A lady related her impression as follows: "Fair and quiet in his twentieth year, he appeared delicate; but his features, although free of all passion, were already developed. Purity, innocence, naturalness, power and depth—these characterized him . . . And with all this easy strength the thin voice of a boy, a voice not yet broken, and the face of a child which any girl could kiss without blushing." Hans von Buelow called him "a candid nature." In 1853 it was said of him: "The purity and firmness of his personality give the assurance that the corruption of the world could do no harm to this man." Schumann called him "one of the most beautiful and one of the most gifted of youths." Eduard Hanslick called him at twenty-one "an ideal Jean-Paul youth." His portrait as a young man, with the long locks of hair, gives an impression of effeminacy;

the high voice remained. According to Specht, in unguarded or excited moments the boyish treble would break through, and all efforts to force his stubborn voice into an artificial manliness were rather ineffectual.

When at the age of twenty Brahms came to the Schumanns, he had never been in love, not counting an innocent infatuation of school days. There he met the woman whom he later called the "only person" he had "really loved."

In his teachers Cossel and Marxen, Brahms learned to know men of superior craftsmanship in music. Later he met the violinists Remenyi and Joachim, Liszt and others, but his meeting with the artists Robert and Clara Schumann was decisive for his life. Many years later he wrote to Clara: "To you I now repeat that you and your husband are the most beautiful experience of my life, that you signify its greatest enrichment and noblest content." Brahms came to know women through their musical husbands, as happened later with Elisabeth von Herzogenberg, or was led to them by their voices or their singing. He could not resist the fascination of a pretty, musically gifted girl; and a beautiful dark voice, like that of Hermine Spiess, charmed him even when he was beyond the age of fifty.

Brahms saw Schumann for the first time in September 1853. The latter not only frankly admired Brahms's compositions and his piano playing but had a friendly feeling toward him and frequently called attention to the beauty of his outward appearance. Schumann at this time showed the first symptoms of his mental disease, i.e., hallucinations, and lived in the fancy that he was having intercourse with higher beings. He instantly discovered the genius of Brahms, invited him to stay with them for some time, and introduced him to his beloved wife with words of praise. Brahms lived with them as their own son. In a way, he had found new and exalted parents. It was like the realization of a fairy tale. Clara especially, in whom outstanding feminine artistry was so harmoniously combined with excellent motherhood (Kalbeck), must have made a deep impression. A mother, a noble woman, and an artist of the greatest understanding, all in *one* person! Schumann almost created Brahms' social existence, for he wrote at the time these enthusiastic words about the young genius: "At his cradle, graces and heroes kept watch" (*Neue Zeitschrift für Musik*). He warmly recommended him to the editor, thereby rapidly increasing Brahms's fame. Only a few months later Schumann, in an attack of lunacy, tried to commit suicide and was taken to the asylum which he was never to leave again. Young Brahms hurried to Düsseldorf to the very shaken Clara, and helped her in those difficult days. At that time began the unique relationship which bound together the lives of an aspiring young man and a woman, fourteen years his senior, the mother of seven children. It was a relationship that varied in intensity. The faithfulness of the wife and the gratitude of the young man toward Robert Schumann made it a friendship of high sanctity. In Brahms Clara again followed step by step a creative artist who, as she said, in daily, hourly company gave her artistic inspiration of the noblest and highest kind, as if strewing precious pearls in her path.

As a world-famous piano virtuoso, Clara often undertook concert tours, and then Brahms gave her news of her children at home. A correspondence began which continued through life whenever they were not together. In this correspondence one can distinctly observe how the relationship became more and more profound and grew to an extraordinary devotion on the part of the man.

In 1854 they came to call each other by their Christian names and the intimate *Du.* "I love him—as dearly as a son" (diary); and Brahms quoted a letter from the *Arabian Nights,* so as to avoid these ardent words as coming from himself:

> Your letter, O my lady, is come and has brought balsam to a soul tormented with longing and desire, and healing to a torn and diseased heart.
>
> [A year later Brahms writes:] What is it you have done to me; can't you release me from this magic? . . . I have dreamt a great deal of you, beautiful things . . . I kiss the boys always as if from you, but I wish I could give the kisses back to you! . . . I am sorry for every word I write to you

which is not a word of love. You have taught me and teach me daily to acknowledge and venerate more and more love, affection and devotion. . . .

[In 1856:] Am I not a good child, beloved (or beloved friend)? Don't throw away a pretty ribbon from your hat or anything like that, but give it to me. I will put it round your letters or something else that is dear to me. Or I will use it as a bookmark.

I wish I could write as tenderely to you as I love you, and do as much good to you as I wish you. You are so infinitely dear to me, more than I can possibly say. I could call you darling and all sorts of things continually and never become tired of flattering you. If it goes on like this, I shall have to put you into a glass-case or save money and have you mounted in gold.

[In 1876, after the death of her son Felix:] Let this earnest love be a comfort to you—I love you more than myself or anyone or anything else in the world.

Brahms's letters in which he so openly confessed his love are an important document to us, though this correspondence represents but a fragment of the total. In the year 1886 Clara and Johannes agreed to exchange their letters. Brahms returned Clara's without having reread them, and she destroyed those that were written up to the year 1858. Brahms, on a Rhine journey, threw those which he had gotten back into the river. But Clara had been allowed to keep for herself a number of letters especially dear to her. It may be assumed that a tendency to concealment played an essential part in the destruction.

It can be seen clearly that Brahms, in a spiritual sense, acted as a substitute for Clara Schumann's husband. Once again there was a man whose art she could share, interpret, criticize and praise. Thus she wrote to him in 1858: "I am often strongly held by your rich genius, you always appear to me as one upon whom heaven pours its finest gifts, I love and revere you for such magnificence."

Our main interest is to understand Brahms's emotions. Only during a certain time can they be characterized as true erotic love. Indeed, he himself said of his Piano Quartet in C-Minor that the first movement is an illustration of the last chapter of the man with blue tail coat and yellow waistcoat (Goethe's *Werther*). Kalbeck called Brahms's life in the years 1854 to 1856 his Werther period for which he has created a memorial in the Allegro of his Quartet Op. 60.

Biographers also speak of Clara's temptations. One of them thought that they must have been tormented by their close yet unfulfilled relationship; that there must have been an hour when they embraced passionately, forgetful of themselves. This, however, can hardly be proved.[1] In any case, it may be assumed that the memory of Schumann restrained them. For Brahms this love grew into something unique: friendship combined with the renunciation of love. It was the only lasting and great friendship in the artist's life, it influenced his whole being, not only as to his remaining unmarried; it left a deep imprint on his life and his music.

We do not believe that Brahms had sexual relations with Clara. Such a relationship with a woman of refinement was not vouchsafed him throughout his life. The objects of his sexual love were only girls of the lower classes, mostly paid prostitutes. Here a division becomes apparent. On the one hand, an exalted love with tenderness and veneration is given to noble women; on the other hand, sexual satisfaction is sought among degraded objects.

Of course Brahms also loved other women, as for instance the much younger Elisabeth von Herzogenberg. We know about this relationship through their correspondence. Brahms met the musical and beautiful lady in her girlhood. For many years her picture stood on his desk. But he refused her as a pupil. Did he feel defenseless against her spell? It became a typically Brahmsian love, with nothing hidden from her husband, a composer. One day he wrote to her: "You must know and believe this, that you belong to the few people whom one loves so much that—as your husband is always there to read and to hear—one cannot tell you. And he himself belongs to the special few!"

---

[1] Just as in the case of Goethe and Frau von Stein, we cannot be sure. But it is immaterial whether nothing happened or something fleeting and disappointing.

Having discussed the relationship with these two happily married women, we must now turn our attention to the unmarried girls whom Brahms has loved. In 1930 a book was published about Agathe von Siebold with the subtitle: *Johannes Brahms's Early Love*. This love experience did not last long and it ended when Brahms, asked by a mutual friend to declare himself, wrote to the girl: "I love you, I must see you again, but I cannot endure fetters!" This confession of his incapacity to marry, even if he loved a woman, appreciated her as a singer, dedicated songs to her, even if he exchanged rings with her, as he did with Agathe— this confession contains the problem why Brahms remained unmarried despite his longing for wife and children: the fundamental problem of this essay.

Brahms's experience with Agathe took place in Goettingen in 1858 and was the profoundest he ever had with an unmarried woman. All he created at that time was meant for her. Clara Schumann also stayed in Goettingen for a few weeks, and her daughter Eugenie wrote in her *Memoirs* of a very pleasant scene when they played hide and seek in the garden, with Agathe, Clara and Brahms taking part. In Michelmann's book about Agathe, it is said that Brahms spoke protestingly about his dependence on Clara. His Werther period had passed. Frau Schumann suddenly left. She was made jealous by Brahms's overflow of good spirits which had to be attributed to his being happily in love with Agathe.

Brahms once said to her: "I can never marry; I could not bear to see my wife suffer, if I did not accomplish the best in music"— a despondent utterance, analogous to others. Later on we shall deal with their interpretation. For the moment we want to quote Michelmann once more: " A certain fear of the fair sex and of his own weakness seemed never to have left Brahms." According to the statement of a witness, Brahms years later said to a friend: "I behaved like a cad toward Agathe." We can imagine that the girl, having received the letter of refusal, was deeply disappointed. They never saw each other again, and a few years later she married a distinguished physician—"consoled." A fact characteristic of Brahms' compositions may be mentioned. His Sextet in G-Major for Strings was a farewell to Agathe, expressing his sorrow but also his release. It is an objective glorification of her personality rather than a personal lamentation of the loss he had suffered (Kalbeck). The work (Op. 36) is dedicated to Agathe. Her name is not shown on the title page but in the context. The motive does not appear as the leading thought of the first movement; it sounds throughout in the notes A G A (T) H E^2 which are woven into the second theme of this movement. Brahms said about it: "Here I freed myself from my last love." Joachim was let in on the secret of the confused play of feelings which are expressed in it.

The thought of marriage with other girls did occur to Brahms occasionally, though with less intensity. He felt, for instance, attracted to one girl but at once turned away when she began to praise a man whom he abhorred. There is also the reflection of a love affair in the Sextet in B-Major. As Brahms relates it, she married someone else, a rich man.

Brahms is a good example for establishing the fact that bachelors have remained unmarried against their will—hindered by unconscious inhibitions—because he, unlike many others, often confessed openly his desire to marry. Most others deny this desire, they hide behind deceptive rationalizations of their inhibitions. Brahms often enough complained that in being without wife and child he "really missed the best in life."

> There is something horrible in the thought [says a biographer] that a man whose eager heart called so loudly for wife and child and who in bitter grief on lonely nights moaned and bit into his pillow so that no one might hear; that he had never called a beloved woman his very own, never held the chosen one in his arms. . . . That one who as man and artist praised women with the tenderest chivalry and who in song knew, as no other did, how to enshrine love in sound, had to content himself with the dregs of humanity; that is the tragedy of his life.

^{2} In the German musical scale, "H" is the same as the English "B."

As an old man Brahms once said: "How I hate the people who have prevented me from marrying!" A year before his death (Clara had already passed away): "Is it a life at all, so solitary? The only true immortality is in children!" Brahms gave many conscious reasons for his bachelorhood. We must seek to discover the unconscious motivations behind them. He had a whole string of reasons which we will supplement. His statements to Widman (in 1887) were:

> I have missed it. When I would have liked to do it, I could not offer a woman what would have been fair . . . at a time when I would have liked most to be married, my pieces were hissed in the concert halls or at best received with icy coldness. I myself could bear that very well, for I knew exactly their worth and how the tables would turn. And if after such failures I came home to my lonely room, I was not too despondent. On the contrary! But if in such moments I had had to face my wife, to see her questioning eyes anxiously fixed upon mine, and had to say to her: "Another failure"— I could not have borne that! For a woman may love the artist whom she has as a husband very much and may, as they say, believe in him, but a certainty of ultimate victory such as is rooted in him she cannot have. . . . And moreover, if she had wanted to console me . . . Compassion of a wife for a husband in his failure . . . ugh! I couldn't think of it, what a hell it would have been, at least as I imagine it.

Here Brahms by no means showed artistic despondency but lack of belief that a woman could love him profoundly or be willing to make sacrifices, and a lack of confidence of his own personality, his manly power of love, which as everybody knows can make a woman faithful, devoted, even a bondslave. He was afraid of a wife, of the matrimonial state. We remember the words: *A certain fear of the fair sex and of his own weakness.*

Marriage meant for Brahms a great deed, something beyond his powers. He put matrimony on a level with the composition of an opera. He wrote to Widman: "Have I ever spoken to you of my fine principles? Among them are not to attempt either an opera or marriage . . . so you can imagine how much money I saved and will have left for my trip to Italy—if I do not marry

before the summer, nor buy a libretto for an opera." Here joking
and seriousness are mingled, but it is hinted that a wife costs
much, there would be nothing left for a trip; the idea that the
wife is expensive and harmful. As if a wife could not be well-off
too, or an agreeable companion for a trip to Italy. Here we have
a deep feeling of inferiority of his manly powers. The unconscious roots are not at first visible. But due to this inferiority, a
strong tie to a female appears alarming, and therefore all kinds
of rationalizations are sought. That Brahms's imagination en-
visaged public disgrace and debasement in front of his wife as a
possibility in marriage proves his pessimistic fantasies and recalls
the similar attitudes of other bachelors who imagine that they
could not be successful with a lady. "In my weakness I am suited
for a simple girl," he may have said when occasionally brooding
over it, "but I cannot expose myself before a noble woman and
stand before her in my failure."

A man who is sexually diffident shrinks from a lady, while he
does not fear a prostitute's criticism of his peculiarities and weaknesses. The exposure of his failure as a musician stands for the
exposure of his failure as a man and is therefore a real obstacle
to marriage. Thus Brahms renounced the greatest and most difficult thing in both love and music, marriage and the composing
of an opera.

Once it is accepted that Brahms wove into his compositions
his feelings, his longings, his gratitude and his memories, that he
set to music his daydreams and that he found expression in the
veiled language of sounds when moved by inner emotions—then
his desire for a life apart and for lonely hours and walks will be
understood.

When the works of an artist or poet, narcissistically highly
estimated by himself, are also appreciated by others, his need for
or his right to isolation makes it, it may be said, a duty to himself.

Herman Levi expressed this about Brahms in enthusiastic
words:

Ordinarily the children of the earth bear the stamp of their time and of its faults upon their foreheads; he alone is able to separate himself from all human relationships and to remain untouched by the squalor and misery of life; to rise to ideal heights, where we can only gaze after him, not follow him. He looks upon us from a royal throne. When we think we are near, he calls to us: "Thou art like the spirit thou canst comprehend, not me" (Goethe, *Faust*, Part I). We are momentarily rejected, hurt, crushed, but again we are drawn toward him by magnetic force.

Some of Brahms's bluntness and wounding harshness is explained by this and, to a small extent, even his bachelordom.

His bluntness [Eugenie Schumann said] hurt his own heart. It constantly kept him in a state of defense against some imagined interference with his way of living and with his independence. If a certain opinion or judgment was assumed of him, he used to assert the contrary. He liked to give, but he thrust back demands or expectations . . . Like all lonely men, Brahms formed his views quietly and without being influenced to any degree from outside; he disliked arguments and tried to avoid them as much as possible.

We excuse as the narcissism of the artist a characteristic of Brahms which has been described rather angrily by his friend Joachim (1854):

Brahms is the most inveterate egoist one can imagine; but he himself is not conscious of it. Everything springs carelessly, impulsively from his sanguine nature, with a want of consideration that is sometimes painful because it betrays a lack of upbringing. Never in his life did he take the trouble to think what others, according to their nature and their development, are bound to esteem highly. What does not suit his enthusiasm, his experience or even his mood is rejected coldly and without sympathy . . . He has a true genius for warding off all unhealthy sensations and imaginary ills of others.

Being of humble origin, Brahms obstinately held to the natural and primitive which others who are more easily influenced and more vain discard as they ascend the social ladder. As he rose from dance-hall player to serious musician and famous composer, he remained simple in his manner of dressing and his way of life. He hated it when he was forced to dress, especially in stiff collar and shirt front. "He was especially bothered by his trousers. He braced them up so high that they did not reach his ankles. It did not help much to ask the tailor to make them longer. Brahms would only draw them up to his shoulders and cut off a piece with his scissors" (Kalbeck). He liked to go to simple inns, had no wants, and lived in moderation. He was easily moved. He remained loyal to his faith and Bible, as his mother had been. "In the Holy Scriptures he finds those words which give him confidence and assurance and which in his mighty, most inspired music have risen to immortal glory" (Specht). Not to be able to lose oneself, this too is narcissism. And here too, his matrimonial inhibitions are rooted.

For many reasons his sexual life remained primitive and restricted mainly to women of the streets—as was well known in Vienna. "He carried the desire of his body, overflowing with strength, into dark alleys or to some nice and obliging 'parlour maid,' like the one whose name he later found scribbled on one of his scores, as a reminder . . ." (Specht).

In this respect, Vienna seems to have appeared to Brahms particularly suitable. He refused a position in Düsseldorf for the reason that in a small town a bachelor is a caricature. "In Vienna one can easily remain a bachelor . . . I no longer want to marry, and yet I have some reasons to be afraid of the fair sex"(1877).

When scarcely thirteen years old, the boy Brahms played in sailors' inns in the evening. Too early he came to know the active, frivolous, purchasable sexuality of the prostitute. He once told of scenes he had witnessed: of the sailors who rushed into the inn after a long voyage, greedy for drinks, gambling and love of women, who, half-naked sang their obscene songs to his accompaniment, then took him on their laps and enjoyed awaking his first sexual feelings. Such impressions, such seductions must be considered momentous in their consequences. Here perhaps we have to deal with an early initiation into the dark secrets of life which at first alarmed and repelled the lad, but forever drew the man back into its net. His sexual life certainly showed a division which could not be bridged or indeed revealed: an embarrassing secret, concealed at least from the ladies of his heart. Sexuality in such cases is reduced to the role of a humble physical function, the tender adoring love for women being kept separate from it, "immaculate." It is clear that this reverential love was in the first place given to his mother. She could indeed not have appeared very attractive to the boy, as she limped from a foot disease and had grown old—she was seventeen years older than her husband—but the treasures of her soul, her goodness and piety, influenced him long afterwards.

Brahms became more and more an old bachelor, whimsical and pedantic, helpless in practical matters. To tie a cravat, or to make up a parcel and post it, was a catastrophe for him. Nor was he skilled as a conductor. He lacked manual dexterity. His powerful and handsome head was set upon a stockily built body. Eugenie Schumann wrote how skillfully and even perilously he once did gymnastics and jumped before the children in Düsseldorf. But later he became stout and clumsy. When asked why he had no wife, he would answer evasively, with a jest. To a pert young lady who had asked him why "Herr Doktor" had not married, he replied with ready wit: "No one has wanted me as yet; and if there were one who did, I would not want her because of her bad taste." In his eighties, he expressed his ambivalent attitude characteristically in the phrase of a humorist: "Unfortunately I never married and am, thank God, still single."

We know the awkward and unpsychological attempts that are made to persuade bachelors to get married. To Brahms too this happened pretty often. We are told of Brahms, going with some ladies for a walk in the country. When they entered an inn, he flirted with the waitress. She was just such a healthy, pretty and fresh creature as always excited in him a happy feeling of living. Someone exclaimed that he ought to get married. Someone else added that he knew two girls who would be quite willing to marry him. The man of sixty-three answered: "I cannot marry

any more, I assure you. I should be forced to despise any girl who
would choose me for her husband. You certainly won't make me
believe that anyone could fall in love with me—as I am now?" By
that time, of course, it was too late. But the enigma why he resisted between the ages of twenty-five and forty-five is our problem.

The psychoanalysis of famous dead men is careful not to overlook anything that might be known about their early childhood.
Sometimes a characteristic moment, a saying of later years, can reveal much. Such a saying of Brahms, when death had just taken
his mother from him, may be quoted here. Florence May writes
in her biography that Brahms, while under the influence of his
mother's death, declared after the burial: "Now that I no longer
have a mother, I must get married." This was reported by eye
witnesses. Kalbeck tells the same story, but, according to him,
Brahms spoke these words at his mother's deathbed. This utterance implies that the loss of his mother brought to life the son's
desire for a wife, or in other words, his attachment to his mother
till then had prevented marriage or at least had made it super-
fluous. This would be a confirmation of the fact often disclosed by
psychoanalysis that a strong mental fixation on a mother may influence and inhibit a son's love life. It may also be a confirmation
of the common experience that men thus inhibited get the desire
to marry after their mother's death. Only by assuming an unusually intense and lasting filial love can we comprehend that
Brahms fell in love with Clara Schumann, a sevenfold mother
who was fourteen years his senior and the happily married wife
of the admired friend to whom he owed his decisive advance
ment. He comforted her and was full of sympathy when Schu
mann went to the asylum. But later Brahms's love became more
passionate, as we see from those letters which have escaped de
struction. It can also be found in the music from that period
which he poured forth with passionate force in an uninterrupted
flow. Later on there seems to have been some crisis, perhaps due
to some disappointment—for one can hardly speak of a passionate
love on the part of Clara—and there began that ideal relation

hip, full of sympathy for one another, mutual stimulation and
rankness of speech, that "amitié amoureuse" of two spirits and
minds of high ethical standards. Eugenie Schumann says Brahms
must have hurt Clara so that she did not quite understand that
change: "Brahms recognized that a task awaited him which required all his personality and which was incompatible with his
devoting himself exclusively to a friendship." They were not always untroubled. When Brahms was harsh and Eugenie had to
comfort her mother, Clara would say: "You don't know how he
used to be; so tender and loving, an ideal man." Thus the daugh-
er (who may not have known everything) described the last time
hey were together in October 1895: Clara played for Brahms
ome Bach and some of his own works. Then she sat there with
lightly reddened cheeks, her eyes shining as if from an inner
ight. Brahms sat opposite her with a look that was gentle and
moved. "Your mother played quite magnificently," he said. The
riends embraced and kissed as they had done for years at every
parting and meeting. Soon afterwards Clara fell ill and died dur-
ng the following May. At first, when bad news came about her
state of health, Brahms wrote to their mutual friend Joachim:
"And when she has gone from us, will not our face glow with joy
whenever we think of her? The lovely woman in whom we have
delighted, throughout a long life, loving and admiring her ever
more and more."

Natures such as Brahms's are capable of very mixed feelings,
omething between love and friendship. They bring to their re-
ations with women that love for their mothers which they have
not overcome; and a love is born which usually excludes sexuality. But friendship then is more tender, more compassionate,
grateful, and more reverential, and it uses the name of love.

"I think I esteem and revere her really no more than I love
her," Brahms once wrote of this relationship, "I believe I can
never love a girl again, at any rate, I have quite forgotten girls.
They only promise the heaven which Clara has opened for us."
Such men love women in preference to girls, and older women
rather than younger ones. They want their guidance and advice,

they love their children too and like to help them in need
Brahms several times in a most tactful way offered Clara a large
sum of money. He always took a kindly interest in her children
Her daughter Julie he seems to have loved, though it only be
came evident when someone else had chosen her. It is thus tha
his lifelong loyalty, his never getting free, are explained as they
occur in relation to Clara and also to her rival "in pocket edi
tion," Elisabeth von Herzogenberg. To such men who have no
overcome the oedipus complex, the beloved woman only substi
tutes for the mother (sister), and the relationship has neuroti
features, changing moods, attempts to escape, and so on. In thi
category may be placed the paradoxical gruffness of Brahm
toward Clara. Resignation and unfulfilled desire, longing and
dissatisfaction, all the favorite daydreams—these bring disturb
ing libidinal agitations into every activity. The artistic creatior
of a genius will be quite under their influence. That explain
Brahms's passionate emotion while composing, the weaving in
of his love, the dedications. The composer escapes into his crea
tion and liberates himself in it. Inner processes are given form
and pattern. We have already spoken of the Piano Quartet in C
Minor as an illustration to the last chapter of *Werther's Leiden*

In a letter to Clara, Brahms said: "I am also painting a por
trait of you; it will be an adagio." In his Schumann Variations h
not only revealed in a middle melody a loving homage to his dea
friend but by interpolating one of Clara's own themes, he se
cretly did homage to her and let a tender message be heard. Th
Sextet in B-Major is the reflection of that story about a girl wh
later married a rich man. For Frau von Herzogenberg he con
fessed his unhappy love in the Piano Rhapsodies which he dedi
cated to her. Kalbeck and Specht again and again know how to
interpret Brahms's works in this way, often enough by followin
the composer's own indications. The *Deutsches Requiem* is com
posed for two persons he loved: Robert Schumann and his own
mother. The tenderness of friendship also finds musical expres
sion. Thus he wrote on the score of his Serenade when he sent i
to Joachim: "Continue your affection for the piece, deares

riend, it belongs to you and sounds for you. For what is the reason of music sounding so friendly if it is not because of the few
one loves like you." Of course, this weaving of stormy emotions
into his compositions is chiefly done unconsciously. Brahms
pointed this out after he had composed the *Vier ernste Gesänge*
(*Four Serious Songs*) without knowing of Clara's imminent danger of death: "Deeply within men something often speaks or
urges, almost unconsciously, and this now and then will reveal itself as a poem or as music."

Brahms's works constitute a diary of the otherwise so reserved
man. His true life was spent apart from the things of the external
world. His work was more important to him than human relationships. It was his consolation, the spiritualization of his wishes,
a sublimation. "I am in love with music, I love music. I think of
nothing but music—or only if it is something that makes music
more beautiful. You will see, I will write love songs again, and
not to A–Z, but to music itself." From early childhood, music
was the center of his being, his ambition. A serious desire to
learn made him read and make excerpts and to buy books. This
was part of his ego ideal, like honesty, frankness, modesty, de-
mocracy, simplicity of living. And it was part of this ego ideal that
sexuality was something low, something that must remain concealed.

Niemann takes the easy way out when he sees in Brahms's
bacherlordom a kind of voluntary renunciation caused by the
fact that he had to wait so long for artistic appreciation. He im-
prudently followed Brahms's own explanations. They do not
seem satisfactory to us. Fortified by our experience, we claim the
right, in spite of Brahms's statement to Widman, to seek for
deeper motives for his unconscious marriage inhibition. We are
guided by the psychological data which are derived from the
analyses of others who remained unmarried.

Statistically speaking, in our civilization marriage is the his-
torically approved, natural solution of life, a tradition forced
upon us by the example of our parents' married life and that of
the surrounding world. It is the foundation on which men de-

velop their careers, free from the disturbance of seeking transient love objects. For the man the founding of a new family, a new center, arises out of his liking for women's motherliness and out of his identification of himself with the father. Matrimony is the consequence of severing oneself from the parents' family. Apart from the social aspect it is the hygienic solution of the sexual problem. Matrimony therefore is the natural solution of life and the union of the sexes. If an individual remains unmarried and without progeny, it is a serious break with the traditions of past generations.

Indeed, when we analyze persons who have not married, we find psychosexual abnormalities or unconscious inhibitions. The wish for an explanation leads them to find secondary, fictitious reasons which, however, often contain a grain of truth, some contributing reality factor. If anyone asserts that he could not marry because appreciation and money have come too late, it may be said that many men marry before being appreciated or becoming well-to-do. The question remains: what are the mental reasons which cause some to renounce marriage and others not?

It is known that creative men, particularly philosophers, very often are not married at all or are unhappy in marriage. Poets and artists belong in the same category. Psychoanalytic works have produced some explanations.[3] Men who contribute to the happiness of mankind are often very unhappy themselves. So, as we know, was Brahms. Now we have to prove that inhibitions of his love life were the main reason for this.

One source of this inhibition, as we have pointed out, was his fixation on the mother. We will now turn to a second similar inhibition. We shall start with the sentence we find in the book about Agathe von Siebold which implies much: *A certain fear of the fair sex and of his own weakness seems never to have left Brahms.* We know of such an inferiority complex which is expressed in the sexual life and causes its victims to doubt their own masculinity; makes them shy and despondent with the female sex; makes them imagine themselves to be unable to satisfy the

[3] Cf. Freud (1910–12), Hitschmann (1919).

"higher" female being, more particularly in the lasting union of matrimony. We call this the castration complex. By this we mean in a literal sense the fixation of fear of being physically incomplete. It is engendered in childhood by impressions, self-accusation, etc. Let us recall the "artistic appreciation, too long denied," which is said to have prevented him from marrying; his fear of a wife, if he should bring her news of a failure; his renouncing both opera and matrimony. The joking remark that he could not marry a girl who would favor him because this would prove her bad taste, reminds us of his diffidence and of his distrust of his own appearance. He did not take much trouble with his exterior, but he wore long hair and a full beard, signs of masculinity, counterbalancing his high voice. His figure was short.

Many a gloomy mood might be traced back to doubts about his own talents. On the other hand, there are quite a few signs of great self-reliance in this respect. Brahms was remarkably intolerant of his contemporaries Liszt, Wagner and Bruckner. Especially toward Liszt he was inflexible, almost maliciously aggressive and incredibly irritable. His judgments, even of the works of his friends, were caustic, jokingly evasive. He treated Wagner skeptically and Bruckner with hostile misunderstanding. If one thinks of his harshness toward his friends, one must say that Brahms could not control his aggressive impulse. He does not appear well balanced and harmonious in this respect, either. "Brahms was sick in a secret corner of his soul, and out of his own restlessness he was bound to hurt others" (Specht). Dissatisfaction and discontent made him sometimes hurt and repel everyone. Brahms, being shy and sensitive, preferred the company of children and animals and liked to make children happy with little presents. Apart from traveling, he had no wants for himself. He had some property, and to Clara as well as to others he offered rather large gifts of money. His will, by which he wanted to leave his property to the *Gesellschaft der Musikfreunde,* was incomplete and unsigned. His attitude toward money does not appear to have been quite unprejudiced. He never accepted money, not even a free ticket. He was fanatically frank, never wishing to seem something that he was not.

His few faults, Eugenie Schumann said, lay on the surface. He displayed them with indifference, leaving the world to lift the thin veil and to discover the heart of pure gold beneath. He made no show in order to capture a woman. He aspired to other glories. In his music his strict honesty, his ingeniousness and his self-control are apparent.

In an essay "Das Ethos bei Brahms," Robert Lach wrote:

> He began as a romanticist and the romanticists gladly claimed him as their own; but very early he became conscious of the dangers of romanticism: the uncontrolled dissipation into excessive emotion and visionary dreamy ecstasy—and with that relentless, strict honesty and sincerity which are present in all phases of his life and work, in his simplicity, truthfulness and frankness that sometimes bordered on brusqueness, he turned to the greater constraint of the Viennese classicists. His self-discipline became sharper and more severe, ever stricter; harsher and more unbending his demand to control his own ego. He turned to the art of Johann Sebastian Bach and to the great masters of counterpoint of the Netherlands, to the polyphony of the sixteenth century. The always existing propensity for simplicity, truthfulness and artless honesty is heightened to an almost ascetic temperance in the use of artistic means of expression. The thought, the experience, and nothing but the thought and the experience—expressed with only the necessary minimum of means—these are the sole purpose of his work, and everything else, every external ornamentation, sensuousness of sound, lustre of shading, has to give way to this purpose. [Lach further speaks of the] inflexible hardness and harshness of the resulting harmonies, the clashing, gnashing counterpoints with their obstinate, defiant syncopes, of the crashing might of the basses, the crafty and thorny rhythms, the relentless logic of the thematic elaboration.

We shall now recapitulate the development of Brahms's life. His most honest, cheerful and ambitious father had a decisive influence upon him. He must have been more than just an average musician, he must have striven for higher goals, showed some passion. Otherwise the son could not have risen above everyday life either. The elder Brahms "out of pure love for music twice ran away from his parents' home." He offered his son a higher musical training. Thus music became the very core of the son's life, the main substance of his aspirations. It filled his days with study, but it also provided him with a private and personal medium to express his emotions. It gave him the narcissistic satisfaction of creation and soon brought him the approval of the world around him.

Father and mother were his models in moral matters. They certainly were the godparents of his strict superego; what was moral was self-evident for him. Music, sincerity and ambition were to be the mainstays of his life. There was little room left for love of women. In sailors' inns he had had many brutal and disillusioning experiences. But he reserved himself for higher aims. His father can scarcely have been an erotic man with a thirst for mere beauty, or he would not have married a limping woman seventeen years older than he. Moreover, the atmosphere of their life was full of cares and darkened by poverty. "Not many," Brahms said later about his youth, "can have had as hard a time as I."

We do not know whether the boy was at first reluctant to study music and was forced to do so. It is more likely that he always enjoyed his father's playing of the bass violin, that it was an object of admiration, and that music was part of the identification with the father, part of the wish to become a man.

His mother, who was absorbed in housekeeping, had nothing to do with all that. She transmitted to her son her tender, kind and pious nature. The son showed throughout his life a particular kindness toward animals and children. Tenderness toward these two kinds of beings is less dangerous than toward men, and timid persons prefer their company to men's. Brahms's mother was primarily a mother and a housewife. She lived for her children, was delicate, more frail than her busily occupied husband. Being perhaps her favorite, Brahms absorbed the image of a mother always nourishing, helping and guiding. This conception was later to be enriched by his meeting with the woman who in music played the part of a mother, nourishing, helping and guiding. She was to remain forever his Egeria.

Any revolt against the parents, any criticism of them, which might have existed, was harmoniously overcome. All his life Brahms remained a devoted and self-sacrificing child.

His life was filled with musical creation, with the knowledge of his ability, his sense of vocation: the erecting of architectonic forms out of well-sounding melodies. "When a nice melody comes to my mind, I prefer it to the Leopold-Medal, and if it should make the writing of a symphony possible, I would prefer it even to being given the keys to the city."

To reach these aims, he clearly learned to esteem solitude, to listen quietly to his own spirit. Company was disturbing and so even marriage was a danger. It was better to think of persons dear to him. Their figures and his feelings for them were part of his daydreams which became music. He could work best on lonely walks. Composing at the piano often became an orgy of violent emotions, narcissistically enjoyed.

Coming from a poor home, Brahms never had learned the manners of society and had seen nothing of elegant dress. He remained diffident and timid. Always cleanly, far from being a dandy, he used to look like someone "who washes with laundry soap at a well" (Specht). Even as a young man he did not make a harmonious impression. Rubinstein gave the following picture of him: "He is not clever enough for the drawing room, not passionate enough for the concert hall, not primitive enough for the country, and not refined enough for the city."

Brahms showed a peculiar diffidence toward women. He never paid court, nor was he a breaker of hearts. He was attracted to several girls but never could make up his mind and never failed to find weighty counter-arguments. Besides, only singers would merit serious consideration. The courage to marry was lacking, just as was his self-confidence to compose an opera. But he longed for wife and children and often expressed his disappointment of his bachelorhood, either sadly or under the guise of sarcasm. His tender love of women remained unsatisfied. Constant longing and resignation were his fate. Connoisseurs sometimes hear in his music the restraint necessary to achieve peace and harmony.

His profound sense of inferiority remained unconscious. Brahms considered as reasons a slow career and perhaps also the fact that he was of small stature and shortsighted. As sexual objects he chose only simple girls of humble origin who could be paid for their love services.

One woman accompanied him throughout his life, from the moment he first met her at the age of twenty. This was Clara Schumann, the great artist, daughter of that severe teacher Wieck, widow of Robert Schumann with whom she had spent many years of untroubled marital happiness. Brahms first admired her as the wife of his patron, of the furtherer of his career, and as the best connoisseur and counselor in music, and he fell in love with the kind woman who treated him like a son blessed with divine talent. Close to her when Schumann died, first mentally and some time later physically, giving her advice, help, comfort and his company—he reached a state of mind in which he could not hide his real love, as revealed in the letters of that time. It was his Werther period and was crowned by his most fruitful work. The virtuoso, fourteen years his senior, caring for seven children, forced to earn her own living, wandering through many countries, acquired worldwide fame. She did not belong to him, except as a loyal friend, understanding him through his art. This friendship filled his life. Clara was the interpreter of his works. He valued her judgment highly and shared with her all the happy and all the sad events (which, alas, were far more numerous) connected with her children. They kissed each other when meeting or parting, and again and again they spoke of their mutual fidelity in spite of the occasional conflicts. "She is the only person whom I have ever loved," he could say of Clara. It was a peculiar state of being bound to a "mother," a spiritually loved woman, a sister in art. He came through his Werther period without taking his own life.

Brahms was not a happy man, and we believe we now know the reason. He was inhibited in his love life and could find no satisfaction in a noble woman's heart. In spite of all longing he remained unmarried and really went through life with love for a woman unfulfilled. Although he liked pleasant and easygoing sociability and enjoyed to spend his evenings smoking and drinking with other men, he was destined to inner isolation. We are not surprised to hear longing and woe sound through his music. He seems to have reveled in grief; he may even have welcomed suffering as an incentive for creativeness which then, in turn, became a substitute for love. The *Song of Destiny* and the Alto Rhapsody speak of fate, of being driven and of never being understood. He always was easily moved. We can better grasp his moods, his harshness, his aggressive mocking and teasing, now that we know how incomplete his life had to be so that his creative work might be whole.

Stilled yearning, satisfied desire, fulfilled wishes, rarely are fortunate gifts for the artist. In his work the forever unattainable lives and resounds and the cruel fate he denounces really means well by him when it withholds that which it so readily bestows on lesser mortals [Kalbeck].

[Walter Muschg said of artists:] There are living beings in nature who react to some imperfection, some painful interference with their organism by producing pearls . . . In the human world similar enigmatic beings exist who respond to a tragic disturbance in their life by creating beauty.

8

Swedenborg's Paranoia*

WHEN an excellent scholar and practical worker in the field of natural science in the fifth decade of his life suddenly one day feels called upon by the Lord to interpret to mankind the inner meanings of the Bible; when he renounces science, resigns his offices and devotes himself solely to these supernatural phenomena and instructions; when he records these revelations with stupendous productivity in a hundred volumes—then we are justified to assume, as an explanation, that he suffered from religious paranoia.

A complete psychoanalytic investigation of Swedenborg has hitherto not been undertaken, probably chiefly because of the enormous extent of his work. It should be noted that even the short data taken from a book by Eugen Sierke, who is not especially interested in psychiatry, form an instructive pathological picture which later can be augmented by additional data.

In the following I shall quote—almost verbatim—some passages which are significant for a psychoanalyst.

Swedenborg (1688–1772) was the son of a Protestant bishop who enjoyed unlimited respect as an able theologian and an honorable, though somewhat irascible man. It is said that the bishop entertained mystical ideas and had planted in the boy the seeds for later mystico-theosophical speculations. This assumption may be correct. Swedenborg himself told a friend that between the ages of four and ten he was constantly occupied with ideas about God, the spiritual condition and redemption of mankind. He said: "I often revealed thoughts which filled my parents with amazement. They said that angels spoke through me." And fur-

* First published in German in *Zentralblatt für Psychoanalyse,* Vol. 3, 1913, and in English in *American Imago,* Vol. 6, 1949.

ther: "From my sixth to my twelfth year, my greatest pleasure was to converse with clergymen about faith . . ."

It seems strange that the boy did not continue in this direction but turned to the opposite extreme, from theology to the exact sciences: mathematics, physics, astronomy and geology. In addition, he pursued classical philology. He finished his studies of natural science and physics at the university in 1709 but continued them during four years of travel. At the age of twenty-six he was considered a polyhistor. As an unusually gifted mining assessor he published a natural history repertorium in 1716 (*Daedalus Hyperboreus*). Besides German he had mastered French, English, Italian and Greek, and wrote poetry in Latin. In 1721–22 he published several scientific works. In 1718 he had become famous with the construction of a mechanism which made it possible to transport two galleys and five big boats for two and a half miles up and down mountains for the purpose of a siege. His *Opera Philosophica et Mineralia* (1733) brought him a membership in the St. Petersburg Academy of Sciences, and the Paris Academy included the work in its encyclopedia. It was the most comprehensive and thorough study about the metallurgy of copper and iron and contained a complete theory of the cosmos based on mathematical laws.

At the age of forty-six Swedenborg was at the zenith of his scientific research and endeavor. But a year earlier (1733) the imminent change in his development was foreshadowed in his book *Prodromus Philosophiae Ratiocinantis de Infinite etc.* It clearly disclosed a return to the old mystical ideas of his youth, ideas which until that time had been resting in the depth of his soul. Swedenborg turned to the realm of theosophic speculation and henceforth attempted to build a new religious theory. He himself told a friend in great detail how this idea came to him.

He was staying in London and had just sat down to a meal in his usual restaurant where he had reserved a private room. It was late in the evening, and he ate with voracious appetite. During the meal a kind of mist spread over his eyes. A lot of horrible crawling reptiles appeared on the floor, snakes, toads, salamanders, and such. In one corner he quite clearly saw a man sitting, surrounded by brilliant light, and the man spoke to him in an awesome voice the words: "Do not eat so much." The apparition disappeared, and Swedenborg, horrified, hurried to his lodgings. The following night the spectre came once more. This time the man spoke these words: "I am the Lord God, Creator and Redeemer. I have chosen you to interpret to mankind the inner, the spiritual meaning of the Holy Writ. I shall dictate what you are to write." The man was dressed in purple, the light that vividly flowed around him was no longer so frightening and painful.

"In that night," Swedenborg said, "my inner eyes were opened and I was enabled to look upon heaven, upon the realm of the spirits and upon Hell. Everywhere I found persons of my acquaintance who had died, some many years ago, some only recently. From that day forward, I renounced all secular occupation and resolved to work only for spiritual goals and to obey the orders I had received. From then on it happened frequently that my spiritual eyes were opened and that I saw, as in broad daylight, what went on in the next world, and I spoke with angels and spirits as with men."

Swedenborg's behavior, his everyday talk and actions remained entirely normal and natural. Only one feature was conspicuous: He asserted that he was able to see spirits and reported with great solemnity his visions of the supernatural world. He resigned all his offices and devoted himself wholly to the mission given him by God Himself, to proclaim to Christianity the hidden truths of the Gospels. His productivity in the religio-philosophical field was prodigious, his capacity for work amazing. Besides the thirteen large printed quarto volumes which comprise his theosophical work, he left a hundred handwritten folios full of gloomy fantasies and mystic visions.

Henceforth his thoughts were concerned only with the next world and with ways to reform the Christian religion, which he considered in a state of utter degeneracy. Nevertheless, he knew how to live as a man of the world, had an adequate income from a private fortune, and was very comfortable in his small, cosy summer cottage. He built a kind of temple at one end of the garden where he could devote himself to his intercourse with the supernatural regions. An angel dictated to him, he said. He was hardly ever ill, except when his "temptations" assailed him. At such times he would stay in bed for days and not see anybody. Once he complained about a bad toothache which he believed to be due to influences of hell and seductive dissemblers who inflicted such suffering upon him by casting a spell from afar. He held loud monologues during the night, referring to evil spirits who had visited him and were permitted to revile him.

He was suspicious of the female sex—though he otherwise liked women. He would receive female visitors only in the presence of the gardener's wife, who was also his housekeeper. "Women are cunning," he said, "they may pretend that I seek a closer relationship with them; and besides, it is well known that such people twist and distort everything they hear and don't understand." After an unhappy experience in his youth, he remained a bachelor. He had been engaged, but his fiancée deceived him so scandalously that he had to break with her.

Swedenborg owed his European reputation not so much to his theological mystical works as to the marvelous accounts he gave of his gift for clairvoyance. He enjoyed vigorous health and was mentally alert and active even in his old age. His habits were simple, he lived mostly on milk, coffee and such, avoiding meat and wine.

In 1771 Swedenborg suffered a stroke; his right side was paralyzed. He lost the ability for "inner visions" and his intercourse with the world of the spirits suddenly ceased. Shortly before his death he regained these powers and again conversed loudly with spirits.

Swedenborg's heaven "consists of three heavens," each different from the others. Each heaven has its own societies. The biggest is inhabited by myriads of angels, the smaller one by some thousands, the smallest only by some hundreds. Some live solitary lives, some in family groups. "I have seen many thousand times with my own eyes that all angels have human shapes and are hu-

man beings. They are by no means bodyless spirits, made of air."
In its landscapes and external forms of life, heaven resembles
earth; banquets, theatrical and musical performances take place.
Only the purely innocent go naked. The damned remain in hell.
The essence of all his mystic and abstruse fantasies can be found
in *Heaven and Its Wonders and Hell: From Things Heard and
Seen.*

Passages which prove that Swedenborg's writings emanate
from a sick mind can also be found in *The Delights of Wisdom
Pertaining to Conjugal Love; to which is Added the Pleasures of
Insanity Pertaining to Scortatory Love.* His heaven, patterned so
closely after the earth, glorifies, above all, human matrimony as
celestial, eternal. In the second part, however, wanton love is
described in such blunt and outspoken manner that one might
assume the real purpose was to excite the senses rather than to in-
timidate.

When asked why he and nobody else had such revelations and
intercourse with spirits, Swedenborg answered that everyone
could experience these, just as in the days of the Old Testament.
There was only one true obstacle: people had become too sensual.

We shall attempt a modest interpretation of these psychic
changes in Swedenborg. We do not pretend to a definitive explanation. In the light of the many missing details, that would be
impossible.

The external cause for the change in Swedenborg is obscure.
The age at which it occurred is not without significance. It may
correspond to a premature climacterium.[1] It began with hallucinations. We obviously have to deal with a regression to
childhood, the love for his father and the father's religio-mystical
influence. "Do not eat so much," points directly to fatherly
admonition. Father and God-Father merge. What the parents
once wished and uttered—"angels are speaking through me"—becomes fact. The horrible snakes, etc., of the first hallucination

---

1 Schreber's paranoia, which Freud was able to interpret completely from the
detailed account given by the patient himself, started at the age of fifty-one.

denote homosexual fantasies. The ascetic factor implied in the admonition not to eat too much, his actually frugal diet, his conviction that sensuality was the obstacle that kept most men from having revelations—all that points to a struggle with sexual temptations. The abundance of these sexual fantasies is shown in the pleasurable descriptions of erotic love and in the depiction of matrimonial love—a state he did not achieve despite his intention, proven by the fact that he once was engaged. The attacks of hallucinations probably correspond to homosexual gratifications.

Swedenborg's insanity appears to be a fulfillment of infantile narcissistic megalomania: to become a son who surpasses his father, a kind of son of God, a redeemer and reformer of Christendom. What an exalted feeling, "to be the sole object of divine miracles." His claim to have clairvoyant powers is part of this. His heavenly bliss has to be understood as an intensification and extension of earthly sensual pleasures.

The disappointment at the deception of his fiancée, which had happened many years earlier, was probably caused by Swedenborg's erotic peculiarities. This disappointment certainly influenced his attitude toward women and estranged him further from heterosexuality. His renunciation of all scientific activity which he had pursued so intensively and so successfully, and the rejection of the ensuing relationships signify a detachment of the sublimated libido. We may assume some kind of disappointment in this field. The significance of the persecution by devils and evil spirits can only be conjectured because important data are missing.

In closing we may quote Freud's important words (1911) which also illuminate this case:

> . . . in paranoia the liberated libido becomes fixed on to the ego, and is used for the aggrandizement of the ego. A return is thus made to the state of narcissism (familiar to us in the development of the libido), in which a person's only sexual object is his own ego. On the basis of this clinical

evidence we can suppose that paranoiacs are endowed with a *fixation at the stage of narcissism,* and we can assert that the amount of *regression* characteristic of paranoia is indicated by the length of *the step back from sublimated homosexuality to narcissism.*

9

New Varieties of Religious Experience[*]

> *Intellectus humanus luminis sicci non est: sed recipit infusionem e voluntate et affectibus: id quot generat ad quod vult scientias: quod enim mavult homo, id potius credit. Innumeris modis, iisque interdum inperceptibilibus, affectus intellectum imbuit et inficit.*
>
> —BACON

IF we were to draw a map of the world in which the area covered by religious people would be white and that of the unbelievers, skeptics and atheists black, we should get a white map of all the continents and only in some capitals should we find some tiny black spots.

About a hundred years ago in the United States of America, "God's own country," a man was born who was deeply interested in the different forms religion assumes in human beings: the saint, the atheist, the converted, and the counterconverted. In his standard work on the psychology of religion, *The Varieties of Religious Experience,* William James had the courage to say that religion does not come from God but is caused by personality and is therefore different in different individuals. He rejected "dogmatic theology" and proposed "a science of religions." James acknowledges the fact that religious feelings are caused or influenced by the unconscious and admits that "the religious are often neurotic."

We shall show in this paper how James's own religious destiny proves this teaching. James mentions Breuer's and Freud's work and writes on the influence of the unconscious:

* First published in *Psychoanalysis and the Social Sciences,* Vol. 1, edited by Géza Róheim. International Universities Press, New York, 1947.

We cannot avoid the conclusion that in religion we have a department of human nature with unusually close relations to the transmarginal or subliminal region. If the word "subliminal" is offensive to any of you, as smelling too much of psychical research or other aberrations, call it by any other name you please, to distinguish it from the level of full sunlit consciousness. Call this latter the A region of personality, if you care to, and call the other the B region. The B region is then obviously the larger part of each of us, for it is the abode of everything that is latent and the reservoir that passes unrecorded or unobserved. It contains, for example, such things as all our momentarily inactive memories and it harbors the springs of all our obscurely motivated passions, impulses, likes, dislikes and prejudices. Our intuitions, hypotheses, fancies, superstitions, persuasions, convictions and in general all our non-rational operations, come from it. It is the source of our dreams, and apparently they may return to it. In it arise whatever mystical experiences we may have and our automatisms, sensory or motor; our life in hypnotic and "hypnoid" conditions, if we are subject to such conditions; our delusions, fixed ideas and hysterical accidents, if we are hysteric subjects; our supranormal cognitions, if such there be, and if we are telepathic subjects. It is also the fountainhead of much that feeds our religion. In persons deep in religious life, we have now abundantly seen—and this is my conclusion—the door into this region seems unusually wide open; at any rate, experiences making their entrance through that door have had emphatic influence in shaping religious history.

William James's father was a very religious man, a sectarian, who not only went through a "salvation from his Calvinism" but was so influenced by the mystic Swedenborg and by Fourier that we may call him twice converted. William refers to his father's conversion at Windsor (1844) as an instance of "panic fear." Henry James was a very kind father who did not influence the choice of profession of his sons. He once told Emerson he wished at times that lightning would strike his "wife and children out of existence and he should suffer no more from loving them." He was enthusiastic and eccentric, a good writer, but paradoxical and obscure in his lectures and books. His relation to morals was not always clear. He may not have really approved of Fourier's interest in free love and Swedenborg's toleration of concubines—this "little fat, rosy Swedenborg amateur."

William James's father was one of those enthusiastic, idealistic, but somewhat obscure sages whom early America produced; "mystics of independent mind, hermits in the desert of business, and heretics in the churches" (George Santayana). The mystic Swedenborg had a potent influence upon these people and especially on the elder James. Swedenborgians still exist as a sect, in spite of the fact that Swedenborg, in his later years, represented an obvious case of religious paranoia. His religious crisis at the age of forty-six is a typical conversion by regression to his childhood. But Swedenborg is not listed among the cases of conversion William James quotes in his book. His name appears only in a footnote.

William James had an idealizing love for his father. He found his place in the world and his career only after a long period of vacillations and doubts, aggravated by neurotic states and ill-health. His work on *The Varieties of Religious Experience* is believed to be an act of filial piety. In spite of the skeptical attitude of his thinking, William James was religious[1] and declared: "I, myself, believe that the evidence for God lies primarily in inner personal experiences." "It seems correct to say," is the opinion of a friendly biographer, "that he did in fact have experiences of the type called mystical." William James named his constitutional disease *Zerrissenheit* (being torn to pieces). According to R. B. Perry, "an inventory of James's pathological traits would embrace tendencies to hypochondriasis and hallucinatory experiences, abnormally frequent and intense oscillations of mood, and an almost morbid alogism, or antipathy to the mode of thinking which employs definitions, symbols and trains of inference." James was periodically depressed, had insomnia and hypochondriasis, not without suicidal preoccupations. He also

---

[1] Janet believed that his own interest in psychology and philosophy was the result of a conflict between two tendencies, the one religious and quasi-mystical, the other scientific.

showed "a pathological repugnance to the processes of exact thought." Santayana calls James an agnostic. James himself never would have admitted this. But Allport's lecture on "The Productive Paradoxes of William James" (1942) seems almost to prove it.

However we interpret and classify "mystical experiences" or "ecstatic states," James wrestled repeatedly in his life with melancholia and a sense of frustration. In his twenties he wrote: "I have always thought that this experience of melancholia of mine had a religious bearing . . . I mean that the fear was so invasive and powerful that, if I had not clung to Scripture texts like 'The eternal God is my refuge,' etc., 'Come unto me all ye that labour and are heavy-laden,' etc., I should have grown really insane." In a letter written at the age of twenty-six James wrote: "The fact is that I am . . . little fitted by nature to be a worker in science, and yet . . . my only ideal is a scientific life."

James was able to find a compromise between faith and the science of religion. "If philosophy will abandon metaphysics and deduction for criticism and induction," he said, "she can make herself enormously useful, frankly transforming herself from theology into a science of religions. Why should a critical science of religions not eventually command as general a public adhesion as is commanded by a physical science! Even the personally non-religious might accept its conclusions on trust." Without being versed in the terms of psychiatry, he emphasized the prevalence of the psychopathic temperament in religious biography. We find in his book on *The Varieties of Religious Experience* the following passage:

Does God really exist? How does He exist? What is He? are so many irrelevant questions. Not God, but life, more life, a larger, richer, more satisfying life, is, in the last analysis, the end of religion. The warring gods and formulae of various religions do indeed cancel each other, but there is a certain uniform deliverance in which religions all appear to meet. It consists of two parts: An uneasiness; and its solution. The solution is a sense that we are saved from the wrongness, from the sense that there is something wrong about us.

James describes those who are predisposed for conversion as "subjects who are in possession of a large region in which mental work can go on subliminally and from which invasive experiences may come." A divine miracle is not necessary for conversion. "But if there be higher spiritual agencies, that can directly touch us, the psychological condition of their doing so might be our possession of a subconscious region which alone should yield access to them." The direct presence of the Deity, however, is not excluded. In his *Will to Believe,* James complains of the paralysis in the academic public of the inborn ability to believe, but he defends the right of the individual to devote himself to his personal faith at his personal risk. He, the son of "the best and most theological" father, had to be deeply religious; but for the people he recommends religion, because it is "pragmatic" to be religious, and he claims that one has "to will" to be religious. The individual should have the right to an individual personal faith.

We do not assume that the conflict between science and faith, between the son's skepticism and the father's profound religiousness alone caused James's neurotic states. But deep differences in their attitudes existed and an anxious letter of William to his wife after his father's death is characteristic: "You must not leave me till I understand a little more of the value and meaning of religion in father's sense, in the mental life and destiny of man . . . I must learn to interpret it alright."

It is not widely known that James met the representative of this new world of the unconscious, Freud, face to face. James really welcomed psychoanalysis. In 1909 he went to Worcester for one day, where Freud gave the well-known five lectures at Clark University. James applauded the aims of psychoanalysis— it was a year before his death—even when he distrusted its individual exponents. We find the following report in a letter to Theodore Flournoy:

> Speaking of "functional" psychology, Clark University . . . had a little international congress the other day in

honor of the twentieth year of its existence. I went there for one day in order to see what Freud was like. I hope that Freud and his pupils will push their ideas to their utmost limits so that we may learn what they are. They can't fail to throw light on human nature; but I confess that he made on me personally the impression of a man obsessed with fixed ideas. I can make nothing in my own case with his dream-theories, and obviously "symbolism" is a most dangerous method. A newspaper report of the congress said that Freud condemned the American religious therapy (which has such extensive results) as very "dangerous" because so "unscientific." Bah!

In another letter he wrote: "I strongly suspect Freud, with his dream-theory, of being a regular halluciné . . . Undoubtedly it covers some facts and will add to our understanding of functional psychology which is the real psychology." Freud—"obsessed with fixed ideas"—"a regular halluciné." James was not exactly a good psychiatric diagnostician! But James's first reaction was indeed a relatively mild one and hopeful for the future of psychoanalysis. "Freud and his pupils should push their ideas to their utmost limits so that we may learn what they are"—this really ensued after James's death.

We have seen how enthusiastically William James, with his interest in novelties, welcomed the great progress in psychology, brought about by the insight into the unconscious psychical processes. It was reserved for Freud to specify the unconscious material that determines the religious *Weltanschauung*. What is rising through the open door is "determined by the situation that subsisted in our childhood . . . A thesis unshakable by any questions of detail," Freud adds.

God-Creator is openly called father. Psychoanalysis concludes that he really is the father, clothed in the grandeur in which he once appeared to the small child. The religious man's image of the creation of the universe is the same as his image of his own creation. The same individual to whom the child owes his existence, the father (or, more correctly, father and mother) has protected and watched over the weak and helpless child, exposed as he was to all the dangers which threatened him in the external world; in his father's care he has felt safe. Even the grown man cannot give up the protection he enjoyed as a child. But he has long since realized that his father is a being with strictly limited powers and by no means endowed with every desirable attribute. He therefore looks back to the memory image of the overrated father of his childhood, exalts it into a deity and brings it into the present and into reality. The emotional strength of this memory image and the lasting nature of his need for protection are the two supports of his belief in God. The same father (the parental function[2]) who gave the child his life and preserved him from the dangers which that life involves, taught him what he might or might not do, made him accept certain limitations of his instinctual wishes, and told him what consideration he would be expected to show toward his parents, his brothers and sisters, if he wanted to be tolerated and liked as a member of the family circle, and later on of more extensive groups. This whole state of affairs is carried over by the grown-up man into his religion. The prohibitions and commands of his parents live on in him as his moral conscience. God rules the world of men with the help of the same system of rewards and punishments. The feeling of security with which every individual fortifies himself against the dangers of both the external world and of his human environment is founded on his love for God and the belief in God's love for him. Finally, he exercises a direct influence on the divine will in prayer, and in that way obtains a share in the divine omnipotence.

We know from the analyses of individuals that the relation to the real father was in all probability ambivalent from the outset, or at any rate it soon became so; that is to say, it comprised two sets of emotional impulses, quite opposite in nature, not merely one of fondness and submission but also one of hostility and de-

---

[2] It is true that Freud limited his investigations to the pecularities of one type of religion; therefore the father motive received a decisive place. But he mentioned the mother or speaks about her parental function. Other psychoanalysts acknowledge the importance of the mother motive and of the narcissistic self-motive, especially H. and K. Schelderup.

fiance. We hold—continues Freud, whom we quote here—that this ambivalence governs the relation of mankind to its deities. This unresolved conflict—the longing for the father, and dread and defiance—explains the fantasy of the Evil Spirit, regarded as the antithesis of God, namely, the Devil. Not all religions have adopted this enemy of God, but it requires no great psycho-analytic insight to guess that God and the Devil were originally one and the same, a single figure bearing opposite characteristics, which was later split into two.

I refer here to Freud's works *Totem and Taboo* (1912/13), *The Future of an Illusion* (1928), the Chapter on "A Philosophy of Life" in the *New Introductory Lectures* (1933), and to his papers on Schreber's paranoia (1911), "A Neurosis of Demoniacal Possession in the Seventeenth Century" (1923), and finally to "Obsessive Acts and Religious Practices" (1907).

We are very fortunate in being able to refer also to the work of R. P. Casey, a professor of Biblical Literature and History of Religions at Brown University in Providence, R.I. In his paper, "Oedipus Motivation in Religious Thought and Fantasy," Casey states in detail his opinion on the influence of the Oedipus Complex. This scholar writes:

> There is a statement of Freud not sufficiently utilized for the understanding of religion, namely, that the Oedipus Complex is unique in being normally and regularly suppressed rather than resolved. It is for this reason that it serves as a foundation for character development and leaves its marks on the adult personality in sickness and in health. The resolution of a complex involves the dissipation of its influence on consciousness, but the Oedipus Complex is habitually not resolved and its influence persists and forms a problem not only in the economy of personal life but in social exchange as well. It is the common possession of this nucleus of conflict that has driven men to find for it a social-ized expression and the result has been the emergence of religious institutions and organizations in the history of all cultures.

The most characteristic symptom of oedipal residuals is responsible for anxiety which betrays itself in two ways: the fear or

suspicion of punishment, however undeserved, and the attempt
to avert such punishment by appeasing the source of the supposed threat. The former appears in imperfectly rationalized
guilt—in religious terms, in an inadequately explained sense of
sin; in the latter an attempt is made to admit the overwhelming
superiority and excellence of the disciplinary figure or to assume that his dispositions are the reverse of those suggested by
the fear.

Alexander's principle of "the bribability of the superego" is
confirmed by the history of religions. Its underlying motivation
is anxiety based on feelings of guilt toward the father; its emotional consequence one of masochistic submissiveness, often covered by unconscious religious attitudes of high and noble character. In the historical sequences of religious ideas and attitudes,
the activity of the oedipus complex can clearly be discerned, having persistently the same unconscious problems for sublimation
in religious patterns of thought, feeling and behavior.

Casey declared in his summary of "The Psychoanalytic Study
of Religion" that "there is a great need for new material of a
kind more susceptible to experimental observation and control
. . . the psychological evaluation of religion in terms of evidence
rather than of hypothesis would represent a substantial gain."

"The structure of most religious beliefs and practices is the
Oedipus Complex." This sentence by Casey I put as motto at the
head of my personal contributions to this subject. We are not
going to discuss the average person, because we are convinced
that their religious destiny is essentially shaped in a general development by public institutions, tradition and education. We
are interested here in the conscious and unconscious development of peculiar religious destinies, peculiar individuals, peculiar religious experiences. We do not exclude psychotic cases,
such as cases of religious paranoia. My varieties of religious
experience have to show that the religious attitude of many normal or seemingly normal people is transparent in its development if we take into consideration their personal oedipus complex. My examples will mostly be writers, people who confess

voluntarily or involuntarily, by writing about themselves; but also some other individuals: an American M.D., an anonymous old maid described in the *Reader's Digest,* a psychoanalyst and others. Writers, poets and artists are the best objects for our investigation because, as Rank (1912) emphasized: "The artist, compelled to an intensive repression of the oedipus complex, sublimates his powerful impulses and indulges in fantasies. The same process takes place in primitive mankind and results in myths and religions."

FRANZ WERFEL

Franz Werfel, the novelist, represented a very interesting type. He was a Jew, but believed he had found the way to genuine Christianity. He did not state exactly when he had had "the religious experience," the revelation, or when his conversion had taken place; but he referred to feelings of his early youth. Orthodox Catholicism rightly claimed the poet as a Catholic. At the age of forty-two, Werfel once lectured to a large audience. "Are We Able to Live without Belief in God?" was the title of his lecture and in it he clearly made propaganda for his own faith. His aim was to convert the audience to divine unity: "The goal of this way is the goal of the world: Joy!" His arguments were partly personal ones. Man will remember death and destruction, especially the death of his mother, particularly the day of her death. More often he may suffer from the fear of annihilation. Werfel added that the idea of God is incomparably older than the patriarchate; but both male and female deities are only interpretations of the divine principle in conformity with the age. The "ecstatic state" is the deepest human experience. "The revolt against metaphysics is the cause of all our misery." Two of Werfel's last novels, *Embezzled Heaven* and *The Song of Bernadette,* deal with religious problems and reveal the dilemma of the writer. The deeply religious persons whom he depicts are described with cool aloofness, even with irony. The little girl who, for some weeks, suffers from visions, reluctantly becomes the origin of the fame of Lourdes and is finally canonized after her

death, which was caused by tuberculosis of the bones. Werfel
deals with her only as a sober historian would. His description of
the inevitable development, the exposure of superstition and
egotism, is masterly. Where does he, in this novel, give proof of
the existence of God or the value of belief? Only toward the end
Lafite, the unbelieving man of letters, admits that he is converted
Lafite probably represents the author. His admission is due to the
influence of a malignant disease. He says:

> I know well that all gods are reflected images of our own
> body structures and that, if the pelicans believed in god, he
> would have to be a pelican. But that is not a proof against
> the existence of a deity; it is only a proof for the narrowness
> of the earthly spirit, which cannot exist outside of images
> and words. I could never have endured the thought of being
> eternally excluded from the knowledge of God, to whom I
> feel, for all that, allied. There are no conversions to belief,
> there is only a return to it. Then God is not a function of the
> soul, but this soul itself in its last nakedness.

Thus Lafite, who had been the arch-skeptic and the Virgin's
proudest foe, was converted when he became gravely ill and then
sank upon his knees before the famous grotto of Lourdes. Here
Werfel unconsciously betrayed his own fear of illness and death.

The original and exceptional religious destiny of Werfel is
easily interpreted by psychoanalytic insight. Feelings of guilt and
anxiety[3] resulting from unusually great hostility against his father, and the influence of a Catholic servant in his youth are
sufficient causes. The conflict between father and son was exceedingly acute in Werfel's life. In his poem, *Father and Son,* in
the novel, *The Murdered Not the Murderer Is Guilty,* and in the
play *Mirrorman*—to quote his biographer, Richard Specht—Werfel has "dramatized the very subtle, horrible and criminal situation that psychoanalysis has formulated as the Oedipus Complex." After the publication of this biography by Specht, Werfel

---

[3] In *Embezzled Heaven,* Werfel formulates the connection between religion
and fear of death: There is an uncanny evening. A mother who fears the death of
her children says: "It is really difficult to believe in God." The writer answers:
"God is exactly that space in us which death does not occupy."

wrote the novel *Family Pascarella* which again describes in detail the damage a vain and aggressive father is able to inflict upon his six children. Verses such as "before our time begins, we become guilty that we are," or "my father, I look now for you!" may have a special meaning. The novel about murder reveals inhibitions similar to those of Hamlet; here the son who hates his father does not kill him, though he threatens him brutally.

The figure of a Catholic servant appears prominently in two of Werfel's novels, in *Barbara* and in *Embezzled Heaven;* in the latter as a bigoted cook who steals from her mistress. The religious persons in Werfel's writings are often very simple. The Catholic servant may have secured her great influence on the boy because the mother had to be supplanted; her picture may have been merged into fantasies about prostitutes, well-known derivatives of the oedipus complex.

Werfel may not have known anything about these interpretations of his strange religiosity. The very paradox of it and the overemphasis that made him a preacher and a propagandist betray its origin in inner conflicts. The storm and stress of Werfel's years of development were violent. He revolted against traditional artistic expression. He chose new forms for his verses, and therefore not all of his poems are intelligible. There does not exists a better proof for Freud's principle that the religious *Weltanschauung* is determined by our childhood.

Certainly Werfel's strange religious attitude was determined "by the situation that subsisted in his childhood." In his works he discloses fantasies of bad and harsh fathers who invariably die or are murdered. It was an archaic, overwhelming hatred against his father that produced these strange reactions. Fear of being punished by God-Father resulted in his fear of dying. Werfel was mistaken in assuming that everybody suffers from such fear of death and in regarding this as a basic motive in religious conversion. Unconscious processes—guilt feelings, anxiety, fear of death—produced in him personally a paradoxical conversion: here was a modern, well-educated man and a Jew, who became a devout Catholic and a propagandist eager to make proselytes.

FREUD'S CASE OF AN AMERICAN STUDENT

In 1928, Freud published a case of conversion, "A Religious Experience" of an American student of medicine who had reported this occurrence years later as follows:

> One afternoon while I was passing through the dissecting-room, my attention was attracted to a sweet-faced dear old woman who was being carried to a dissecting table. This sweet-faced woman made such an impression on me that a thought flashed through my mind: "There is no God. If there were a God, he would not have allowed this dear old woman to be brought to the dissecting-room." When I got home that afternoon, the feeling I had had at the sight in the dissecting-room made me determine to stop going to church. Before this, the doctrines of Christianity had been the subject of doubts in my mind. While I was meditating on this matter, a voice spoke to my soul that I should consider the step I was about to take. My spirit replied to this inner voice by saying: "If I knew of a certainty that Christianity was truth and the Bible was the Word of God, then I would accept it." In the course of the next few days, God made it clear to my soul that the Bible was His Word, that the teachings about Jesus Christ were true and that Jesus was our only hope. Since then God has revealed himself to me by many infallible proofs.

Freud suggests the following hypothetical explanation: The aspect of the naked body of a woman or of one destined to be exposed reminded the young man of his mother and awakened in him a longing for his mother which originated from the oedipus complex. This longing included rebellion against the father. The desire to kill the father can become conscious as a doubt in the existence of God, and it can be accepted by reason as indignation about the mistreated mother object. The child sometimes regards what father does to mother as an assault. The new emotion displaced to the religious realm is only a repetition of the oedipal situation and therefore has the same destiny. It succumbs to a mighty counterwave. The conflict seems to have assumed the form of a hallucinatory psychosis; inner voices resounded in order to dissuade the student from resistance. The end of the conflict appeared again in the religious realm. It is the complete subjection to the will of the Father-God, as predestined by the oedipus complex. The young man now believed and accepted everything he had been taught since childhood about God and Jesus Christ. He had had a religious experience, had been converted, and then tried to convert friends. Theodore Reik, in "A Note to Freud's Paper: A Religious Experience," remarks: "The most important precondition for a conversion is the unconscious emergence of hostile and aggressive impulses against the father, which appear as doubts, respectively as unbelief in God. The conversion follows upon a break-through of an impulse which actualized the hate tendencies against the father; it represents a reaction caused by unconscious anxiety and tenderness."

A CASE OF COUNTERCONVERSION

The following case of counterconversion is reported in James's book: The impression of a husband violently assaulting his wife produced in a girl of nineteen the idea "I have no use for God who permits such things." Since this painful experience she never again had any personal relation to God. From early youth, she had always been more or less skeptical about "God," had felt shame and remorse for a long time when, at sixteen, she joined the church and was not sincere about it. Her actual story reads as follows:

> At nineteen, I had an attack of tonsilitis. Before I had quite recovered, I heard a story of a brute who had kicked his wife downstairs and then continued kicking her until she passed out. I felt the horror of the thing keenly. Instantly the blasphemous thought flashed through my mind.

No further recollections are told, nothing about her father and his relation to her mother. But in all probability our assumption is justified that an originally loved father had disappointed his daughter by violence and had become the origin of her negation of God the Father. Generally, religious persons do not make God responsible for violent actions of brutal people,

THE MAGAZINE CASE

I think I should discuss a case of a rather amazing conversion of a young woman, although we do not know anything about her childhood. A religious writer who has published a book, *Have You a Religion?* commented on her way of conversion in an article in the *Reader's Digest*. The woman, who was neither pretty nor gifted, became a happy and religious person when she happened to read the brief magazine suggestion: "Try religion for a day—a single day!"

We are told that the girl praised this change by which she lost her fears of life, of death, of old age, of sickness, of losing her job, of the future. She gave up anger, hatred, greed, lust, cruelty and pride, as well as suspicion and intolerance of people around her. She tried the suggestion for a day and then for another day. Success came to her increasingly. Tolerance, kindness and love won the upper hand. She seemed to have become positive instead of negative and felt she was at last a genuine human being.

No doubt this girl was in a chronic state of anxiety, isolated and disappointed. A scene in her office in which she had been made the scapegoat had occurred just before she read the notice in the magazine. She was not especially attractive. Thus we have to assume a certain readiness for an escape from herself, and the suggestion of the magazine came just in time. The flight into faith may have rescued her from suicide; a new life began. But how many readers of that magazine were in such readiness? Fear, isolation, despair and frustration provide the most fertile ground for a conversion, if childhood has prepared the way.

Santa de Sanctis writes in his book on *Religious Conversion:* "Suffering in advance is to be found in every case of adult conversion. Liberation and the sensation of victory, feeling the nearness of God and finally tranquility are experienced afterwards."

THE SWISS PSYCHOANALYST

A scientific opinion can be changed by a kind of conversion. Maeder, a Swiss psychoanalyst, reported in his paper, "Healing

ld Development of the Soul" (1918), that a sentence of Christ—
I am the way, the truth and the life"—which he had as a child
arned by heart but had never comprehended, all of a sudden
ecame meaningful. A feeling of new power and new trust in his
uman nature and destination was caused by his discovery of the
:eleological function of dreams," of this entirely unconscious
id incontrovertible phenomenon. This made an overwhelming
npression on him. For the first time his positivism and his me-
ianical conception of life were shaken.

From the general circumstances we described, we must sup-
ose that Dr. X was in a state of inner readiness for his conversion
id that his alleged discovery—incidentally, not accepted by
reud—was conditioned entirely by his unconscious readiness.[4] It
really a return from science to faith, to the emotional religious
npressions of his youth. We quote here a passage from the paper:
Sensual enjoyment and greediness for money took possession of
ie hearts and enslaved the world. The word of Christ claims
iat every really born or newborn living personality looks for its
wn path."

C. G. Jung, once an enthusiastic follower of Freud, wrote:
Every one of my patients in the second half of life—that is to
.y, over thirty-five—fell ill because he had lost that which the
ving religions of every age have given their followers; and none
: them has really been healed who did not regain his religious
utlook." If you read this, you may well remember that Jung is
ie son of a minister and may have gone the way of regression,
ke his colleague. He once wrote a paper about "The Impor-
ince of the Father for the Destiny of the Individual." It is very
istructive to read what Professor Casey wrote about Jung's
iethod, which erroneously still goes under the name of psycho-
ialysis: "Freudian analysis is different from other analytic pro-
:dures which rely on suggestion and instruction, as, for example,

4 Even a conversion which is reported as sudden has been prepared uncon-
ously. Starbuck speaks of "subconscious incubation," James of a state of being
uned aright."

Jung's analyses which end in conversion to Jung's ideas an
ideally at least, in a graduate course in his philosophy of life."

ALBERT SCHWEITZER

Even if a man is already religious, a conversion is still possibl
it is then a conversion to a higher ethic, to a perfection near
that of a saint. Such was the conversion of Albert Schweitzer,
man of varied talents: theologian, preacher, student of Jesus ar
of Bach, expert in organ music and virtuoso, philosopher ar
finally missionary and doctor in Africa. Schweitzer describes h
conversion at the age of twenty-one as follows:

> One brilliant summer morning at Guensbach, during the
> Whitsuntide holidays, there came to me, as I awoke, the
> thought that I must not accept this happiness as a matter of
> course, but must give something in return for it. Proceeding
> to think the matter out with calm deliberation, while the
> birds were singing outside, I settled with myself, before I got
> up, that I would consider myself justified in living for
> science and art till I was thirty, in order to devote myself
> from that time forward to the direct service of humanity.
> Many a time already had I tried to settle what meaning lay
> hidden for me in the saying of Jesus, "Whosoever would
> save his life, shall lose it, and whosoever shall lose his life for
> my sake and the Gospels', shall save it." Now the answer was
> found. In addition to the outward, I now had inward happi-
> ness.

Schweitzer, too, was the son of a minister. He describes h
childhood and youth as a very happy one, "unclouded but for tl
frequent illnesses of the father." In the Gymnasium (Hig
School) he was "slack and dreamy," yet mastered what did n
come easily to him and learned strict discipline and fulfillment
duty.

"It struck me," he said later, "as incomprehensible that
should be allowed to live such a happy life, while I saw so mar
people around me wrestling with care and suffering." What ra
feelings of compassion and guilt!

Schweitzer wanted to work with abandoned or neglected ch

dren, with tramps or discharged prisoners; but he did not like to work with an organization. What he wanted was an absolutely personal and independent activity, free from interference. By chance, "one day in 1904," he read that there was the "need of the Mission of the Congo," to find some of those "on whom the Master's eyes already rested" and who had only to answer the Master's call: "Lord, I am coming." Schweitzer decided to begin his medical studies and in spite of the fact that his friends and family warned him and said that he was "not quite in his right mind," he accomplished "the most irrational thing." In 1913, he left with his wife for "the direct human service (as a doctor) in Equatorial Africa."

It is disappointing not to find more details about his youth in his all too short autobiography *My Life and Thoughts*. We have here the typical formula for conversion: "Once on a sunny day . . ." We see a moral conversion to a more highly appreciated occupation than could be offered by the work of a writer, theologian, musician, scientist or artist. The God of Schweitzer prefers "direct service of humanity," and only thereby does Schweitzer achieve security and inner happiness. External happiness in which not all people participate in equal degree he experiences as sin. Since this feeling is not a general one, we assume the existence of an unconscious guilt feeling which originated in early years and was revived by regression.

GOTTFRIED KELLER

Gottfried Keller, the well-known Swiss poet, had a complicated relationship with his father. At the age of five he lost his beloved and esteemed father. At the age of seven he hated his stepfather; but this marriage of his mother lasted only a few years. She often spoke about his father, and the son was full of longing and nostalgia for him. The father had been an enthusiastic and learned man, interested in arts and literature and in a moral and religious education.

Idealized father images appear in Kellers' autobiographical novel, *Der grüne Heinrich,* and the writer and passive hero is continuously struggling with the problem of divinity. God is for him a kind of father, the supporter who takes care of him. The father's noble image is growing to "a part of the great infinite." He has to sanction his son's work as a painter. The son "had won a mighty and grand patron who invisibly stalked over the dusky world." The son inherited from his father the delight in festivals and in the ringing of bells in church, as well as the sense of freedom from encroachments of ultra-Montanism and from the intolerance of orthodox and hypocritical priests. The penitential sermon at his confirmation drove the son from the church for many years, but he kept an unsophisticated belief in God. He wrote to his mother: "I always need to remain in an easily trusting relation with God." While studying with Feuerbach, he came to deny God and immortality, but later he changed again and returned to God the Father.

He imagined the dead father as an intellectual mentor. Great men of genius are his father substitutes; Jean Paul, an older poet, influenced him and was venerated and loved. It is said in the novel: "At that time I entered into a new alliance with God and Jean Paul who took the place of a father for me . . . I will never disown him as long as my heart does not dry up. With other spiritual heroes one is only a guest, with him one is united forever." Keller was indebted to his father for his liberal faith in God.

As a little boy—was it at the time when his stepfather appeared? —Keller committed compulsive blasphemies, succumbing to the temptation, especially before falling asleep, of calling God nicknames, even invectives. The hero of the autobiographical novel calls it "an unconscious experiment with the omnipresence of God." It is interesting that the boy imagined God as a weathercock or picture-book tiger.

AUGUSTE COMTE

Auguste Comte's life history can be regarded as an example of a character development, where scientific interests are in opposition to early religious trends. His work reminds one of Sweden-

borg, inasmuch as during twelve years of his life he examined
"the total state of the wisdom of his time for its concrete and positive contents, removing its theological and metaphysical ingredi-
ents." Originally the *Positive Philosophy* was intended as a
"harmonic and systematic whole of all science." But Comte experienced in later years a change in personality and was converted
from science to faith. By regression to deep religious impressions
of his youth, he even changed his work to a religious one.

Auguste Comte was a descendant of an exceedingly pious
family. His mother especially went to extremes in order to vali-
date her principles, even at the risk of his life. That explains why,
in the last period of his life, he returned by regression to the religious state, although it was in complete opposition to his previous axioms.

At the age of twenty-eight, Comte was psychotic for a certain
period. He was divorced at forty-four. In his forty-seventh year
he again went through a "nervous crisis." His new sweetheart,
Clothilde de Vaux, was the origin of his conversion to a renewed
religion. However, after a year they spent together she died. Here
a regression to childhood, to the mother and the early influence
of her bigotry, brought about the conversion to Catholicism. It
was Wilhelm Ostwald who, in his biography of Comte, pointed
out this mechanism of regression. As a result we have "Comte's
conviction of the inevitability of religious institutions and sentiments in a world enlightened by science": a compromise.

SELMA LAGERLÖF

If we wish to collect more "religious experiences," I may use
at random the psychoanalytic supplements to biographies I have
published. The famous Swedish writer Selma Lagerlöf, for instance, was a very pious lady. She was charitable, full of mercy
and pity, and showed traits of saintliness. Her novels deal all too
often with the themes of guilt and punishment, atonement and
redemption. As a child she was full of feelings of guilt and anxiety. In her writings she preferred to deal with harsh and unjust
stepmothers, or mothers-in-law, or with witches. Even in later

years she was frightened by the hallucination of a gruesome old female beggar.

Here we see that the feeling of guilt arising from the oedipus complex, by the roundabout way of anxiety, produced the over-religious character. A very kind father was the prototype of God who, represented by Christ or by a priest, acts in this world as a mild, forgiving, understanding authority. Some of the memories of her childhood, particularly the mention of some little acts of sacrilege, verify Selma Lagerlöf's development. At the age of fourteen, Selma listened with curiosity to a conversation her uncle had with a lady who was interested in positivism and seemed not to believe in God. Selma felt obliged to assert that she herself did believe in God. But she was too shy to profess it in the way the old Christian martyrs did. She doubted whether God could ever forgive her for this omission and feared she would be punished by Him with many severe disasters. She developed into a very religious personality, and her characters, in reaction to her early stubbornness, avarice and irascibility, display compassion, charity and kindness.

KNUT HAMSUN

How will the religious reaction to the oedipus complex develop in an individual who as a boy had had a phobia of an uncanny, threatening, devilish man, toward whom the boy felt guilty? The Norwegian novelist, Knut Hamsun, in his work manifests his hatred of his father, in addition to the recurrent problem of the fear of "castration." Incidentally, he lets all father images, the mighty, impulsive and sensual types, lose their fortune and potency in later age. The motive of jealousy and of "the damaged third" demonstrates the fixation to the mother. In the entire work of this ingenious writer we do not find the description of any noble woman, but psychoanalysis teaches us that the exalted image of the mother may be symbolized by Mother Earth or by nature. Actually, Hamsun and his heroes flee from the struggles and worries of life to the outdoors, the forest, the beach —to nature. They enjoy living in a warm, lonely cavern. Hamun's description of nature shows its maternal origin and its symbolic character. For instance, he describes a locality: "It is not really a slope of a hill; it is a breast, a lap, so smooth . . . a big slope, so full of tenderness and helplessness, like a mother it allows itself to be fondled in every way." Nature appears as a place where one has already been, as a *déjà vu*, combined with feelings of reincarnation. He said once:

Many years have passed since I felt such peace around me, maybe twenty or thirty years, maybe it was in an earlier life. I must have once felt this peace, though, as I now walked around here . . . and cared about every stone and every blade, and these in turn, seemed to care for me. We knew each other . . . I walked through the wood, I was moved to tears, I was enchanted, and I said constantly: God in heaven, that again I should come here! As if I had been here before.

Hamsun's much praised sentimental descriptions of nature result from his longing for the innocent time of paradise with the mother. We know of his fixation to his homeland. *Mother Earth* is the title of one of his novels. He liked country life and ran a farm. Is it too dogmatic to assume that he built up a kind of religion of nature, that he found security only at the breast of the mother, symbolized by nature, that he achieved the fulfillment of an unconscious longing only in a pantheistic union with her? He worshiped nature. The "oceanic feeling," the feeling of an indissoluble union with nature, the *Naturgefühl*—they all may replace a religious feeling for a God, substituting the beloved mother for the father and nature for the mother. The mother does not only represent tenderness, warmth and beauty. She is the nourishing principle too.

Hamsun obstinately refused to give biographical data about himself. But in a well-concealed place in his writings he mentions his childhood: "We had an unusual mother who often turned back and pretended to have forgotten something when she caught us in the store-room." Although Hamsun had the tendency to keep all details about his development to himself, we may quote here the Norwegian analyst, Trygve Braatoy, who ascribes one

striking trait to the main characters in several of Hamsun'
books: "Love and hatred, contempt and veneration in turn are
felt toward the same object—toward God and existence.''

MAX DAUTHENDEY

I discussed one of the most striking examples of our problem in
my paper on the German poet, Max Dauthendey. In his autobiography the ambivalent relation to his domineering father is
described very lucidly: "My father's spirit rules all I do. He comes
and goes (a long time after his death) as if alive. For me his spirit
still rises daily with the sun and stays with the stars in the nocturnal sky."

Too hard and too strong to be loved unambiguously, these
superfathers are so attractive and imposing, so efficient in everything, and represent such perfect models for ambition that the
children are not able to reject them with indifference. The sons
remain in feminine dependency, in fetters, for a long time or
forever: or they break loose fighting in heroic love for their
mother or her representatives, thereby fighting the omnipotent
fathers.

Max Dauthendey demonstrates clearly the psychoanalytic concepts of conversion and counterconversion or apostasy. For three
months he had hardly spoken a word to his father. Finally he
left the house, thoroughly fed up with the tyrant. A single remark
of a friend made him a pantheist who could imagine the heavens
empty and could dethrone the old God. The apostasy from the
father made the son able to sustain the apostasy from God. "A
human being is not the slave of a master; he is a master himself;
the master of his life and of all future lives," he said. His words—
"The feeling of love will also then be richer. You will not value
God any higher than the heart of the woman whom you will
choose"—seem to illustrate the libido change as the basis of the
conversion by regression to the mother's image.

Dauthendey's conversion from Father-God to Mother-Nature,
from a homosexual attitude to a heterosexual one, is a regression
to his earliest love, the love for his mother. Her early death

urthered the later substitution by his father's personality. In his
works the poet characteristically indulges in his great enjoyment
of nature, which he intimately describes.

I have interpreted some telepathic phenomena Dauthendey
experienced and in this context had to point out his ambivalence,
his hostility to his father, his death wishes and repentance. When
his father died, and he received the message abroad, he felt relief.
Later he found it vicious and low "that the death of the beloved
old father made him feel relief in his distress." But the son was
relieved from veritable hunger and was enabled to live on the
inheritance. He says: "In the wild disdain I felt in this tragic
situation, I said: to inherit is cannibalism."

His flight from his homeland may be characteristic for his escape from the father, who seemed to have been the cause of the
suicides of his first wife and of a second son who suffered from
delusions of persecution. Perhaps this psychosis was caused by a
parallelogram of the same forces of different intensity—fixation
in love and hatred. A dream Max Dauthendey had in his forty-
seventh year may here be cited as proof of an intensive father
fixation:

> I stood beside my father and embraced him and pointed
> to a little child who wore a little cap on his head and was
> held on somebody's arm. "Ah!" said I, "Papa, let all of us
> wear such little nightcaps, you and me too, and let us then
> sit under the plumtrees, you and me, and let us speak about
> Mama!" My father smiled and I felt in the dream that what
> I had said was childish and tired. Then I threw my arms
> around him, drew him to me and said: "Ah, Father, let me
> at least imagine this, even if it is not at all possible, I like to
> imagine it, that is already enough, and it does me good to
> imagine it." I awoke and felt my heart sweetly beating, my
> chest sobbing and my eyes wet with tears which I had shed
> in the dream on my father's shoulder, half in delight, half
> in great suffering and inexpressible grief.

MAHATMA GANDHI

If I choose Mahatma Gandhi as a further example, I know
well that he belongs to a nation with a very different religion, one

inclined to asceticism; e.g., it is forbidden to eat meat because i
is a sin to kill animals.

Gandhi did not show a sudden conversion but a gradual one
He was a rebellious son, stubborn and arbitrary. He had to take
care of his sick father for several years, and the main reason fo
his intense guilt feelings was that by having intercourse with hi
wife, he missed being present at his father's death. At one time he
attacked his wife and drove her away. His dietetic asceticism wa
hidden behind health theories, but the doctors advised him a
least to take goat's milk in addition to his vegetables. His prin
ciple of "nonviolence" in politics, by its fundamental and over
emphasized nature, looks suspiciously like a reaction to a ver
strong personal aggression impulse. His methods of hunger strike
or civil disobedience are aggression under a new mask. His figh
against the English government had a rare tenacity; he was the
admired leader of the Indians, he who fought for them as a mar
tyr.

Gandhi proves once again that a very aggressive boy may, by
repression and reaction formation, develop into the most altru
istic, ascetic, and pious man. But the repressed aggression of the
"original sin" will return, accompanied by feelings of guilt, mani
festing itself by submission to God and reactive masochistic traits
such as the preference of a simple life, asceticism, periods o
silence or fasting. He did not mind being imprisoned many
times. Thus he represented "the fighting soul of India" and
aroused in the Indians a sense of nationhood and courage. He
stressed the importance of religion and fought for the "Untouch
ables"; they call him "India's Noblest Son." Some obstinacy
against natural cultural progress, such as railways, or his fight for
the "spinning wheel" and for "India-made cloth," reveal that he
sometimes was "absolutely irreconcilable," like compulsive neu
rotics or psychopaths.

His religion shows a development similar to conversion. Origi
nally "entirely Hindu," he was influenced by the Christian fa
ther-son religion. He admitted that he owed to his Christian
friends in South Africa the awakening of his religious quest. To

him, "all religions are like different roads leading to the same goal."

Gandhi's saintliness was characterized by fanaticism, purity, charity and asceticism, all furthered by unconscious masochism. This masochism was based on repressed aggression which broke through in his tenacity, irreconcilability and consistent fight against the "stepfather" England. Noncooperation and civil disobedience are the substitutes for "violence." There seems to be some hypocrisy in the principle of "nonviolence." All these paradoxes and the overemphasis betray the repressed aggression, which here leads to slow conversion, by way of unconscious guilt feelings, anxiety and ingratiation with God. All the prayers, the fasting and the self-ordained silence were compulsive means to expiate his sins. Let us call Gandhi a borderline case, an abortive saint with peculiar character traits.

SAMUEL JOHNSON

One of the most instructive cases of "religious experience" is that of the famous English writer and moralist, Samuel Johnson (1709–1784).[5] He was a model of morality and religiousness. A volume of his prayers and meditations was published after his death. His charity was well known. He used only one third of his royal pension for himself and the rest he spent for indigent people. We may be justified in calling him an abortive saint. It would, at least, have been his ideal to represent one, as he described the wise man Imlac in his novel *Rasselas*.

Religion was, as a biographer rightly found out, "the nightmare of his life." His parents were very religious and his mother had told him about heaven and hell at an early age. But he denied any lasting impression from this information. The real cause of his anxiety, which increased enormously toward the end of his life, was a deep feeling of guilt about his aggressive behavior against and early hatred of his father, about his later offenses against decency and moral religious commands, especially about an irreligious period in his boyhood. Such a period is a frequent

5 For a more extensive discussion, see pp. 175–185.

occurrence as a result of hatred against the father, originating from the oedipus complex. It was the son's everlasting reproach that the father was a miser and guilty of hiring the tuberculous nurse who infected him. Thus it was small wonder that the boy was very aggressive and had to repress this aggression; and that this caused his severe neurosis. Johnson's was indeed a severe neurosis. The compulsion neurosis normally has as its basis the oedipal hatred against the parent of the same sex. Anxiety and guilt feelings with self-punishment result. In their childhood these patients often show periods of irreligiosity, blasphemic utterings or little acts of sacrilege—an early expression of identifying God with the parent. Self-punishment, masochistic tendencies and remorseful actions result. The compulsive neurosis is, so to speak, a substitute for a religion. The painful repetition of repentant acts as an aid against anxiety, as self-punishment and masochistic enjoyment, is compulsive, as are the repetitions of rituals and prayers. (We know, for instance, that Johnson once returned in contrition to a place where he had offended his father fifty years earlier by obstinacy and arrogance.) Johnson also displayed the symptom of irrepressible, loud, short prayers, offering them in spite of the presence of other people. Freud in 1907 published a paper on the similarity of "Obsessive Acts and Religious Practices," both called ceremonials. Johnson manifested both.

ARTHUR SCHOPENHAUER

Since the conception of God and religious belief and practice are so essentially dependent on the child-parent relation in their structure, I would like to add at least one more proof that "the need of conceiving a universe and the character ascribed to any universe," the philosophy of life or *Weltanschauung,* depend on the same unconscious development. In Schopenhauer's main work, *The World as Will and Idea,* his pessimism and misogyny are striking features in this brilliant and highly educated man.

As previously pointed out,[6] his pessimism derived from his

6 See pp. 35–125.

peculiar childhood influences exercised by a father of a hard and violent nature and a mother who was tender in the beginning and then rejecting. There are no reports with full details, but many characteristic memories. Schopenhauer was approximately eighteen when he said: "A God is said to have created this world? NO! Rather a devil! . . . I had to suffer a great deal in growing up, through my father's strictness." Behind this conscious remark of the young man, we have to assume an unhappy childhood. We know that the boy considered the two happiest years of his youth those he spent with another family, where the foster father was "a dear, kind, pleasant man." Schopenhauer showed anxiety, feelings of guilt and hypochondriacal symptoms and suffered from strong, mostly suppressed sexual desires. A second root of his pessimism may be seen in the deep disappointment in the changing behavior of his mother who rejected her son, preferring her lovers who lived with her. Schopenhauer became, of course, irreligious early in life, but his ideal was the saint who has overcome will, hostility and sexuality. "Schopenhauer idealized compassion and chastity because he suffered most from their opposites" (Nietzsche).

Schopenhauer's philosophy is an unconscious confession and projection. He projected the power of his father, which he felt in childhood so superior to himself, as a symbol into the universe; as will.

He was not in sympathy with the supernatural element, but valued the moral doctrines of Christianity and Buddhism. In his dialogue on religion, he admits the practical value of religion, which is metaphysics of the masses, on the intellectual level. But the other partner in this dialogue predicts euthanasia of religion in the future. Religion will take its leave from European humanity, like a nurse whom the child has outgrown. Philosophy and science will then be instructors and tutors. We find many of Schopenhauer's argumentations in Freud's *The Future of an Illusion*.

It is again Professor Casey who formulates it clearly:

The assumption of a good universe depends on a disposition to affirm the successful survival of positive elements in the Oedipus Complex, that of a hostile or indifferent universe represents their extinction or defeat by negative elements, reflecting experiences of hostility or indifference in the parents or parent-substitutes in the formative years.

GOETHE

Goethe, in his universality, greatness and comprehension of all human affairs, is not easy to understand.[7] His faith was influenced by a strong father whom he experienced as overwhelming, often manifesting intense rivalry with and resistance against him. The victorious overcoming of this father was revealed in his poetry.

> Could I but be replete
> With Thee, Eternal One—
> Alas, this deep torment
> How it endures on earth.

These verses reveal feminine-passive emotions and a humble longing. The poem *Ganymed* shows a glorification of being merged with the universe. The poem *Prometheus* discloses open rebellion, the defiance of the Titans. In the son, the father's Protestantism became a more comprehensive, impersonal, pantheistic religion, a kind of overcoming of the paternal principle. Yet all his life Goethe remained religious in a wider sense. The father had been relatively tolerant toward his son: "Though more old-fashioned in his religion, he did not take offense at my views and speculations," says the son. One may remember the peculiar altar that the son once built, in a rather heathenish manner, from products of nature, and dedicated to the God of nature, as a burnt-offering. "The God who was closely connected with nature . . . He seemed to him the real God . . . The boy could not bestow a definite shape on this deity . . ."

Perhaps we may ascribe the uncertainty, the doubt about God and the denial of a personal God, to this ambiguous relation to the father and to a kind of longing for the mother, interwoven with a specific "feeling of nature." The circumstances in this case

7 For a more extensive discussion, see pp. 126–151.

are complicated because nature represented for Goethe something divine. His religious feeling merged with the "feeling of nature." It is for him a "pure, deep, innate and familiar perception to see God in nature and nature in God." Faust's creed, too, is that of a pantheist. "Neither the philosopher nor the theologist is able to arrive at a satisfactory idea about Goethe's God and Goethe's nature" (Chamberlain).

We may quote here once more Goethe's letter to his friend Jakobi:

> As a poet and an artist, I am a polytheist; as a natural scientist, I am a pantheist. I am as decidedly one as I am the other. And if I need a God for my own person, as a moral being, this, too, has been taken care of. The celestial and terrestial matters are so vast a realm that only the organs of all beings together are able to grasp it.

The rebellion against the father is known from Goethe's autobiographical novel. The kind mother, to whom the son was always very much attached, often had to intervene. In his book on the incest-complex, Rank points out the unconscious continuation of this rebellion against the father.

SUMMARY

The series of "religious experiences" I reported here may be tiring, but only "the regularity of occurrences" proves a law and "the technique of proving a particular law is the demonstration of the frequency of similar events, disregarding individual differences" (Aristole).

Freud calls the thesis that the religious *Weltanschauung* is determined by the situation that subsisted in our childhood "unshakeable by any question of detail."

I think I should close my demonstration with one significant passage, quoted from the posthumously published papers of the famous, though neurotic theologian and philosopher Sören Kierkegaard:

> I never knew the mirth to be a child because of the dreadful tortures I suffered . . . But often it seems to me as if all

would come back again. Then, how unhappy *my father* has made me, it seems as if I would live to see it *now in relation to God:* to be a child; and all my earliest life may have been so awfully lost and wasted in order to undergo it a second time, more true in relation to God.

Here I end my presentation of a new group of varieties of re ligious experience. I have to expect the criticism that I have deal with the problem of religious feelings only from a psychoanalytic point of view and have not shown insight into the broader aspects of religion as a sociological, historical, cultural problem. But my intention was merely to reaffirm the importance of the oedipus complex, which is ubiquitous, yet through differences in intensity and character creates varieties of character types, neuroses and incidentally, different religious types. To understand these types will also further our practical work with patients.

Another reproach may be more justified: that I did not bring more extensive psychoanalytic material. If I had dealt with patients, discretion would explain the restriction. My biographical studies contain further data. In this chapter on personality I intended to summarize the results.

We have seen how effective the oedipus complex, the "original sin," is in forming the varieties of our experience, and have only to add an explanation of how the multitude of normal, average people solve it without doubts and difficulties. Most of the members of the many hundred creeds in the melting pot America develop, after successful repression of a moderate oedipus complex, an independent, strong and reliable ego and superego. They do not suffer from guilt and anxiety, but are influenced by tradition, models and the atmosphere of the formative years. Incidentally, the problem of the followers of the founder of a new sect is one of mass psychology and sociology.

All the unconscious developments caused by the oedipus complex or its consequences, are now easy to understand. James felt that there was an open door to the unconscious; but not till Freud did we learn what comes up through this door. James knew where, but Freud found what comes up. James described the varieties of religious experience, Freud taught us to understand them. James knew what they are like, Freud why they are so. We do not yet know where the psychotic process begins and what the mystic and ecstatic states represent. As paranoia or fixed idea, a conversion does not change the whole personality, especially not the intelligence or ability to work. Even the religious paranoia of Swedenborg with all its psychotic symptoms did not prevent his followers from regarding him as a great man. It is the overemphasis of the phenomena that is so convincing. Saints are rare, but ascetic, overcharitable types with self-sacrificing tendencies exist also without having a particular religious belief.

I do not pretend to have revealed something basically new and am satisfied if I have offered stimulation and suggestions regarding the problem of personality. The insight that religious attitudes have unconscious personal roots will create an atmosphere of tolerance.

What we have pointed out as the norm in special religious attitudes is also valid for the two great minds and contrasting personalities of James and Freud.

I am not able to evaluate James's eminent achievements in other realms of science. He represents "the great philosopher of America" and was the most beloved philosopher of his time. He did not found any school, left practically no disciples in the strict sense of the word. His was a neurotic belief, developed after inner struggles and mystic experiences. He gave a description of religion, as Santayana points out, "that showed religion to be madness"; characterizing James's uncertainty, he says that James did not really believe, he merely believed in the right of believing, that you might be right if you believed. The focus of James's outlook was moral heroism. He adopted the belief in the freedom of will and has frequently been blamed for systematic lack of system.

Freud's psychology is based on rigorous determinism, he is rational and believes only in logos. He was the most hated psychologist of his time, but he found enthusiastic followers and founded a school that spread all over the world. He himself must have gone through a very intensive oedipus complex[8] which prompted him to write, at the age of seventy-two, *The Future of an Illusion,* his polemic treatise against religion. It presented a personal point of view; he himself said that his pupils may think differently about the problem. But let us stress the main thesis "unshakable by any question of detail": The religious *Weltanschauung* is determined by the situation that subsisted in our childhood.

[8] Cf. Hanns Sachs (1944).

Bibliography

Abraham, K. (1921–25), Psycho-Analytical Studies on Character Formation. *Selected Papers on Psycho-Analysis.* London: Hogarth Press, 1927.

Andrews, C. F. (1931), *Mahatma Gandhi at Work.* London.

Auernheimer, R. (1923), Hundert Jahre Eckermann from the *Neue Freie Presse.* Vienna (June 10).

Arnim, B.v. (1906), *Goethes Briefwechsel mit einem Kinde.* Jena.

Bebel, A. (1907), *Charles Fournier.* Stuttgart.

Bergler, E. (1944), Psychopathology of Impostors. *J. Crim. Psychopath.,* V.

Bloch, I. (1902/3), *Beiträge zur Aetiologie der Psychopathia Sexualis.* Dresden.

—— (1908), *The Sexual Life of Our Time in Its Relation to Modern Civilization.* London.

Bode, W. (1917), *Weib und Sittlichkeit in Goethes Leben.* Berlin.

Boswell, J. *The Life of Samuel Johnson.* London.

Brandes, G. (1922), *Goethe.* Trans. from the Danish by Erich Holm. Berlin.

Brill, A. A. (1931), Poetry as an Oral Outlet. *Psa. Review,* XVIII.

Carlyle, T. (1847), *Critical and Miscellaneous Essays.* London.

Casey, R. P. (1933), The Psychoanalytic Study of Religion. *J. Abn. & Soc. Psychol.,* XXVIII.

—— (1942), Oedipus Motivation in Religious Thought and Fantasy. *Psychiatry,* V.

—— (1943), Religion and Psychiatry. *Psychiatry,* VI.

Castle, E., ed., *Gespräche mit Goethe. Kommentiert.* Berlin.

Chamberlain, H. S. (1912), *Goethe.* Berlin.

Chitamber, J. R. (1933), *Mahatma Gandhi.* Philadelphia.

Craig, W. H. (1895), *Dr. Johnson and the Fair Sex; a Study of Contrasts.* London.

Damm, O. F. (1912), *Arthur Schopenhauer. Eine Biographie.* Berlin: Reklam.

Ebstein, W. (1907), *Arthur Schopenhauer. Seine wirklichen und vermeintlichen Krankheiten.* Stuttgart.

Eckermann, J. P. (1836), *Conversations with Goethe in the Last Years of His Life.* Boston: Millard, 1839.

Emerson, R. W. (1886), *Essays; Representative Men.* London.

Engel, E. (1916), *Goethe. Der Mann und das Werk.* Berlin.

Ernest, G. (1930), *Johannes Brahms.* Berlin.

Evans, B. I. (1944), *English Literature.* London.

Ferenczi, S. (1912), The Symbolic Representation of the Pleasure and the Reality Principles in the Oedipus Myth. *Sex in Psychoanalysis.* New York: Basic Books, 1950.

Feuerbach, L. (1846–1866), *Sämtliche Werke.* Leipzig.

Fischer, K. (1898), *Schopenhauers Leben, Werke und Lehre.* Heidelberg.

Fitzgerald, P. H. (1912), *Boswell's Autobiography.* London.

Forman, H. J. (1942), One Day Can Change Your Life. *Reader's Digest.*

Foster, G. (1945), The Psychotherapy of William James. *Psa. Review* XXXII.

Frauenstaedt, J. (1854), *Briefe über die Schopenhauersche Philosophia.* Leipzig.

—— (1862), *Schopenhauers Leben und Lehre.* Leipzig.

Freud, A. (1936), *The Ego and the Mechanisms of Defense.* New York: International Universities Press, 1946.

Freud, S. (1900), The Interpretation of Dreams. In: *The Basic Writings of Sigmund Freud.* New York: Modern Library, 1938.

—— (1904), The Psychopathology of Everyday Life. *Ibid.*

—— (1907), Obsessive Acts and Religious Practices. *Coll. Papers, 2.* London: Hogarth Press, 1924.

—— (1910/12), Contributions to the Psychology of Love. *Coll. Papers, 4.*

—— (1911), Psychoanalytic Notes upon the Autobiographical Account of a Case of Paranoia (Dementia Paranoides). *Coll. Papers, 3.*

—— (1912/13), Totem and Taboo. In: *The Basic Writings of Sigmund Freud.*

—— (1917), A Childhood Recollection from *Dichtung und Wahrheit. Coll. Papers, 4.*

—— (1923), A Neurosis of Demoniacal Possession in the Seventeenth Century. *Coll. Papers, 4.*

—— (1928a), *The Future of an Illusion.* London: Hogarth Press.

—— (1928b), A Religious Experience. *Coll. Papers, 5.*

—— (1928c), Dostoyevski and Parricide. *Coll. Papers, 5.*

—— (1930), *Civilization and Its Discontents.* London: Hogarth Press.

—— (1931), Libidinal Types. *Coll. Papers, 5.*

—— (1932), *New Introductory Lectures on Psychoanalysis.* New York: Norton, 1933.

—— (1937–39), *Moses and Monotheism*. New York: Knopf.

Friedlaender, B. (1904), *Die Renaissance des Eros Uranos*. Berlin.

Ginsberg, M. (1948), National Character. In: *Reason and Unreason in Society*. London.

Girgensohn, K. (1921), *Der seelische Aufbau des religiösen Erlebens*. Leipzig.

Glaser, R. (1929), *Goethes Vater. Sein Leben nach Tagebüchern und Zeitberichten*. Leipzig.

Greenacre, P. (1945), Conscience in the Psychopath. *Am. J. Orthopsychiat.*, XV.

Grisebach, E. (1897), *Schopenhauer. Eine Geschichte seines Lebens*. Berlin.

Grossmann, S. (1928), Eckermanns Schicksal. From the *Neue Freie Presse,* Vienna (May 3).

Gundolf, F. (1918), *Goethe*. Berlin.

Gwinner, W. v. (1910), *Schopenhauers Leben*. Leipzig.

Harnik, J. (1912), Psychoanalytisches aus und über Goethes Wahlverwandtschaften. *Imago,* I.

—— (1919), Nachtrag zur Kenntnis der Rettungsphantasie bei Goethe. *Int. Zeitschr. f. Psa.,* V.

Haym, R. (1857), *Hegel und seine Zeit*. Berlin.

—— (1870), *Die Romantische Schule; ein Beitrag zur Geschichte des deutschen Geistes*. Berlin.

Hartmann, R., Kris, E., and Loewenstein, R. M. (1946), Comments on the Formation of Psychic Structure. In: *The Psychoanalytic Study of the Child,* II. New York. International Universities Press.

Heinemann, K. (1895), *Goethe*. Leipzig.

Hermann, I. (1924), Die Regression zum zeichnerischen Ausdruck bei Goethe. *Imago,* X.

Hertolet, W. L. (1910), *Schopenhauer-Register*. Leipzig.

Hinrichson, (1911), *Zur Psychologie und Psychopathologie des Dichters*. Wiesbaden.

Hitschmann, E. (1913), Goethe als Vatersymbol. *Int. Zeitschr. f. Psa.,* I.

—— (1915–16), Ein Dichter und sein Vater. *Imago,* IV.

Hohenstein, F. A. (1929), *Goethe. Die Pyramide* (Ein neuer Weg zu Goethe). Dresden.

Hohlfeld, A. R. *Eckermanns Gespräche mit Goethe*. Reprint from the Year Book 1925 of the Monatshefte für deutsche Sprache und Paedagogik; Milwaukee, 1926.

Houben, H. H. (1925), *J. P. Eckermann. Sein Leben für Goethe*. Leipzig.

In Commemoration of William James 1842–1942. New York: Columbia University Press.

James, W. (1898), *The Will to Believe.* New York.

—— (1902), *The Varieties of Religious Experience.* New York.

Jenner, G. (1930), *Johannes Brahms als Mensch, Lehrer und Künstler* Marburg a.d. Lahn.

Jezower, I. (1928), *Das Buch der Träume.* Berlin.

Joel, K. (1905), *Nietzsche und die Romantik.* Jena.

Jones, E. (1923), Kälte, Krankheit und Geburt. *Int. Zeitschr. f. Psa.* IX.

—— (1949), *Hamlet and Oedipus.* London.

—— (1950), *Essays in Applied Psychoanalysis.* London.

—— (1953, 1955), *The Life and Work of Sigmund Freud,* Vols. I and II. New York: Basic Books.

Juliusburger, O. (1912), Psychotherapie und die Philosophie Schopenhauers. *Zentralbl. f. Psa.,* III.

Jung, C. G. (1938), *Psychology and Religion.* New Haven.

—— (1949), *Die Bedeutung des Vaters für das Schicksal des Einzel nen.* Zürich.

Kalbeck, M. (1910), *Johannes Brahms.* Berlin.

Keyserling, Graf H. (1910), *Schopenhauer als Verbilder.* Leipzig.

Kinkel, J. (1922), Zur Frage der psychologischen Grundlagen und des Ursprungs der Religion. *Imago,* VIII.

Kraepelin, E. (1897), *Ueber geistige Arbeit.* Jena.

—— (1909–1915), *Psychiatrie; ein Lehrbuch für Studierende und Aerzte.* Leipzig.

Kretschmer, E. (1929), *Geniale Menschen.* Berlin.

Kroh, O. (1929), *Experimentelle Beiträge zur Typenkunde.* Leipzig.

Kronenberger, L. (1947), *The Portable Johnson and Boswell.* New York.

Krutch, J. W. (1944), *Samuel Johnson.* New York.

Ladell, R. MacDonald (1929), The Neurosis of Dr. Samuel Johnson. *Brit. J. Med. Psychol.,* IX.

Lagerborg, R. (1926), *Platonische Liebe.* Leipzig.

Lander, I. (1942), The Pubertal Struggle against the Instincts. *Am. J. Orthopsychiat.,* XII.

Leuba, J. A. (1925), *The Psychology of Religious Mysticism.* New York.

Levi, H. (1910), *Johannes Brahms im Briefwechsel mit Hermann Levi, Friedrich Gernshein, sowie den Familien Hecht und Fellinger.* Berlin.

Lindner, E. O. and Frauenstaedt, J. (1863), *Arthur Schopenhauer.* Berlin.

Litzmann, B. (1909), *Clara Schumann*. Leipzig.

Macaulay, T. B. (1905), *Life of Samuel Johnson*. New York.

Mallory, G. (1912), *Boswell the Biographer*. London.

Matte-Blanco, I. (1941), A Psychoanalytic Comment on English Manners. *Psychiatry,* IV.

May, F. (1905), *The Life of Johannes Brahms*. London.

Mayreder, R. (1913), *A Survey of the Woman Problem.*

Menninger-Lerchenthal, E. (1932), Eine Halluzination Goethes. *Zeitschr. f. d. ges. Neurol. u. Psychiatr.,* 140.

Michelmann, E. (1930), *Agathe von Siebold, Johannes Brahms' Jugendliebe.* Goettingen.

Mises, R.v. (1939), *Kleines Lehrbuch des Positivismus.* Chicago.

Moebius, P. J. (1903), *Goethe.* Leipzig.

—— (1904), *Schopenhauer.* Leipzig.

Muschg, W. (1930a), *Psychoanalyse und Naturwissenschaft.* Berlin.

—— (1930b), *Tragische Literaturgeschichte.* Berlin.

Nicholson, H. (1927), *The Development of English Literature.* London.

Niemann, W. (1922), *Brahms.* Berlin-Stuttgart.

Nietzsche, F. W., *Collected Works.* New York.

Nock, A. D. (1939), *Conversions and Adolescence.* Muenster.

Obphuels, G. (1921), *Erinnerungen an Brahms.* Berlin.

Ostwald, W. (1914), *Auguste Comte.* Leipzig.

Paulsen, F. (1900), *Schopenhauer. Hamlet. Mephistopheles. Drei Aufsätze zur Naturgeschichte des Pessimismus.* Berlin.

Perry, R. B. (1935), *The Thought and Character of William James.* Boston.

Petersen, J. (1924), *Die Entstehung der Eckermannschen Gespräche und ihre Glaubwürdigkeit.* Berlin.

Rank, O. (1911), Schopenhauer über den Wahnsinn. *Zentralbl. f. Psa.,* I.

—— (1912), *Das Inzestmotiv in Dichtung und Sage.* Vienna.

Reich, W. (1925), *Der triebhafte Character.* Vienna.

Reik, T. (1929), *Warum verliess Goethe Friederike?* Vienna.

—— (1940), *A Note on "A Religious Experience."* New York.

Reynolds, Sir J. (1952?) *Portraits.* Character Sketches of Oliver Goldsmith, Samuel Johnson and David Garrick. New York.

Richert, H. (1909), *Schopenhauer. Seine Persönlichkeit, seine Lehre, seine Bedeutung.* Leipzig.

Riehl, A. (1898), *Friedrich Nietzsche, der Künstler und der Denker.* Stuttgart.

Roback, A. A. (1942), *William James, His Marginalia, Personality and Contribution.* Cambridge, Mass.

Roberts, S. C. (1926), *Dr. Johnson in Cambridge; Essays in Boswellian Imitation*. Cambridge.

Ruemcke, H. C. (1924), *Zur Phänomenologie der Glücksgefühle;* Monographien aus dem Gesamtgebiet der Neurologie und Psychiatrie.

Rzewuski, Count St. (1908), *L'Optimism de Schopenhauer. Etude de Schopenhauer.* Paris.

Sachs, H. (1944), *Freud, Master and Friend.* Cambridge; Harvard University Press.

Sanctis, S. de (1927), *Religious Conversions.* New York.

Santayana, G. (1934), *Character and Opinion in the U.S.A.* New York.

Sarasin, P. (1929), Goethes Mignon. *Imago,* XV.

Schelderup, H. & K. (1932), *Ueber drei Haupttypen der religiösen Erlebnisformen und ihre psychologische Grundlage.* Leipzig.

Scheler, M. (1912), Ueber Ressentiment und moralische Werturteile. *Zeitschr. f. Pathopsychologie,* I.

Schemann, L. (1894), *Gespräche und Briefwechsel mit Schopenhauer.* Leipzig.

Schewe, K. (1905), *Schopenhauers Stellung zu der Naturwissenschaft.* Berlin.

Schopenhauer, A. (1909), *Tagebücher.* Leipzig.

Schopenhauer's Werke. Nachlass. Briefe. Leipzig.

Schreber, D. P. (1903), *Denkwürdigkeiten eines Nervenkranken.* Dresden.

Schumann, C., *Johannes Brahms, Briefe 1853–1896.* Berlin.

Schumann, E. (1925), *Erinnerungen.* Stuttgart.

Schweitzer, A. (1933), *My Life and Thought; An Autobiography.* London.

Sedlitz, C.v. (1872), *Dr. Arthur Schopenhauer vom medizinischen Standpunkt aus betrachtet.* Dorpat.

Seillère, E. (1912), *Arthur Schopenhauer als romantischer Philosoph.* Berlin.

Sierke, E. (1874), Schwaermer und Schwindler zu Ende des 18. Jahrhunderts. Leipzig.

Simmel, G. (1907), *Schopenhauer und Nietzsche. Ein Vortragszyklus.* Leipzig.

Specht, R. *Johannes Brahms.* Hellerau.

—— (1926), *Franz Werfel.* Berlin.

Springer, B., *Der Schlüssel zu Goethes Liebesleben. Ein Versuch.* Berlin.

Stamm, I. S. (1935), *Religious Experience in the Works of Franz Werfel.* Cambridge: Harvard University Press.

Starbuck, S. D. (1899), *The Psychology of Religion.* London.

Strunk, W., Jr., ed. (1895), *Macaulay's and Carlyle's Essays on Samuel Johnson*. New York.

Tewes, F., ed. (1905), *Aus Goethes Lebenskreise*. Berlin.

Theilhaber, F. A. (1929), *Goethe. Sexus und Eros*. Berlin.

Trueblood, D. E. (1942), *The Logic of Belief*. New York.

Voelkelt, J. (1900), *Arthur Schopenhauer. Seine Persönlichkeit, seine Lehre, sein Glaube*. Stuttgart.

Vulliamy, C. E. (1936), *Mrs. Thrall of Streatham. Her Place in the Life of Dr. Samuel Johnson and in the society of her time, Her Character and Family Affairs. Reviewed in the Light of Newly Assembled Evidence*. London.

—— (1946), *Ursa Major; A Study of Dr. Johnson and His Friends*. London.

Wagner, C. F. (1909), *Encyclop. Register zu Schopenhauers Werken*. Karlsruhe.

William James, The Man and The Thinker. Addresses delivered at the University of Wisconsin, 1942.

Winterstein, A. (1912), Zur Psychoanalyse des Reisens, *Imago*, I.

Witkowski, G. (1899), *Goethe*. Leipzig.

Wuertz, H. (1932), *Goethes Wesen und Umwelt im Spiegel der Krüppelpsychologie*. Leipzig.

Bibliography of
Edward Hitschmann's Writings

Key to Abbreviations

A	Almanach der Psychoanalyse
Am. Im.	American Imago
Bw.	Psychoanalytische Bewegung
Im.	Imago
J.	International Journal of Psycho-Analysis
Jb.	Jahrbuch der Psychoanalyse
Päd.	Zeitschrift für psychoanalytische Pädagogik
Q.	Psychoanalytic Quarterly
R.	Psychoanalytic Review
Y.	Yearbook of Psychoanalysis
Z.	Internationale Zeitschrift für Psychoanalyse
Zb.	Zentralblatt für Psychoanalyse

Internal Medicine

1903

Zur Kenntnis der Tuberkulose des lymphatischen Apparates (with O. Stross). *Deutsche medizinische Wochenschrift*

Ein Fall leukämieartiger Erkrankung mit schewerer megaloblastischer Anämie und eigentümlichem Exanthem (with H. Lehndorf). *Zeitschrift für Heilkunde*

1904

Über Venenpulse an den Vorderarmen bei atrophischer Lebercirrhose. *Zentralblatt für innere Medizin*

1926

Zum Gebrauch der Injektiorsspritze. *Wiener klinische Wochenschrift*

1931

Die schonende Entlehrung des Rectums. *Biologische Heilkunst*

Psychiatry and Psychoanalysis

1910

ur Kritik des Hellsehens. *Wien. klin. Rundschau.* English: *Psychoanalysis and the Occult,* ed. G. Devereux. New York: International Universities Press, 1953.

1911

in Fall von Symbolik für Ungläubige. *Zb.*
eiträge zur Sexualsymbolik des Traumes. *Zb.*
ckermann (über Goethe und Träume). *Zb.*
ebbel kennt auch die Rolle des Unbewussten im Künstler. *Zb.*
omment on Möricke: "Erstes Liebeslied eines Mädchens." *Zb.*
Velche hohe Wertung Hebbel den Träumen entgegenbrachte. *Zb.*
reuds Neurosenlehre. Wien: Deuticke. Second edition: 1913.

1912

eitrag: *Die Onanie.* Wiesbaden: Bergmann.
ine sehr durchsichtige Symbolik. *Zb.*
riedrich Nietzsche über den Wahrheitssinn des Künstlers. *Zb.*
um Farbenhören. *Im.*
eligiöse Ekstase und Sexualität. *Zb.*
um Werden des Romandichters. *Im.*

1913

reud's *Theories of the Neuroses.* New York: Nervous and Mental
    Disease Publishing Co.
chopenhauer, Versuch einer Psychoanalyse des Philosophen. *Im.*
wedenborgs Paranoia. *Zb.* English: *Am. Im.,* 1949; *Y.,* 1950.
inderangst und Onanie-Entwöhnung. *Zb.*
esteigertes Triebleben und Zwangsneurose bei einem Kinde. *Z.*
    English: *J.,* 1924.
aranoia, Homosexualität und Analerotik. *Z.*
wei Fälle von Namenvergessen. *Z.*
in wiederholter Fall von Verschreiben bei der Rezeptierung. *Z.*
oethe als Vatersymbol. *Z.*
Veitere Mitteilung von Kinderträumen mit spezieller Bedeutung:
    Z. Ein Nachtrag, 1914.
um Thema Enuresis, Harnreiztraum, psychische Hemmung. *Zb.*
reuds psychoanalytische Behandlungsmethode. Berlin: *Jahreskurse
    für ärztliche Fortbildung.*
exualsymbolik in Bildern. *Z.*

1914

Trieblehre. *Jb., Bw.*, 1921.
Über Träume Gottfried Kellers. *Z.*
Über Nerven- und Geisteskrankheiten bei katholischen Geistliche
und Nonnen. *Z.*
Dichterausprüche zur Beurteilung der Sexualverdrängung. *Z.*

1915

Ein Fall von Zwangsbefürchtung vom Tode des gleichgeschlech
lichen Elternteiles. *Z.*
Franz Schuberts Schmerz und Liebe. *Z.* English: *Am. Im.*, 1950.
Gottfried Keller. *Im.*
*Gottfried Keller: Psychoanalyse des Dichters, seiner Gestalten ur
Motive.* Leipzig: Bach.

1916

Ein Dichter und sein Vater (Dauthendey). *Im.*
Thomas Mann über Friedrich den Grossen. *Im.*

1919

Eine literarische Verwertung des Vatermordes. *Z.*
Maurus Jokai über den Traum. *Z.*
Über einen sporadischen Rückfall in Bettnässen bei einem 4 jährig
Kinde. *Z.*
Über eine im Traum angekündigte Reminiszens an ein sexuell
Jugenderlebnis. *Z.*

1920

Zur sexuellen Natur des Lutschen. *Z.*
Urethralerotik und Zwangsneurose. *Z.* English: *J.*, 1923.

1923

Telepathie und Psychoanalyse. *Im.* English: *J.*, 1924; *Psychoanalys
and the Occult,* ed. G. Devereux. New York: International Ur
versities Press, 1953; Italian: *Arch. gen. Neurol. Psichiat.*, 1925.
Zum Tagträumen der Dichter. *Im.*
Experimentelle Wiederholung der infantilen Schlafsituation z
Förderung analytischer Traumdeutung. *Z.*

1924

Die Indikation zur psychoanalytischen Behandlung. Wien: Ars M
dici.

1926

in Gespenst aus der Kindheit Knut Hamsuns. *Im.;* also as book:
Wien: Internationaler psychoanalytischer Verlag.
er sittliche Gehalt der Lehren Freuds. Prague: *B'nai B'rith Mitteilungen.*
ine natürliche Schwierigkeit der Aufklärung. *Päd.*

1927

eitrag zu einer Onanie-Diskussion. *Bw.*
iskussion der Laienanalyse. *Z.;* English: *J.*
ie gröbsten Fehler der Erziehung. *Päd.*
uf der Höhe der Entmannungsangst. *Päd.*
ie Heilbarkeit der weiblichen Geschlechtskälte. *Ars. med.*

1928

ur Psychoanalyse des Misanthropen von Molière. *Im.; A.,* 1929
on, um und über Knut Hamsun. *Im.*
ber einige praktische Ergänzungen der psychoanalytischen Behandlung von Impotenz und Frigidität. *Allgem. Zeitschrift für Psychotherapie.*
sychoanalyse trotz Hormonen. *Ibid.*

1929

in geborener Bildhauer. *Päd.*
nut Hamsun und die Psychoanalyse. *Bw.*
om Zwangsimpuls, zum Fenster hinauszuspringen. *Ars med.*

1930

erjüngung durch Psychoanalyse. *Ars. med.*
ie Bedeutung der Psychoanalyse für die Biographik. *Bw.*
himose und Neurose. *Zentralblatt für Psychotherapie.*
ur Psychologie des jüdischen Witzes. *Bw.*
erhütung und Heilung der Ehehemmungen. *Berichte des Int. Kongresses für Sexualreform.* Wien: Elbemühl Verlag, 1931

1931

athographie und Psychoanalyse. *Int. Tagung für angewandte Psychopathologie und Psychologie*
Vandlungen der Traumsymbolik beim Fortschritt der Behandlung. *Z.*

Die Zwangsbefürchtung vom Tode des gleichgeschlechtlichen Elter
teils. *Päd.*
Eine unverstandene Frau der vorpsychoanalytischen Zeit (Mrs. Ca
lyle). *Bw.*
Josef K. Friedjung zum 60. Geburtstag. *Z.*
Die Angst um den Tod des geliebten andersgeschlechtlichen Elter
teils. *Bw.*
Das Strafen aus analerotischen Motiven. *Päd.*

1932

Psychoanalytisches zur Persönlichkeit Goethes. *Im.;* also as boo
Wien: Internationaler psychoanalytischer Verlag
Über die Psychoanalyse einer hypochondrischen Todesangst. *B*
logische Heilkunst
Freud über Menschentypen. *Bw.*
Goethe über die Psychoanalyse (publ.: Multaretuli, pseudonym). *B*
Die Psychoanalyse der Zwangsneurose. *Zeitschrift für die gesam*
Neurologie und Psychiatrie
Zehn Jahre Wiener psychoanalytisches Ambulatorium. *Bw.*
Kindheitseindrücke und Homosexualität. *Päd.*
Franz Werfel als Erzieher—der Väter. *Bw.; A.,* 1933
Vom Junggesellen, dem "unbekannten Neurotiker." *A.*
Zur Geschichte des Ambulatoriums (1922–1932). *Z.*
Kann ein Psychoanalytiker (religiöser) Christ sein? *Bw.*
Können wir ohne Gottesglauben leben? *Bw.*
Ein tschechischer Almanach. *Bw.*

1933

Nemo propheta in patria. *Bw.*
Die Bindung Eckermanns an Goethe. *Bw.*
Johannes Brahms und die Frauen. *Bw.* English: *Am. Im.,* 1949. Ita
ian: *Arch. gen. Neurol. Psichiat.,* 1934
Die Psychoanalyse der nervösen Sexualstörungen. *Wien. me*
Wochenschrift
Soll man bei psychischer Impotenz Hormonpräparate anwende
Ars. med.
Gedankenübertragung während der Psychoanalyse (publ. anor
mously). *Bw.*
Die Psychoanalyse der Spermatorrhoe. *Wien. med. Wochenschrift*
Johann Peter Eckermann. *Bw.*
Sandor Ferenczi (publ. anonymously). *Bw.*
Eines Psychoanalytikers Dankgedicht an den Uhrzeiger. *Bw.*

Gerichtliche Medizin und Psychoanalyse. *Bw.*
Kain- und Oedipus-Komplex in musikalischer Produktion. *Bw.*

1934

Die Geschlechtskälte der Frau: Ihr Wesen und ihre Behandlung.
(with E. Bergler). *Ars med.* English: New York: Nervous and Mental Disease Publishing Co., 1936; Japanese: 1938
Der narzisstische Gatte. *A.*
Beiträge zu einer Psychopathologie des Traumes. *Z.*

1935

Beiträge zu einer Psychopathologie des Traumes. *Z.*
Der Vater als Eindringling. *Päd.*
Einschlafen nach Coué. *Ars med.*

1936

Triebdurchbrüche bei Neurosen. *Der österreichische Arzt*

1937

Zur Entstehung des Kinderbuches von Selma Lagerlöf *Wunderbare
Reise des kleinen Nils Holgersson mit den Wildgänsen. A.* Dutch:
1938
Todesangst durch Tötungsdrang. *Zeitschrift für Kinderpsychiatrie*
Bemerkungen über die Platzangst und andere neurotische Angst-
zustände. *Z.*

1938

Psychogene Spermatorrhoe. *Psychiat. en Neurol. Bladen*

1939

Selma Lagerlöf, ihr Wesen und ihr Werk. *Z.*

1940

Beiträge zur Ätiologie und Konstitution der Spermatorrhoe. *Z.*

1941

Freud in Life and Death. *Am. Im.* Spanish: *Rev. Psicoanal.,* 1944

1942

Psychoanalytic Characterology. Lecture, New York Psychoanalytic
Society

1943

Neurotic Bashfulness and Erithrophobia. *R.*

1945

Samuel Johnson's Character. *R.*

1947

New Varieties of Religious Experience: *Psychoanalysis and the Social Sciences,* ed. G. Róheim. New York: International Universities Press.

The History of the Aggression-Impulse. *Samiksa; Y.,* 1948

1948

Boswell: The Biographer's Character. *Q.; Y.,* 1949.

1949

Frigidity in Women: Restatement and Renewed Experiences (with E. Bergler). *R.*

Fear to Die by Wish to Kill. *Zeitschrift für Psychoanalyse* (Berlin)

1951

Freud's Conception of Love. *Q.; J.,* 1952; *Y.,* 1953

1955

Some Psycho-Analytical Aspects of Biography. Lecture, Int. Psychoanalytic Congress, Geneva